Thames Valley Landscapes: The Windrush Valley, Volume 1
(Series Editor: Ellen McAdam)

An Iron Age and Romano-British Enclosed Settlement at Watkins Farm Northmoor, Oxon.

by T. G. Allen

GW00503125

Oxford University Committee for Archaeology
1990

Published by the Oxford University Committee for Archaeology
Institute of Archaeology
Beaumont Street
Oxford

Distributed by Oxbow Books
Park End Place, Oxford, OX1 1HN

© Oxford Archaeological Unit 1990

ISBN 0 947816 80 1

Origination and Layout by Oxbow Books
Printed in Great Britain at
The Short Run Press, Exeter

Preface

Thames Valley Landscapes

Since its formation in 1973 the Oxford Archaeological Unit has carried out a series of major excavations on sites in the Thames Valley ranging in date from Neolithic to the early modern period.

Most of these have been what are sometimes called 'rescue' excavations in advance of gravel extraction, housing and roads schemes, funded by English Heritage. These threatened sites were not dug just because they happened to be there. Our aim has always been to pursue specific problems in the context of research into the settlement history of the Thames Valley.

For this reason certain areas within the Thames Valley were selected for long-term investigation — through aerial photography, field survey, large-scale and more selective excavation. Within these areas sites are often chosen for their 'group-value', their relationship with their neighbours, or their place in the landscape. Emphasis has also been placed on investigating well preserved sites, particularly those with waterlogged deposits, and on systematic sampling for biological data.

In the past the OAU's excavation reports have been published by the Council for British Archaeology, English Heritage and in local or national journals. The aim of this new series, *Thames Valley Landscapes*, is to present results in as consistent a way as possible and to allow them to complement one another. They will be grouped into their various sub-regions, usually based on the Thames confluences: the rivers Coln/Leach, Windrush, Evenlode and Ock. This first volume will be a companion to forthcoming accounts of other Windrush Valley Sites: the Devil's Quoits henge monument, the Mingies Ditch banjo enclosure and the Gravelly Guy Iron Age settlement with its storage pits and fields.

Each of these reports will stand alone but each will also fit with the others like the cubes of a mosaic to build up a picture of a changing landscape with its shifting economies and societies. It is hoped that in this way a complex picture will gradually come into focus.

The series is a co-operative venture between the Oxford Archaeological Unit, English Heritage and the Oxford University Committee for Archaeology. I am grateful to Professor Barry Cunliffe, Dr Geoffrey Wainwright, Mr A J Fleming and Mr David Brown for their help in inaugurating the series, and particularly to Dr Ellen McAdam for her sisyphean labours as the series editor in making it a reality.

David Miles
Director
Oxford Archaeological Unit

Contents

List of figures and plates in the text

List of tables in the text

List of tables in the technical appendix

List of figures in the technical appendix

Summary

Excavation of a Middle Iron Age enclosed settlement and Romano-British enclosures was carried out in advance of gravel extraction over three short seasons between June 1983 and January 1985. The site was not visible from aerial photographs, and first appeared during topsoil stripping by ARC Ltd. It lay on low-lying First Gravel Terrace E of the river Windrush (SP 426 035), and the occupied areas lay upon a slightly higher gravel island than the surrounding land. Because of the high water table waterlogged remains were preserved in the deepest features.

Within the main settlement, Site A, the Iron Age settlement consisted of at least four small penannular enclosures, probably surrounding houses, all of which had more than one phase of use and several of which may have been contemporary. There were only two pits and no definite four-post structures, and the environmental evidence suggests that arable agriculture was not practised close to the site. The animal bones indicate predominantly cattle, horses and sheep; a high percentage of horses compared with other sites in the region suggests that horse-breeding was a significant part of the economy. A relict stream course just S of the settlement may have been active at this time; there was also a shallow well c 2.0 m. deep within the main enclosure. Pottery and C14 dates suggest that occupation fell entirely within the later part of the Middle Iron Age, most probably between 250 BC and 50 BC.

After a break in occupation the main Iron Age enclosure was reused in the late 1st/early 2nd century AD. A series of ditch circuits was dug respecting the main enclosure, and these were followed by a trackway and field system incorporating a subrectangular enclosure which cut across but overlay the main Iron Age enclosure. There was a succession of these subrectangular enclosures, apparently dating between the early 3rd century and the mid 4th century AD. The only features within the Romano-British enclosures were a few shallow pits and short lengths of gully, a scatter of postholes and one or two wells. The density of Romano-British pottery suggests that domestic occupation lay close by, but there was no firm evidence for structures within the excavated area.

Two hundred metres to the NE another area of Romano-British enclosure boundary ditches and wells was uncovered (Site B). The pottery indicates 2nd-century occupation close by, with much smaller scale activity in the 3rd and 4th centuries AD. Again, no evidence for structures was recovered, though one probable domestic enclosure was seen. In the medieval period Site A was cultivated. Finds from one or two of the wells suggest these may have been medieval and that there was an early 11th-12th-century phase of pasture before arable cultivation began. On Site B one pit of the 11th-12th century was found, and several ditches forming rectilinear enclosures were possibly also of this date.

Acknowledgements

Thanks are due to Mr Jeff Williams, who discovered the site, and to ARC, Ltd, without whom the work could not have taken place. I would particularly like to thank Mr Terry Jones and Mr Bob Turner of ARC by whose good offices free machining was provided for the 1984 season, and whose co-operation was very helpful throughout. The work was carried out by a team of six or seven MSC scheme employees, and I am deeply indebted to the untiring efforts of Ashley Coombes, Robert Bailey and Hugh Cameron in the most testing conditions.

Many thanks to all the contributors to the report. The Iron Age pottery was drawn by Simon Pressey, the Romano-British pottery by Sheila Raven and the medieval pottery and other finds by Wendy Page. For the pasting up I would like to thank Elinor Beard. The plans and sections were drawn by the author, Figures 1 and 33 by Paul Hughes and the cover illustrations by Simon Chew. I am very grateful to Jackie Carvell and Georgina Griffiths for their patience in typing and amending the report. In the final stages of preparation and editing, the assistance of Ellen McAdam was invaluable.

I would also like to thank Tom Hassall for his support in ensuring that all of this underfunded site was excavated and David Miles for encouragement in the post-excavation stages. I am grateful to Simon Palmer for allowing me to use pottery data from the excavations at Claydon Pike ahead of publication, and to George Lambrick for the benefit of his advice throughout the writing of the report.

The excavation was funded by English Heritage and by the Manpower Services Commission, the preparation of the report and its publication by English Heritage alone.

Chapter 1

Archaeological background and Iron Age features

INTRODUCTION

Watkins Farm was investigated because of its potential interest as one of a group of sites in the Stanton Harcourt area. There had been recent excavations within a 4 km radius at Farmoor and Mingies Ditch, Hardwick, both floodplain Middle Iron Age settlements (Fig. 1 and Fig. 34; Allen and Robinson forthcoming; Lambrick and Robinson 1979). Mingies Ditch was an enclosed settlement, and a comparison between it and Watkins Farm was thought likely to be very informative. Together with the Second Gravel Terrace arable settlements at Gravelly Guy and Beard Mill (Lambrick 1985; Williams 1951, 5–22) excavations in this area represent a coherent landscape study.

The development of this landscape in the Romano-British period has not been the subject of such intensive study, but excavations have taken place at Farmoor, Smithsfield, Gravelly Guy and Vicarage Field (Lambrick and Robinson 1979; Allen 1981, 28–31; Lambrick 1985; Thomas 1955, 1–28).

Since the excavations at Watkins Farm, another Iron Age site at Gill Mill, Ducklington has been investigated by the Oxford Archaeological Unit (Fig. 1) and several Romano-British settlements have been excavated, notably at Eagle Farm, Standlake and Old Shifford Farm in the parish of Acton, Bampton and Shifford (see Fig. 1). These sites will form the subject of future reports in the 'Thames Valley landscapes: the Windrush Valley' series.

GEOLOGY AND TOPOGRAPHY (Fig. 1)

For a general description of the local geology see Allen and Robinson (forthcoming). The site sits upon low-lying First Gravel Terrace shelving very gradually onto the floodplain of the rivers Thames and Windrush. The limits of floodplain and First Terrace are difficult to define; a map showing the maximum recorded extent of flooding in 1947 (Lambrick and Robinson 1979, 4, Fig. 1) reveals that while the whole of the terrace around the settlement was inundated there was an oval 'island', including both the Iron Age and Romano-British sites, which was not. The site thus occupied a very slight eminence. The Pleistocene gravels were overlaid by an oxidised non-calcareous silty clay; this soil becomes sticky very quickly when wet, but because of the underlying gravel also dries rapidly.

S and E of the Thames is the Oxford clay which also underlies the gravel terraces, giving way on its E to the Corallian sand and limestone beds, with small outcrops of Lower Greensand on the tops of Boars Hill and Cumnor Hurst. To the N the second terrace gives way to the third, which tends to be thin and poorly drained, before the gravels run out onto Oxford clay some 6 km from the site. Beyond the clays are the limestone beds, from which was derived the limestone used on the site (Technical appendix section 2: Stone objects, Table T8). Deposits of the Unbedded Glacil Drift are common on the Oxford clay to the N and on Wytham Hill only 6 or 7 km from the site, and from these could have derived a variety of quernstones, quartzitic and other pebbles and other exotic rocks.

AIMS AND STRATEGY

Stripping for gravel extraction exposed two areas of archaeological features. Site A was the more coherent, centred around a large ditched enclosure of Iron Age date; Site B, some 200 m further N, was a scattered collection of Romano-British pits and ditches (see Fig. 2). Excavation was concentrated upon Site A because of its Iron Age origins, and because the large enclosure provided a defined settlement unit for investigation.

On Site A, the S and E parts of the main enclosure were the areas first uncovered. When first visited these had been stripped of topsoil and ploughsoil, and at this stage a measured sketch plan of the visible features was made. Unfortunately, deeper stripping took place over this area before excavation began, resulting in the loss of the shallower features (see Fig. 3). The sketch plan has provided some extra information which is shown in dotted outline, but does not represent all that may have been present, as the site was not cleaned at the time.

Since this half of the enclosure had been heavily stripped, objectives were initially limited to recovering a plan, enough pottery to date the occupation and a spectrum of environmental samples.

Four weeks' salvage work achieved two of these objectives, but very little pottery was recovered, though what there was suggested a Middle Iron Age origin for the settlement. It was decided to strip the other half of the main enclosure archaeologically and excavate this in greater detail. A medieval headland had protected a strip across the middle of the enclosure; N of this medieval and modern ploughing had truncated the gravel somewhat. Despite limited time and resources most features in the second half of the interior were excavated, and enough pottery and bone were recovered to allow direct comparison with other large-scale excavations in the region. The best-preserved area provides an index of loss of information elsewhere on the site (see Fig. 4 and

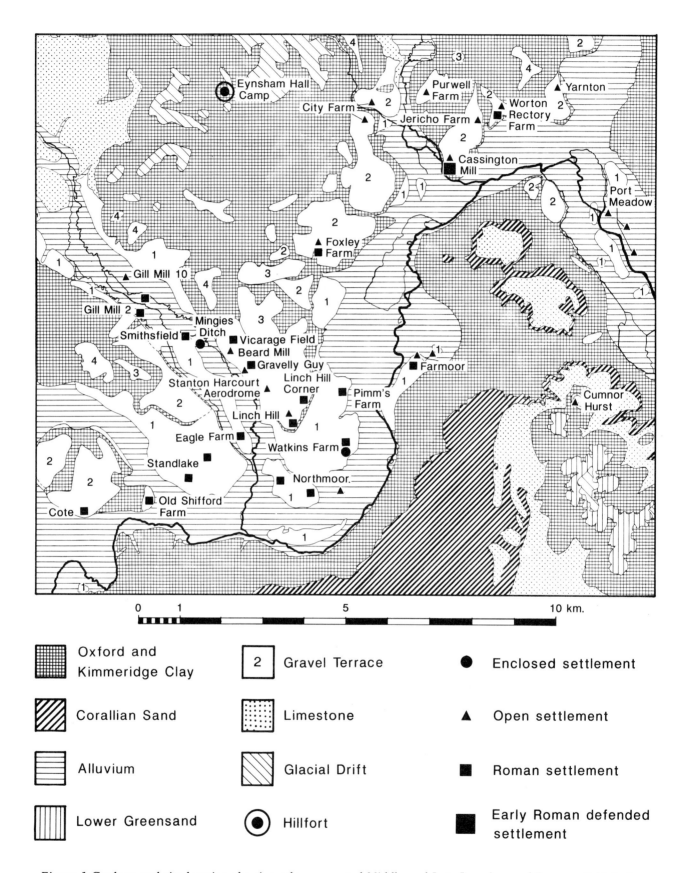

Figure 1 Geology and site location showing other excavated Middle and Late Iron Age and Romano-British sites

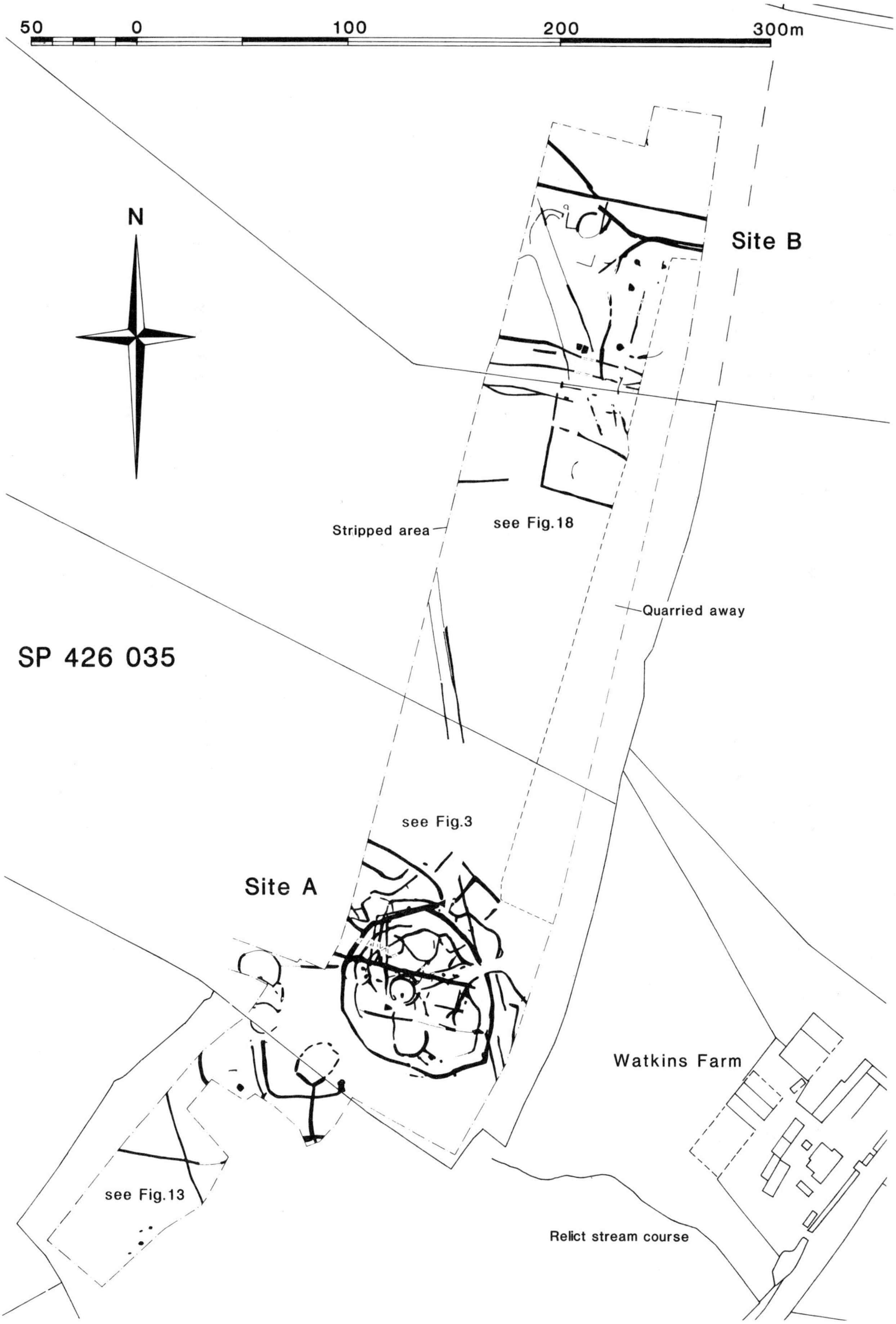

Figure 2 Overall site plan in relation to modern topography

Chapter 5: The interior: preservation), and a sizeable Iron Age pottery sequence was obtained from the central roundhouse. Effort was concentrated on the Iron Age features, as this was the period when domestic occupation was evident.

THE EXCAVATION: IRON AGE FEATURES, SITE A

Summary

The Iron Age settlement lay within a large elliptical enclosure with entrances on the E and the S. In the centre of the interior were the penannular ditches surrounding a central roundhouse, whose numerous recuts denote a long life. This house at first faced S, but was later enlarged and reoriented to face the E entrance; parallel trackway ditches were dug defining a path leading from the main enclosure entrance to the central house.

Around the southern half of the interior and facing towards the central house were three other penannular or U-shaped enclosures, which probably also surrounded houses. The southern U-shaped enclosure apparently shared a common forecourt bounded by linking gullies with the central house in its earliest phase. SW of the central house was a triangular well. The western enclosure, which was joined onto the main enclosure ditch, contained one of only two cylindrical storage pits on the site, and also surrounded another well which contained a human burial accompanied by wooden and leather objects.

The northern half of the interior was open, but was encroached upon by further enclosure ditches at a late stage in the occupation. A small enclosure butted up to the main enclosure ditch on the outside on the N, adjacent to a boundary ditch running off north-westwards. SW of the main enclosure was a smaller one made up of short lengths of ditch, joined onto another field boundary.

The main enclosure ditch (Figs. 3, 4, 5)

This described a rough ellipse 75 m × 67 m, long axis NW-SE. There was one entrance midway along the E side, 6.5 m wide. The ditch was V-profiled and in the best-preserved areas was between 1.00 m and 1.10 m deep and 1.8-2.00 m wide. Generally the sequence of fills was as follows:

a) grey clay and gravel spills down the sides, peat or peaty clay with gravelly spills in the bottom. At the SE corner and northwards towards the E entrance several deposits of peat were distinguishable.

b) overlying the peat in some areas was a very gravelly grey clay; elsewhere thin spills of gravel covered the peat.

c) These layers and spills were followed by clean clays, grey, orange-brown and brown. On the E side of the

enclosure gleyed clay just above the peat contained aquatic molluscs, and was clearly of alluvial origin (see Chapter 4: The environment of Site B, Romano-British: conditions in the contexts investigated).

In the heavily scraped areas nothing survived above this level. On the NE, N and W, however, the top of the ditch was backfilled with gravelly clays. The gravel is very unlikely to have derived from the sides, and was mixed throughout the layers; on the NE (Fig. 5 Section 1-155) there were small pockets of pure sandy gravel, which suggests that this was deliberate backfilling using material from freshly dug features. This backfilling can be dated to the Roman period, as it is cut through by ditch 155 on the NE, and by enclosure ditch 450 and wells 412 and 478 on the N. Roman pottery was also found in both the clean clays and in the more gravelly spills beneath them directly over the peat, and one or two sherds of Roman pottery came from the black upper peat near where ditch 5 cut across. It seems probable that the upper peats here belong to a Romano-British recutting.

On the S side there were apparently two phases of ditch, the earlier of which survived as a slightly out-turned terminal (Fig. 3 and Fig. 5 Section 1C). No corresponding terminal was found further W. The second phase of ditch continued but ran out over an area of concreted hard pan; where this ditch began again was also perhaps the position of the first phase terminal. There is no dating evidence for the narrowing or blocking of this entrance, but a small Iron Age enclosure just inside, 22-23, also had two phases of ditch, one of which had an entrance facing S towards the main enclosure ditch (Fig. 3). This was subsequently dug through and the enclosure reoriented, and it is plausible that the cutting through of the southern gaps in both 1 and 22 was linked. There was a short gully 44 just outside the main enclosure ditch terminal (Fig. 3). There was no dating evidence, but it was perhaps connected with the entrance in ditch 1. W of these ditch 1 was shallower so this stretch of ditch did not contain peat.

A radiocarbon date of 2340 ± 90 bp was obtained from bones in the bottom of the main enclosure ditch. When calibrated this gives a date range of 580 BC to 330 BC (68% confidence; see Table 8 for further details). On the W the bottom fills of 1 were cut by a small Iron Age enclosure ditch 517. The first phase ditch of this enclosure 513 stopped just short of and apparently respecting 1. 517 was overlaid by later silting and backfilling layers in the main enclosure ditch (Fig. 6).

On the NW the main enclosure ditch was contemporary with ditch 479 (Fig. 5), which was apparently backfilled before slow silting in 1 began. Romano-British pottery came from silting above the backfill layers in 479. All the adjacent ditches just outside 1 were Iron Age, and this is probably also the date of 479.

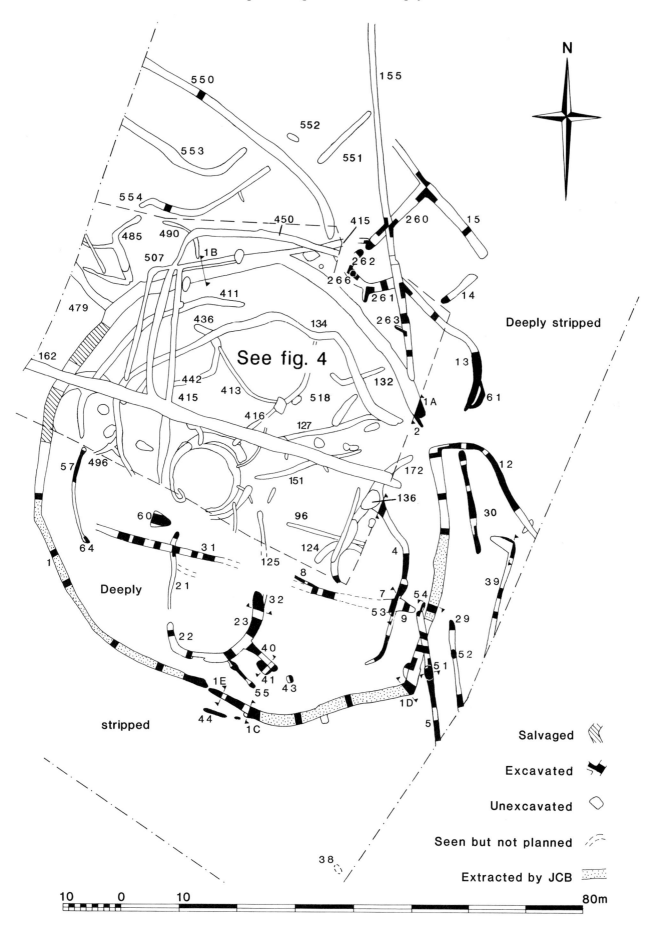

Figure 3 Site A: Plan of the main enclosure showing areas not excavated in detail

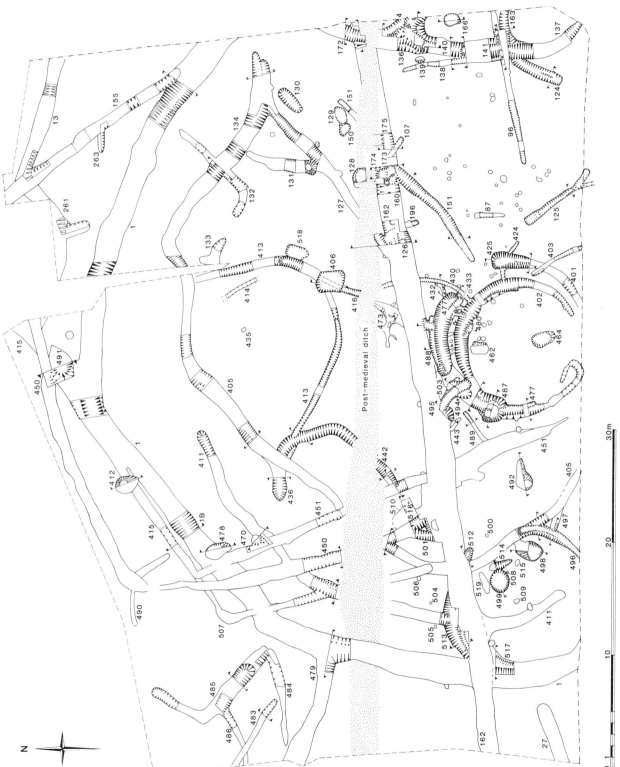

Figure 4 Detailed plan of the well preserved half of the main enclosure

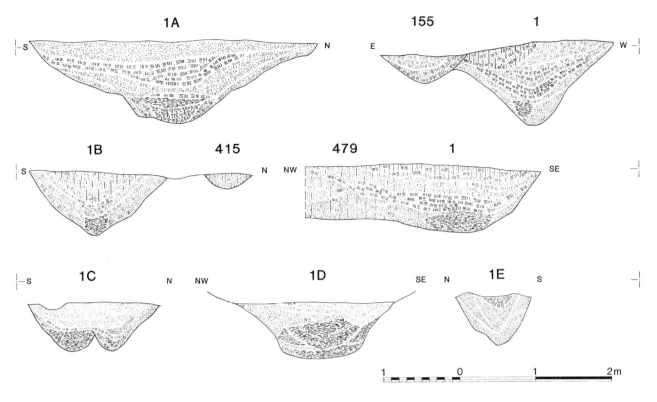

Figure 5 Sections across the main enclosure ditch

The main enclosure was thus Iron Age in origin, but was still largely open and was partly recut in the early Romano-British period. It was, however, backfilled during the Romano-British occupation, and was overlaid by later Roman enclosure and boundary ditches, 5, 155, 450 and 126–162 (see Chapter 2: The later Romano-British occupation, and Figs. 4 and 35).

The E entrance was narrowed by gully 2 projecting S from the northern enclosure ditch terminal. The gully did not show in section cutting through the ditch fills, and could have been contemporary with either the Iron Age or early Romano-British use of the enclosure, or may have been a marking-out ditch.

An antenna ditch 12 ran E from the southern terminal of 1. The upper fills of both had been heavily disturbed, but the fills of 1 were darker and probably cut those of 12. Since, however, 12 ended within 1 it is likely that it was the Romano-British recut of 1 that cut 12, so that 12 was contemporary with the original Iron Age enclosure ditch.

The interior

The interior contained a number of small ditched enclosures.

Enclosure 496–512

Just inside the main enclosure ditch 1 on the W was a penannular enclosure 11.5 m across internally, with an

entrance just over 4.0 m wide facing E towards the main enclosure entrance. The N arc of ditch had two cuts, the earlier of which, 513, ended just short of 1, showing that this small enclosure was added to the main enclosure. The recut 517 ran straight into the main enclosure ditch, cutting through primary silting down its side (Fig. 6). Both 513 and 517 were cut away by Romano-British ditches 411, 126 and 162, but the terminal survived as feature 512. There was a distinct angle shortly before the western terminal of 513, and it may have been made up of a series of straight lengths, like enclosures at Little Waltham, Essex (Drury 1978, 11–124). 517 on the contrary curved too gently to describe a circle, suggesting more an oval shape.

The S arc 496 only survived on the E and at the very western end, the rest having been destroyed by deeper stripping. The eastern part was truncated by a Romano-British ditch 405 = 134. The enclosure ditches were in general 0.6–0.7 m deep, but 496 increased to 1.17 m deep at the terminal.

Primary gravelly fills were followed by much cleaner silts once the eroding sides had stabilised. Black layers with much charcoal and occupation debris survived at the terminals, in 496 overlying a dump of burnt limestone. The density of occupation material in both S and N ditch arcs fell off away from the terminal.

Midway between the terminals of the enclosure was a large posthole 500. This contained Iron Age pottery

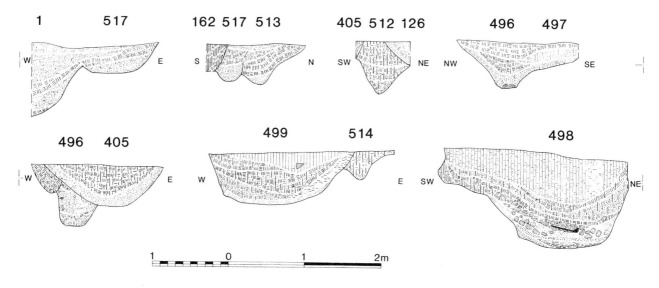

Figure 6 Sections of enclosure 496–512 and features inside it

and was probably contemporary. The interior of the enclosure was damaged both by 405 and by 411, another large Romano-British ditch. The back (western) half was, however, devoid of features, while the E half was occupied by a waterhole 498, a circular pit 499, gullies or shallow pits 514 and 519 and a few postholes, of which 508 and 509 were possibly Iron Age. The surviving postholes did not form any recognisable structure (see Fig. 4).

499 was one of only two sizeable pits on the site, the other being 166 (see section on Enclosure 124–163, below, and Fig. 10). It was circular, with steep sides and a flattish bottom, and most of the pit was filled with dark soils and occupation debris. This included the articulated lower foreleg of a cow. Such deposits may be simply refuse from butchery, but articulated limbs in pits at Gravelly Guy have been shown to have been deliberately and carefully buried (Lambrick 1985, 108). N of 499 was a soilmark, 519, similar to 514, but with darker fill.

Well 498 and its burial (Figs. 6, 7, 7a)

498 was a tadpole-shaped soilmark with head to the SW, cut at the NE end by Romano-British ditch 405. The shallow 'tail' sloped downwards into the 'head', which was oval and had vertical or undercut sides all the way round (Fig. 6). The peaty clay on the bottom was overlain by sandy and gravel spill and clay lenses. This was overlain in turn by a thick deposit of gleyed clay and burnt grey limestones. Over this was another lens of gravelly peat, localised to the very middle of the pit. Immediately above it were several pieces of waterlogged wood, two of which were shaped objects (see Fig. 7 and Chapter 3: Wood), and on top of one of these were the remains of a large amorphous patch of leather (Fig. 7).

Extended around the S and E sides of the pit just above these objects was an adult human skeleton, head at the S end and facing westwards into the pit. The skeleton was articulated, but one arm and the lower right leg were absent. Both the objects and the burial were covered by a layer of black sticky clay which was slightly organic.

The top of this clay corresponded roughly with the bottom of the shallower part of the pit, and layers above this covered the entire floor area. These were dumps of dark silty loam blackened by charcoal and ash containing many burnt limestones, interspersed with backfill layers of gravel. The top of the pit was filled with a homogeneous silty loam, probably also backfill.

This pit is similar to other waterlogged features on the site, which have been interpreted as shallow wells with steps or a slope leading into them (see Chapter 2: Site A: pit 492, and Site B: wells, pits and other features within the eastern enclosure). The peat layers show that it was open for some time before the burial was inserted, and was probably dug for water. The limestone layer contained no charcoal or ash, and may therefore have been a deliberate deposit rather than simply rubbish from burning. The thin layer of organic material between this and the wooden objects suggests a slight interval between deposition of the burnt stone and the burial, during which the feature was no longer functioning as a well.

The position of the body indicates that it was placed in the pit, not simply thrown in, and the objects lay within the curve of the body. The organic layer directly overlying the objects might suggest that the pit was left open after the burial had been deposited, but the articulation of the body and the environmental evidence argue otherwise (see Chapter 4: Iron Age burial). The organic layer may represent an organic covering, but it was not sufficiently well-preserved to be identified.

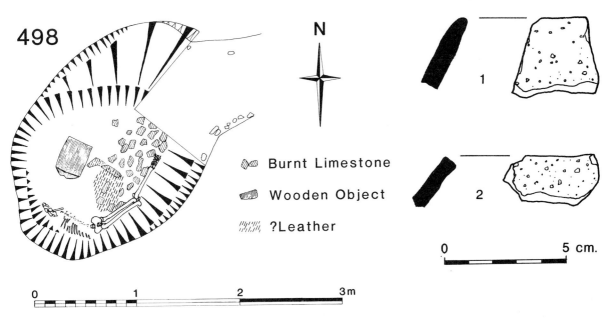

Figure 7 Plan of well 498 showing human burial and associated objects within it

Fig. 7a Detail of well 498 from the NW showing human burial and associated artifacts

A radiocarbon date of 3060 ± 60 bp was obtained from fragments of wood from one of the objects accompanying the burial. When calibrated this gives a date range of 1400 BC to 1250 BC (68% confidence; see Table 8 for further details).

Three small sherds of pottery were found in the pit, all from the upper backfill layers overlying the burial. These were:

Fig. 7 No. 1   Reduced fabric — abundant shelly limestone, ill-sorted, frequent grog inclusions.

Fig. 7 No. 2   Oxidised fabric — abundant flint, well-sorted. Very hard fired.

Body sherd   Reduced fabric — abundant grog, well-sorted, occasional calcareous inclusions.

Neither rim is chronologically diagnostic, but the flint and grog fabrics occur very rarely in the Iron Age pottery assemblage (see Chapter 3: The Iron Age pottery, Table 1), and both are more characteristic of Bronze Age assemblages from the Middle and Upper Thames (De Roche and Lambrick 1980, 45–59).

Environmental evidence for the date of well 498
The waterlogged plant and invertebrate assemblages from well 498 were similar to those from the Iron Age enclosure ditch (see Chapter 4: The charred plant remains and the waterlogged seeds, insects, molluscs and other biological evidence). Such assemblages could plausibly be of Middle Bronze Age date, but the presence of carbonised spelt wheat in the deposit suggests a date no earlier than Late Bronze Age. The only known occurrence of spelt in a pre-Iron Age context has hitherto been in Neolithic material from Hembury said to have been shown to Helbaek, but a recent re-examination has failed to identify spelt in these samples (Moffett et al. 1989, 247).

More significantly, the level of the top of organic preservation in the pit sediments was identical to that in the Iron Age enclosure ditch. There is evidence for a rise in the permanent water table on the floodplain of the Upper Thames Basin (including the Lower Windrush Valley) between the Late Bronze Age and the Middle Iron Age (Bowler and Robinson 1980; Robinson and Lambrick, 1984). This provides the strongest evidence for an Iron Age rather than Middle Bronze Age date for well 498.

The use of pits for burials in the Iron Age is now known to have been common in central southern Britain. Burials with accompanying blocks of stone or chalk are listed by Wilson (1981, 141 and Table 5), and both human and animal burials associated with dumps of burnt limestone are known from Gravelly Guy only 2–3 km away (G Lambrick pers. comm.). Conditions

allowing the preservation of wooden or leather artefacts are rare, and this burial demonstrates that there may have been more grave goods placed with these pit burials than the surviving evidence would usually suggest. One burial at Gravelly Guy was accompanied by a spindle whorl, but most contained no detectable artefacts; Gravelly Guy was well above the water table (Lambrick 1984, 108). The presence of carrion feeder beetles (Chapter 4: Iron Age burial) suggests the possibility that the body was exposed for some time before burial. The evidence for excarnation in the Iron Age is very slight, but the practice does appear to be represented at Danebury and Winklebury (Wilson 1981, 148–9). However, the small number of carrion beetles in well 498 makes it possible that they were not associated with the burial, and were derived from the surrounding settlement.

Enclosure 21–23 and 32 (Figs. 3, 8)
Just inside the main enclosure on the S side was another small enclosure framed by gullies 21, 22, 23 and 32, enclosing a subrectangular area. 21 was sectioned when the site was first stripped of ploughsoil (see Table 13 for dimensions), but further stripping before excavation proper began removed another 0.4 m of stratigraphy, and with it almost all of the feature. The sketch plan drawn after ploughsoil removal (see Fig. 3) suggests that there was a ditch running towards 23 from 21 (marked in dotted outline on the plan).

21 was cut through by Romano-British ditch 31. At the W end it petered out just short of ditch 22; the two may originally have been linked, but the bulbous end of 22 shows that there was a terminal here at one stage. 22 and 23 were broader and deeper ditches than 21. The enclosure here had two phases, one of which had an entrance on the S side, probably corresponding to the gap in the main enclosure ditch adjacent. The other phase ditch ran straight through this gap. As both cuts were shallow no relationship was established, but on the analogy of the sequence in the main enclosure ditch adjacent it is suggested that the entrance was primary (see section on the main enclosure ditch, above).

Towards the N end the later cut deepened and obliterated the earlier one, which was curving back inwards, and its terminal contained much occupation refuse. Just before the terminal was a sump. Close to the terminal the deeper cut was 0.90 m deep and the shallower 0.65 m; at the sump the ditch would have been 1.25–1.30 m deep. 23 cut a shallow gully 32 on the E side, which was running due N. This gully did not survive the further stripping, but possibly continued N to join a similar gully 125, running parallel to 21 (Figs. 3 and 8). 125 was cut away to the S by deep stripping. Just before it was obliterated it split into two, one arm turning SE, the other continuing southwards towards 32.

125 contained burnt limestone and other domestic refuse all the way along, but this was concentrated

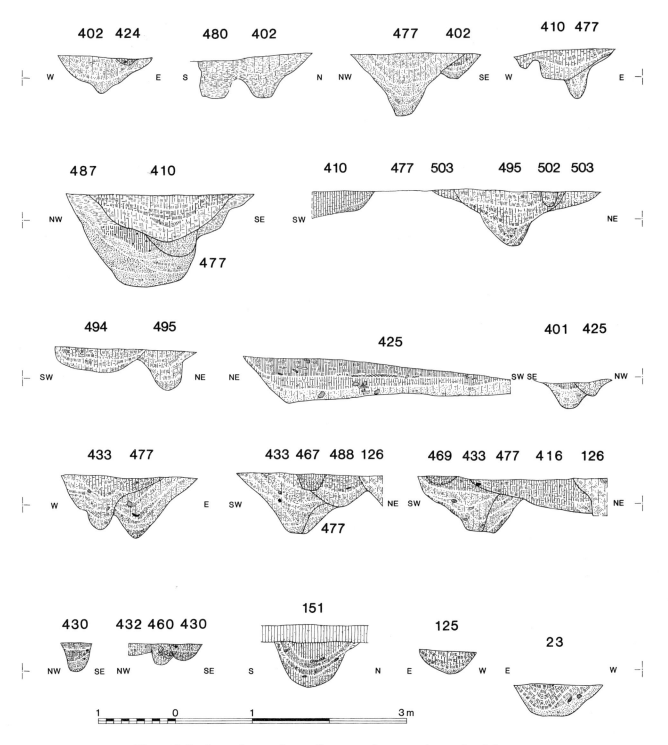

Figure 8 Sections of central roundhouse enclosure and associated features

towards the N end, where the fills were also darker. Debris thus increases with proximity to the central roundhouse, with which 125 was therefore probably contemporary.

Running SE from 23 and 22 were parallel soilmarks, 40 and 55. 55 was in general very shallow, but had a U-profiled sump just outside 23. Its fill was like that in the earlier cut of 23, with which it was probably contemporary; the junction was too shallow to establish a relationship. 55 ended opposite the first phase terminal of the main enclosure ditch, and may have been related to use of this (see Fig. 34).

Feature 40 was very shallow and had indistinct edges. Just S of it was a large subrectangular pit 41, which

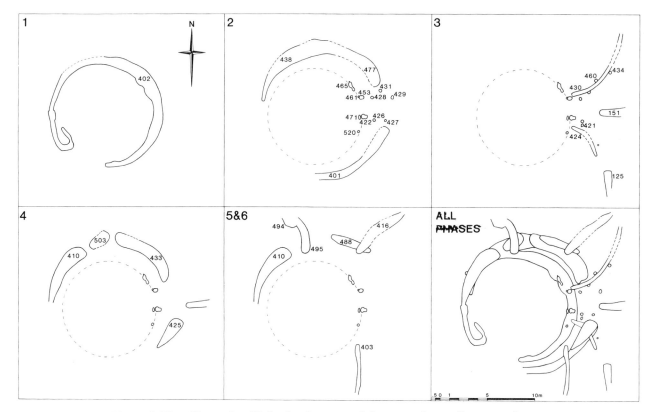

Figure 9 Plan illustrating likely development of the central roundhouse enclosure

was Romano-British, and some 3.0 m beyond its end was another smaller pit 43, also Romano-British (see Fig. 3 and Fig. 26 Nos. 1 and 2). No relationship could be established with 23 or 41, but 41 was parallel to 40 and so perhaps contemporary. Faint traces of a continuation were observed c 4.0 m W of 23.

There were no features within the area bounded by 21, 22, 23 and 125. Comparison with levels on the better preserved areas demonstrates that no postholes or shallow gullies would have survived the heavy stripping, and when first seen after removal of the ploughsoil the area was not sufficiently clean to distinguish these.

The central house enclosure (Figs. 4, 8, 9 and 9a)

Phase 1
N of enclosure 23 were the successive ditch cuts of a central penannular enclosure. The earliest of these, 402, surrounded an area c 10 m in diameter, and had a wide entrance gap on the S and SE. On the W side 402 was obliterated by later cuts of an enlarged circuit, 477 and 410. On the E and N it was filled with gleyed and very gravelly primary silting overlaid by thick and mottled homogeneous soils. These upper fills were probably either slipped upcast or deliberate backfilling. The fills at the E terminal and on the SW were truncated by post-medieval ditches.

There were no postholes in the southern half of this enclosed area, and those on the NE were all probably associated with a later phase, as four of them, 442, 453, 461 and 471, cut into the top of 402. A horse burial 464 in a shallow subrectangular pit lay inside mid-way between the crook end and the SE terminal of 402, but this is suspected to be Romano-British or later (see Chapter 4: Skeletons of late or uncertain date).

Phase 2
The central enclosure was enlarged and 402 was replaced by 401 on the E and 477 = 438 on the W, with a new entrance facing E directly onto the main enclosure entrance. The former entrance was maintained, but may have shifted from S to SW, as 438 ended several metres N of the crook end and the end of 401 was removed by the deep stripping (Fig. 4; Fig. 9).

The enlarged enclosure ditches were steeper-sided and deeper than 402 (Fig. 8 Section 477–402). Close to the terminal of 477 gravelly primary silts were followed by dark occupation-rich layers. Sherds of a large storage jar spread along the ditch show that rubbish was being dumped into it. The fills of 401 had mostly been removed by recut 425 at the terminal opposite 477, and 438 was truncated by 410 at its S end. Nevertheless, the finds suggest that more occupation debris was being deposited at the eastern entrance than at the southern

Figure 9a Central roundhouse viewed from the S in the process of excavation

one. On the W side the top of the ditch was infilled with gravel and silty clay; at the E terminal, however, 477 contained occupation debris right to the top.

On the W 438 cut into a large, deep, subrectangular pit 487 (Fig. 8). This pit was largely backfilled; the surface of the backfill was uneven, and was overlain by black fine silty loam and charcoal. This soil contained the only sizeable assemblage of carbonised seeds from the Iron Age occupation (see Chapter 4: The charred plant remains, and Fig. 31). The top of the pit was filled with a thick layer of clayey silt very like the surrounding subsoil. Unlike 498, there was no trace of waterlogging in 487, despite their similar depths; presumably 487 was not open for long, or was not allowed to become overgrown.

A radiocarbon date of 2210 ± 90 bp was obtained from bone in the lowest backfill of the pit. When calibrated this gives a date range from 420 BC to 170 BC (68% confidence; see Table 8 for further details). No

relationship with 402 was obtainable, as 438 and 410 had completely removed the early ditch.

Phase 3

Cutting into 402 on the E and ending within it were gullies 424 and 430. 424 was cut by 425 but appeared to cut 401, and ended opposite the end of gully 125. 430 was deeper and longer, cut by Romano-British ditches 126 and 162 and by a post-medieval boundary ditch, beyond which it did not reappear. 430 did not intersect with 477 and 433. Unlike 424, which only had one fill, 430's narrow vertical-sided slot was filled with several occupation-rich silts. 430 cut a posthole 460 on its W side, and both 460 and 430 cut a shallow gully 432 (Fig. 8). 432 did not reappear E of 430, and ended just short of 477 at the W end.

Gullies 42 and 430 perhaps represent a pair of gullies flanking the approach to the door of the house.

Phase 4

Recutting 477 and 401 were shorter ditches 433 and 425 respectively. Both were slightly shallower than their predecessors but had similar V-profiles, and both were deepest at the E entrance to the house. They were filled with dark silts containing much occupation debris; erosion from the sides shows that this was a gradual process (Fig. 8). 425 may have been removed by the deeper stripping at the S end. The top fill of 433 contained several iron objects (Fig. 28 Nos. 4 and 5), but this was seriously disturbed by features 457, 459, 467 and 469, which were probably animal burrows, (see Fig. 8 and Technical appendix Fig. A1), and these objects may have been intrusive.

433 was only c 7.5 m long. Some 3.0 m W of it was a shallower ditch 410 cutting along the top of 477=438 (Fig. 8). It ran on S of 438, but it is not clear whether 410 or 402 is represented by the crook-ended ditch. Fills were dark at the N end, lighter further S. Its top fill contained medieval as well as Iron Age pottery, and was probably disturbed by extensive animal burrowing beneath the medieval headland.

Between 433 and 410 was linear pit 503, also cut into 477. This was c 2.0 m long and equidistant from both 410 and 433 (Figs. 4 and 9).

Phases 5 and 6

Pit 503 was largely cut away by the terminal of a steep-sided ditch 495, which began just inside the edge of 402 and ran NW until obliterated by Romano-British ditches 126 and 162. 495 was darkest and contained most finds closest to the house at the SE terminal. Scattered along the ditch were fragments of a human skull and other bones of a skeleton (see Chapter 4: The human bones). Further human bones which could belong to the same individual were found in ditch 410 adjacent; this could represent a disturbed or disarticulated burial. Pottery joins between 410 and 495, together with the human bones, show that 495 and 410 were open at the same time (Fig. 9, Phase 5). 495 was cut on its W side by feature 494 (Fig. 8). This was broad and shallow at the SE, but deepened to the NW. It too was obliterated by Romano-British ditches 126 and 162. In the top of 495 was a series of shallow 'gullies' 493, 457, 502, etc., probably animal burrows.

S of 425 and cutting 401 was gully 403. At the N it stopped just inside 401 short of 402, and at the S it was removed entirely by the heavy stripping. Steep-sided and flat-bottomed, it contained a little Iron Age pottery in its dark silt fill, and may well have been Iron Age, respecting the roundhouse; possibly it was contemporary with 425, which appeared to end just short of it (see phase 4).

The central enclosure was recut again on the N side, 433 being cut by 488. Like 433 and 477, 488 was disturbed by later features 467 and 457, and its S edge was cut away by Romano-British ditch 126. It was also cut through by ditch 416.

Ditch 416 ran NE from just inside the outer edge of 433. Since it ended within the house enclosure ditch, although this had silted up, the central roundhouse may still have been standing.

Enclosure 416-413 (Fig. 4)

416 was obliterated by 126 and 162, but continued NE to meet ditch 413. At their intersection a shallow Romano-British pit 406 had removed 413 and almost all of 416, but N of 406, 416 was overlain by a shallow cut of the same depth as 413, so 413 probably cut 416. 416 ended only 2.0–3.0 m beyond this, but 413 continued N. Just N of 406 both 413 and 416 were cut by another shallow pit, feature 518. There was no dating evidence for this (but see Chapter 2: Later Romano-British occupation: other features inside the main enclosure).

413 formed the W, S and E sides of a U-shaped enclosure. There were two phases on the W and S, where a narrow and very steep-sided cut similar to 416 was overlaid by a shallower and slightly wider cut. The primary cut of 413 ended c 3.0 m short of the junction with 416, and was probably contemporary with it, with an entrance gap between them. Subsequently 413 was recut and blocked off this gap, running northwards along the line of 416. At the NE end 413 petered out just S of Romano-British ditch 405. Alongside 413 here and converging southwards towards it was gully 414, of which only a few metres survived. There were no finds from this, but it was perhaps another phase of this enclosure. At the W end 413 cut into and ended within ditch 436–442 (Fig. 10).

Within the area surrounded by 413 there was only one feature, posthole 435, which was undated.

Well 60 (Fig. 3)

SW of the central house through the gap between the crook end of 402 and ditch 21 was a large triangular pit 60. This survived 1.15 m deep, with near-vertical sides and a flat bottom. The bottom 0.4 m was waterlogged, and contained a succession of gleyed clay silts and three peat layers. On the interface between the second and third peats was a wooden plank c 0.5 m long; the peat fills also contained bones of a pike.

Above this 60 was backfilled with thick layers of clay and gravel. Both these fills and the peats below contained burnt limestones but no pottery. Wood from the plank has been radiocarbon-dated to 2160 ± 70 bp, which when calibrated gives a date range from 310 BC to 130 BC (68% confidence; see Table 8 for further details). Well 60 presumably supplied water for the central enclosure and for enclosure 23.

The trackway ditches 151 and 127 (Figs. 4, 8, 15)

Just outside the E entrance of the central house enclosure was ditch 151, which ran E towards the entrance to the main enclosure. For the four or five metres closest to the central house its fill was a succession of very dark silts containing much burnt limestone and charcoal. An oval spread of charcoal in the ditch top a few metres from the house appears to have been the site of a fire. Charcoal from this has been radiocarbon-dated to 2190 ± 70 bp, which when calibrated gives a date range of 350 BC to 160 BC (68% confidence; see Table 8 for further details). Further E the fill became progressively lighter and cleaner, consisting largely of eroded subsoil mixed with Iron Age topsoil. Here 151 was cut through by Romano-British ditches 161/175 and 162. At the E end it had a sump; the ditch bottom sloped all the way along towards this sump.

Parallel to 151 and c 4.0 m N of it was ditch 127. Steep-sided and flat-bottomed, and 0.15–0.20 m deeper than 151, it too sloped down from W to E and filled by gradual silting. It was cut away at both ends by Romano-British ditches 134 and 126–162 (Fig. 4), and was also cut by the post-medieval ditch and by a curving Romano-British gully 196 (Fig. 15). 127 contained few finds, but where not disturbed by later features these were Iron Age, and it is suggested that 127 was paired with 151, forming a ditched roadway leading from the main enclosure entrance up to the central house enclosure (see Chapter 5: The trackway in the interior, and Fig. 34). Both ditches stopped well short of the main enclosure ditch, allowing entrances to the northern and southern parts of the enclosure.

Between these two ditches were the shallow pits or hollows 129, 130 and 150 (Fig. 4). All three features contained dark spills and occupation debris. These pits were presumably earlier than the trackway 151–127.

S of 151 and between it and 125 was a short and shallow gully 87, filled with dark grey to black silty clay loam and burnt limestone. It contained only one sherd of pottery, which was Iron Age.

Enclosure 436–442 (Figs. 4, 10)

This formed another U-shaped enclosure open on the W side. It was cut through by the post-medieval ditch, and N and S of this was numbered 436 and 442 respectively. 436 was cut by ditch 413, which terminated within it. Finds were generally more prolific in 442, where there was also a spread of charcoal.

This enclosure ditch produced almost as much occupation material as did enclosure 496–512, and could have surrounded yet another separate house (see Chapter 5: The interior: preservation, and Table 14). However, its small size and the concentration of occupation debris towards the SW end, closest to 496–512, may indicate that the rubbish derived from there. There were no features inside the enclosure, but since this area was truncated by medieval ploughing only very deep postholes would have survived. There were several postholes W of 442 and just N of 513/517, numbers 505, 504, 516 and perhaps 506. These were roughly in line, but none produced any dating evidence. Other postholes may have been removed by the Romano-British ditches and by the post-medieval ditch.

N of 442 and W of posthole 516 was a dark reddish-brown layer with lighter orange mottles, 510, filling a very shallow and broad E-W hollow in the gravel (Fig. 15). This produced several large Iron Age sherds. On the W, 510 was cut away by Romano-British ditches 162–126.

Enclosure 124–163 (Figs. 4, 10)

In the SE quarter of the main enclosure a curving ditch 124–163 survived on the edge of the heavily stripped area. This had two cuts. Both cuts silted up, the fills of the later one being generally darker. These ditches contained much occupation debris.

Ditch 124 was cut through by Romano-British ditch 137 = 141, and E of that is numbered 163. Here the fills were lighter in colour and contained much less occupation debris, 163 was removed by deep stripping

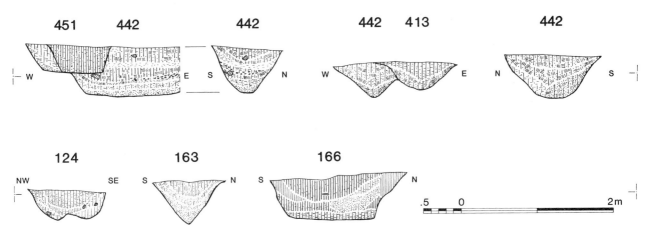

Figure 10 Sections of enclosures 442 and 124–163 and their associated features

further E. Iron Age pottery, including some decorated sherds, was found in ditch 137 = 141 where it cut through 124–163, and is probably attributable to this enclosure (Fig. 24 No. 18; Fig. 25 No. 31).

124–163 was probably part of another penannular enclosure; the concentration of occupation debris at the terminal suggests that this was the site of a house (see Table 14). S and E of 124 the only possibly Iron Age feature was gully 8, only surviving up to 0.20 m deep. This produced several sherds of an Iron Age vessel, but could have been associated with a Romano-British boundary ditch 31 adjacent. Its alignment (see Fig. 3) does not correspond with the likely position of a second terminal to a penannular enclosure.

There were no features in the area surrounded by 124–163, much of which had been heavily machined and cut through by later features.

Just N of 124 the terminal of Romano-British ditch 141 cut ditch 140, which ran off northwards. There was a scatter of Iron Age finds and of charcoal in its lower silty fills, but backfill layers in the ditch top contained Romano-British pottery. Despite this 140 is considered to have been Iron Age in origin. After a few metres 140 was cut away by 136, the large sub-rectangular terminal of ditch 4 (Fig. 14). Beyond 136 ditch 172 continued on the line of 140 to within 3.0 m of the main enclosure entrance, but stratigraphically appears to have been contemporary with ditch 4 (see Chapter 2: Ditch circuits). There were, however, signs of an earlier cut on the E side of 172, and this may have been a continuation of 140, as the pottery from 172 was wholly Iron Age. Just E of 140 was a sub-circular pit 166, which contained some charcoal but few finds (Fig. 10). The W edge of this pit was disturbed by animals.

The postholes
(Iron Age and Romano-British) (Fig. 11)
Postholes were scattered within and to the E of the central enclosure. Another smaller group occurred within and N of enclosure 496–513/517 (see section on enclosure 496–512, above, for description). Their distribution is partly an accident of survival, as the Iron Age ground surface N of the post-medieval ditch had been truncated by medieval and later ploughing (Fig. 4), and was 0.12–0.18 m lower than in the central strip under the headland. However, any deeper postholes in this area would have survived; postholes would only have been obliterated completely in the most northerly 20 m of the main enclosure. The southernmost 2.0–3.0 m of the area stripped under archaeological supervision (Fig. 4) had several post-medieval ditches running along it, effectively removing all but the deepest postholes. No postholes survived in the deeply stripped areas S and E of this.

Within the central strip there was a lower density of postholes W of the central enclosure than further E. Similarly, even deep postholes were absent N of this, probably indicating a genuine concentration in the central strip. Fig. 11 illustrates the postholes in this area, and differentiates between three basic types of fill. Burnt limestone and burnt clay occurred in all three, and the fills do not seem to correspond to any differences in size or location of the postholes. Very localised groups of postholes did have similar fills, suggesting that varying loads of spoil or localised patches on the contemporary ground surface were used in backfilling. Only one posthole, 89, contained Romano-British pottery, and only 460 and 431, which were cut by 430, were definitely Iron Age. 106, 86 and 439 also contained Iron Age pottery, but 106 was disturbed by animals.

No obvious structure is apparent and comparison of posthole depths is unhelpful. The common occurrence of two or more postholes close together suggests renewal.

It is possible that inside the central enclosure two large postholes 422 and 453, which lay slightly back from the entrance between 433 and 425, represent the door of a roundhouse inside it. 422 was a double posthole, 453 cut another posthole 461 on its W side. Double postholes like 422 are commonly found at the doorway of roundhouses, as at Danebury (Cunliffe 1984b, 72–80 and Figs. 4.20–26), and the narrow oval posthole 471 behind 422 is also characteristic. At Mingies Ditch, Hardwick, Oxon. (Allen et al. 1984, 94 and 99, Fig. 6.8) houses of stake wall and other lightly bedded construction were found in which the only apparently structural postholes were those at the door. In at least two of these houses, groups of postholes were found behind and to the right of the doorway, usually in pairs, and postholes 419, 420, 423, 439 and 440 may have performed a corresponding function here (Fig. 9 Phase 3). Postholes immediately E of 422 and 453 perhaps supported fences or a porch, the group along the line of gully 430 reflecting a boundary perpetuated by the gully, or a fence linking 477 to the end of ditch 127.

Most of the other postholes are contained within the area bounded by ditch 151 and 140, gullies 87 and 125 and the penannular gully 124, and were possibly therefore related to the use of this open area between the trackway and the three penannular enclosures in the Iron Age.

There were also small hollows 139 and 115 on the fringes of the posthole area, both of which are undated.

Enclosures adjoining
the main enclosure on the NW (Figs. 3, 4, 12)
Just outside the main enclosure on the NW was a series of enclosures contained between ditches 479 and 550. 550 began 5.0 m N of the main enclosure and ran NW

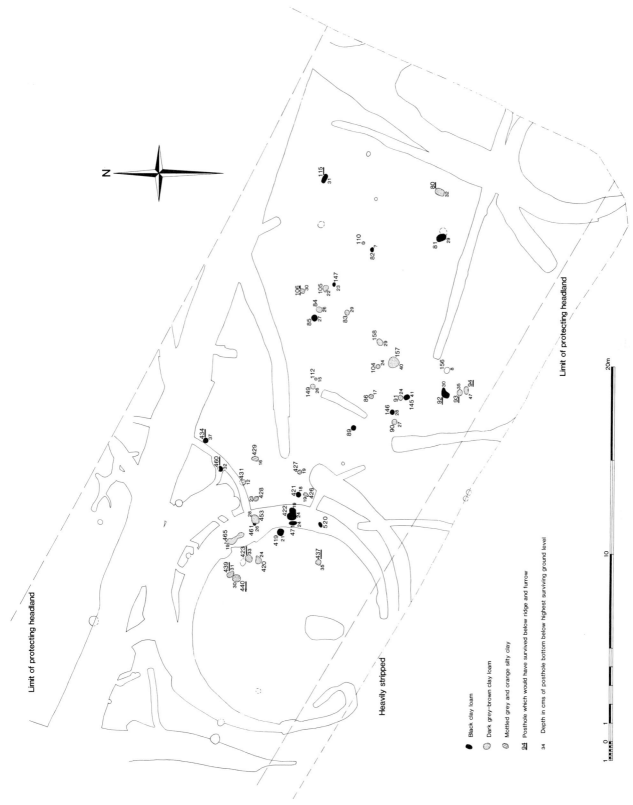

Figure 11 Plan of postholes protected by headland inside the main enclosure (both Iron Age and Romano-British)

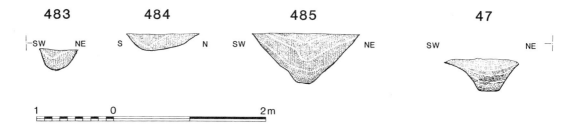

Figure 12 Sections of enclosure 485 etc. outside the main enclosure

roughly parallel to 479. The gap between 550 and ditch 1 probably represents an entrance.

Within this area ditches 485 and 490 formed a small enclosure abutting the main enclosure. 485 was deep and steep-sided. Originally it began only 2.0 m from the main enclosure ditch; when silted up it was recut to end 3.0–4.0 m away. The fills of the first phase were more gravelly and lighter in colour than those of the recut, but the sequence in both phases was similar (Fig. 12). The primary fill of the recut was darkened by occupation debris including charcoal and clay daub with wattle impressions, after which the ditch silted up. Just S of the corner in 485 a slightly shallower ditch 486 ran off W. This was contemporary with the recut of 485. Gully 490 also began just N of the main enclosure, and ended 4.0 m from 485. 490 was cut by one of the later Romano-British enclosure ditches, 450.

Just outside 490 and parallel to it ditch 553 curved eastwards and stopped just short of 550. A circular deposit of charcoal and black soil in its top was probably a temporary hearth, and has been radiocarbon dated to 2060 ± 80 bp. When calibrated this gives a date range of 200 BC to 0 AD (68% confidence; see Table 8 for further details). W of 553 and partly surrounded by it was curving ditch 554, forming another small enclosure attached to 550. 554 contained a very little coarse pottery, probably Iron Age.

486 was cut across by a narrow ditch 483 roughly parallel to 485. At its S end 483 stopped just short of ditch 484, which ran westwards from the S end of 485 and ended just short of 479. Although continuous with the earlier phase of 485, 484 was very shallow at the junction, so that their relationship was uncertain. No cut was visible in plan, however, and perhaps 484 was contemporary with both 485 and 479.

The little pottery that came from this group of ditches was Iron Age. 479 also appears to have been Iron Age,

being backfilled by the Romano-British period (Fig. 5). 550, however, survived into the 1st century AD, when another group of small enclosures was added to its N side (see Chapter 2: Features outside the main enclosure entrance).

The enclosure on the SW (Figs. 12, 13)
This was a sub-rectangular enclosure, two-thirds of which lay in the heavily stripped area, and showed as a series of separate short lengths of ditch with gaps of c 1.5 m in between, features 17, 58, 59, 319, etc. The southernmost third was better-preserved, and here the ditch lengths were either almost touching or were intercutting (Fig. 13). The enclosure may therefore have been continuously ditched, but was dug as a series of short, deep lengths with shallower joins. This may reflect the use of gang labour.

Most of these ditch lengths had peaty clay and gravel in the bottom, overlaid by a light gleyed clay, often with much gravel (Fig. 12, Feature 47). In the better-preserved pits this was overlain by clean oxidised clay silting, with ploughsoil in the very middle of the top. The few sherds of pottery from this enclosure were Iron Age.

At the SE corner a shallower ditch 320 ran off S from 319; the upper fills of 319 were continuous with those of 320. On the edge of the stripped area 320 intersected at right angles with ditch 321. This intersection was not investigated, but S of it the continuation of 320 was much narrower than to the N, and 321 E of the intersection was also much narrower than it was to the W. Most probably at one stage 320 turned westwards into 321.

320 was cut part of the way along by Romano-British ditch 303. On the basis of this relationship and of the few sherds of Iron Age pottery this group of features is thought to have been Iron Age.

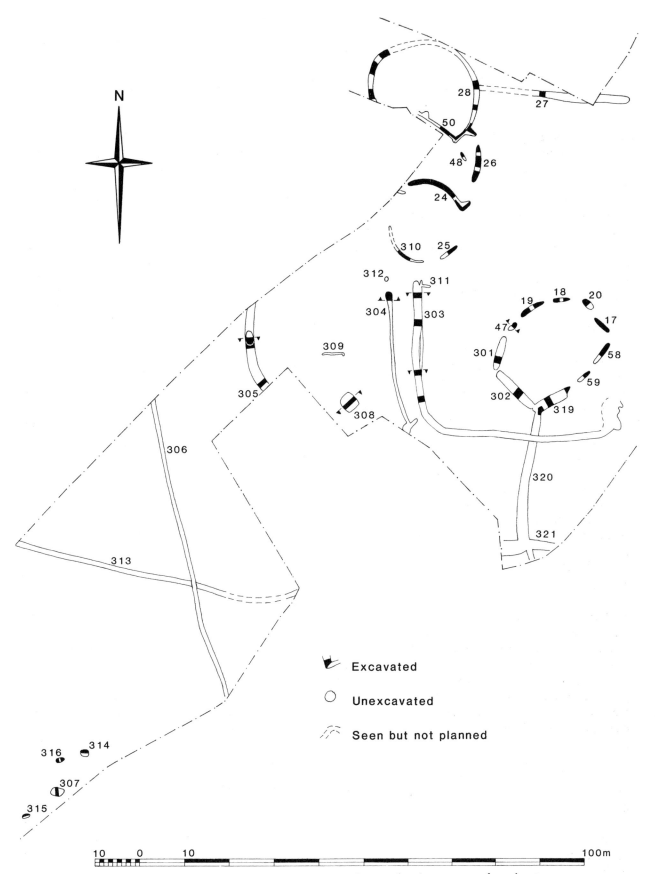

Figure 13 Plan of features W of the main enclosure showing excavated sections

Chapter 2

The excavation: Romano-British features

SITE A: INTRODUCTION

In this period the site had two main phases, the first characterised by a cellular cluster of enclosures based around the former Iron Age enclosure (Fig. 36 Stages 1–3), the second consisting of a trackway with sub-rectangular enclosures and fields alongside it (Fig. 36 Stages 4–7). The first phase began in the late 1st or early 2nd century AD, the second superseded it not later than the early 3rd century AD.

THE EARLY ROMANO-BRITISH OCCUPATION

Summary (Fig. 3)

The main enclosure ditch was reused, and in the interior was abutted on the NE by ditches probably forming a small enclosure, but was soon supplemented or replaced by concentric ditch circuits on the inside. There were no surviving structures in the interior, but ditches defined a small enclosure on the SE; the only other features were scattered pits, wells and postholes.

The E entrance was flanked on the outside by antenna ditches, with small rectangular pens attached to the northernmost. These abutted a large boundary ditch running off NW. W of the main enclosure was a large rectangular enclosure whose W side was formed by a group of intercommunicating sub-circular enclosures, probably also connected with stock management. S of these, behind the field boundary, was a trackway leading S.

The main enclosure ditch (Fig. 5)

The sequence of fills in the main enclosure ditch after peat deposition had ceased suggests a short period of heavy erosion followed by slow silting in stable conditions, after which the ditch was backfilled. Roman pottery came from all these stages, and clearly the ditch remained in use during the Romano-British occupation, and was not immediately replaced by other ditch circuits such as 134 or 411. This is also suggested by gully 132, which appears to respect 1 but is cut by 134 (Fig. 4).

In the clay and gravel immediately overlying peat there were aquatic molluscs, showing that this clay was originally alluvially deposited. It is possible that there was a short period of slight alluviation at the beginning of the Romano-British occupation, but there does not appear to have been any further alluviation until the end of the Roman period. The large proportion of gravel in this clay may indicate cleaning out of the ditch just prior to this, and the finds also imply activity on the site. If

alluviation occurred this was probably not during a period of abandonment. Mark Robinson believes (Chapter 4: The environment of Site B: conditions in the contexts investigated) that this alluvial clay is redeposited, probably coming from a stream channel nearby. It is difficult to see this as deliberate backfilling, in view of the silting above it, but it is possible that it had been incorporated into a bank inside or outside the enclosure, which was now collapsing into the ditch. If so the subsequent slow clean silting would imply that ditch and bank soon stabilised.

Ditch circuits 4, 134, 405 and 57 (Figs. 3, 4, 14, 15)

Inside 1 and running roughly parallel to it were ditches 4, 134, 411 and 57. 4 and 134 formed opposite sides of an entrance corresponding to that in the main enclosure ditch, with their terminals turned outwards towards it.

Ditch 4 was deep and V-profiled. For most of its length nothing but primary silting and gravel survived, but at the N end (Fig. 14) slower clean clay silting followed, with intermittent further erosion. This was overlaid by recent ploughsoil. Halfway along 4 was cut across by Romano-British ditches 7 and 9 (Fig. 14). To the S ditch 4 petered out opposite the corner of ditch 1; the sketch made before heavy stripping suggests that it continued parallel to the main enclosure ditch. To the N it ran into feature 136; at the junction there was a slight rise in the gravel bottom of 4, but fills were continuous (Fig. 14), and 136 is seen as the terminal of ditch 4, turned at right angles to it. Along the E side of 136, however, an earlier and shallower cut of 4 continued NW.

136 cut Iron Age ditch 140 (Figs. 4, 14). Continuing the line of 140 N from 136 was another ditch, which shelved up very gradually from the terminal. Despite slight differences in fill it was probably open together with 136, and was not a continuation of 140. This ditch ran alongside the earlier cut of ditch 4 and cut it.

N of the post-medieval ditch their continuation was numbered 172 (Fig. 14). There may have been an early cut on the E side where the primary silt was darker. The upper fills on this side were apparently cut through by a layer of almost pure gravel (Fig. 14 Section 172), which cannot have derived from the ditch side, so may represent a further recutting with upcast on the E side. Similar material then came in from the W side, but was followed by slow clean clay silting. The ditch was eventually backfilled with homogeneous clay loam and gravel.

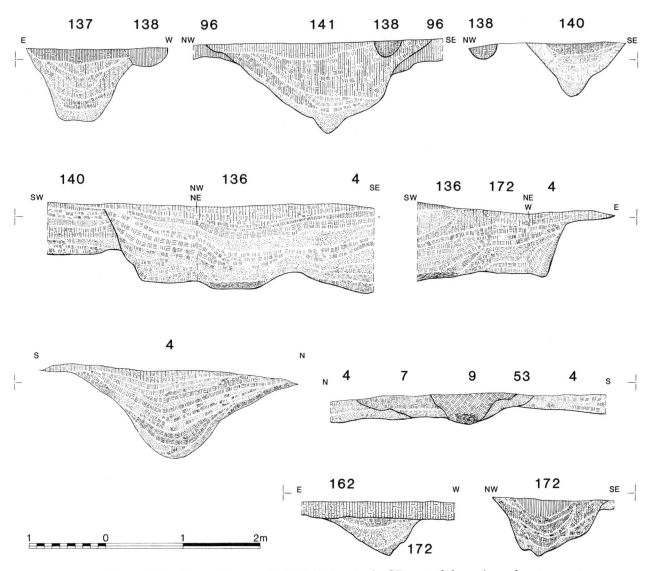

Figure 14 Sections of Romano-British ditches in the SE part of the main enclosure

A sherd of Romano-British pottery came from the clean clay silting well down in 136. Only three sherds were found in ditch 4, all of them Iron Age, but it seems likely that these were residual and that 4 was only dug in the Romano-British period, and corresponds to ditch 134 on the N side of the E entrance (see Fig. 36 and below). 172 also contained only Iron Age pottery. It is conceivable that ditches 4 and 136 ended where removed by the post-medieval ditch, but more likely 172 is a continuation of these. The Iron Age pottery may, however, indicate that Iron Age ditch 140 had originally continued this far, and possibly survives as the earliest cut in 172.

Starting 3.0 m S of 136 ditch 141 was deep and steep-sided, wide at the N end but narrowing as it ran S to a nearly vertical-sided slot called 137. 141 continued the line of ditch 140, whose S end it cut away completely. It was filled with a succession of very dark silty clay loams, interspersed with gravelly layers from erosion. Further S along 137 the fills were lighter and browner.

In the top was a black layer 170 of almost gravel-free clay loam, equivalent to the top fill in 136. This was soil accumulated from the surrounding ground surface before gully 138 was dug through the top of the ditch (Fig. 15). 141 seemed to cut E-W gully 96, but since the fill of 96 was also black this is not certain.

At the S edge of the better-preserved area 137 was turning eastwards. There was no relationship with the W-E ditch 31, and it is possible that 137 was ending. 141 and 137 probably formed a small enclosure with ditch 4, with an entrance between 141 and terminal 136.

Like 4, ditch 134 was of two phases. The earlier cut was visible at the E terminal and on the NW (Fig. 15). Its fills were more gravelly than those of the recut, but followed the same silting sequence, very gravelly gleyed clay silting overlaid by less gravelly and more loamy slower silting. In its top was generally a darker clay loam with some gravel. On the W the ditch was almost completely filled by dark grey to black clay loam silting and charcoal (Fig. 15 Section 405). The profile of both cuts varied considerably.

Close to the eastern terminal of 134 ditch 131 ran up to its edge as if respecting it. Away from 134 131 deepened, ending after c 8.0 m in a sump just short of ditch 127. Its fills were dark; the sump was filled with very gravelly gleyed clay silts.

N of 131 ditch 134 cut a shallow gully 132 (Fig. 15). This flat-bottomed gully had only one fill. Just before the S end 132 turned a 90 degree corner; at the other end 132 was obliterated by a medieval furrow, and did not reappear adjacent to or cutting into the main enclosure ditch. In line with the S terminal of 132 was a short length of similar gully 133 forming another corner; possibly these gullies marked a small enclosure. The only finds were one Romano-British and one intrusive medieval sherd.

Between 134 and the main enclosure ditch on the N and W was ditch 411. This ran parallel to the main enclosure at a distance of c 3.5 m except at its ends, where it turned away slightly. It was deep and steeply V-profiled; on the W two cuts were visible, the earlier and slightly deeper cut on the E side. This was filled with sandy clay loam and some gravel. The later cut had an unexceptional silting sequence. The top fill was generally a dark grey gravelly clay loam, but on the NW this was browner and more gravelly. Fills were darker on the W but were not as dark or loamy as those of 134 = 405 in the same area.

Both 134 and 411 were cut by N-S enclosure ditches 451, 450 and 415, and by the E-W ditches 126 and 162. Where 451 crossed 411 a small pit 470 cut into the side of 411 (Fig. 15). On the W 411 cut through Iron Age enclosure ditches 513 and 517 (Fig. 4) but ended not far S of that; 134 cut both 512 and 496 (Fig. 6) and continued SE to the edge of the heavily stripped area, where it had been completely removed.

S of 411 and continuing parallel to the main enclosure ditch was ditch 57 (Fig. 3). Only the very bottom survived, filled with grey clay and gravel. At the N and S ends were bulbous and slightly deeper terminals. SE of this only amorphous patches of dark gravelly soil were seen in the stripped surface.

The function and relative chronology of these ditches is not easy to determine. 4 and 134 were presumably contemporary, and may originally have formed a complete enclosure within the main one. 411 and 57 may simply have been dug to provide extra material for a bank inside the main enclosure ditch, but as with 4 and 134 the apparent absence of the ditch S of 57 may not be genuine. 134 has an unusual bend at the NE corner; this was not investigated, but perhaps indicates a change

between its original and final course. Possibly 134 originally only ran from the E entrance up to 411, with an entrance between them, but later a smaller circuit was required, and 134 was extended running inside 411 (see also Figs. 35 and 36).

Insufficient pottery was recovered from either ditch to establish their relative dates. Their differing fill on the W, however, suggests that 134 and 411 were not open at the same time, and the darker fill of 134 makes it likely that this is the later ditch. This dark fill reflects the general intensity of occupation, particularly burning, in the area, and its relative absence in 411 suggests that this activity had not developed when 411 was dug.

Inside the larger area enclosed by 4, 134 and 57 there was a scatter of Romano-British pits and gullies, but since these cannot be attributed securely to this phase, they will all be described after the second phase enclosure ditches. The postholes have already been dealt with in the Iron Age description.

Features outside the main enclosure entrance

Just S of antenna ditch 12 was ditch 30, which ran straight for c 20 m approximately parallel to 1. Bowl-profiled, it was silted with clay and gravel; at the N end there was a little peat in the bottom. One medieval and one post-medieval sherd were found in the top fill close to the intersection with post-medieval ditch 11; these may be intrusive.

E of 30 and S of 12 was ditch 39, which ran S, parallel to the main enclosure ditch and 12 m from it. At the N end it turned 90 degrees W for c 6.0 m towards 30. The ditch was steep-sided and V-profiled, and was filled with clay and gravel fills which were generally mixed, so was possibly backfilled.

Corresponding to 12 on the N side of the E entrance were ditches 13 and 61. Both began c 8.0 m from the main enclosure ditch opposite the point at which 12 began to curve away SE. 61 only survived to a depth of 0.25 m; 13, which seemed to cut it, was deeper and wider, with a wide bowl profile near the S terminal but steeper sides and a flatter bottom elsewhere. The ditch drained towards the S terminal, but it was towards the N end that peat was preserved in the bottom.

Peat was overlaid by gleyed and then oxidised clay, then eroded clay and gravel spills, and this was followed by further clean clay silting. The top 0.25 m of the ditch was backfilled with sandy clay and gravel.

Towards the N end 13 turned towards 1, and then split into two, one arm terminating just short of the main enclosure ditch. Fills in both arms were the same. Possibly 13 originally ended at the terminal, but was soon extended (see also Figs. 35 and 36).

N of this 13 was cut by a slightly deeper circular pit 266. Just beyond 266 a shallower ditch 262 ran off at right-angles. This was only 0.07 m deep where it intersected with 13, and no clear relationship was

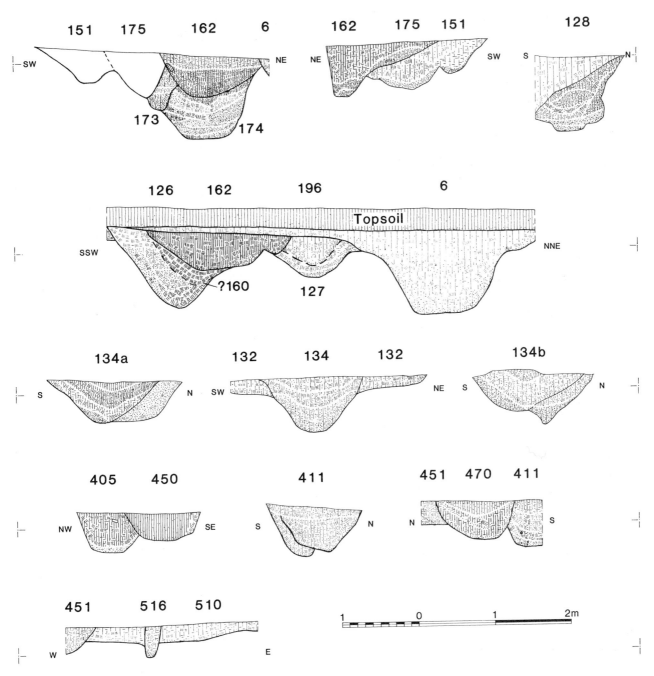

Figure 15 Sections of Romano-British ditches across the northern part of the main enclosure

obtained. At the N end 262 deepened to 0.47 m 13 was then cut by enclosure ditch 450, and beyond this ran into or was cut by another Romano-British enclosure ditch 415. 13 did not reappear beyond 415, but ditch 550 began c 1.0 m from 415 and continued the line of 13; probably 13 ended beneath either 450 or 415, with a narrow entrance between it and 550. 550 was the boundary respected by Iron Age ditches 553 and 554, but appears to have remained open into the early Romano-British period. This ditch silted up at first, but like 13 was finally backfilled with gravelly clay.

Ditch 260 continued from 262 after a gap of only 1.0 m, and at the end ran into ditch 15, which ran roughly parallel to 13. Fills in 15 and in 260 were identical, and very similar to those of 13. At either end of 15 and parallel to 260 were ditches 14 and 551, forming the fourth sides of small subrectangular enclosures. 551 was not dug into, but 14 had a profile and fills similar to those of 15 and 13. It was not, however, as deep, so there was no organic material in its bottom. There were entrances at both ends of 14 and between 551 and 550, but 551 was almost contiguous with 15. W of 551 and a little way N of 550 was an oval pit or hollow 552, which was not investigated.

No Iron Age pottery came from this enclosure group. Romano-British pottery was found in the upper layers of 13 and 15, together with a coin of Trajan. This dates the backfilling of the ditches to the 2nd century AD, as 13 and 260 were also cut across by 155, a later Romano-British boundary ditch (see Fig. 5 and section on trackway 5-29 and boundary 155, below). The pattern of silting in these ditches is like that in the main enclosure ditch, but it is unlikely that these shallower ditches had been open since the Iron Age. More probably they were added early in the Romano-British period onto the pre-existing boundary formed by the main enclosure and by ditch 550.

THE LATER ROMANO-BRITISH OCCUPATION

Summary (Figs. 3, 35)

The early Romano-British main enclosure went out of use: it was cut across the middle by parallel boundary ditches on a WNW alignment, which ended on the E against a N-S boundary ditch and trackway. The N-S boundary, however, lay along the line of the E side of the former enclosure, and seems to have utilised it as part of the boundary; no later ditch was dug along the stretch where the boundary coincided with the former enclosure ditch.

The N half of the early Romano-British enclosure continued in use, redefined by further ditches which closely followed the line of its N side. These formed a succession of subrectangular enclosures in the angle between the N-S and WNW ditches, and appear to have maintained the position of the original entrance. The interior of the enclosures contained only a few deep pits or unlined wells, except for a single burial which was not excavated. At one stage the S boundary of the enclosure appears to have been the more southerly of the WNW ditches; the area between these parallel boundaries was also divided by a cross ditch towards the E end.

Trackway 5–29 and boundary 155 (Figs. 4, 5, 14)

Running NNW from the eastern edge of the stripped area were parallel ditches 5 and 29, roughly 5.0 m apart. 5 ran across the main enclosure ditch and ended just inside it, adjacent to the E end of ditches 7 and 9. 29 ended outside the main enclosure, also in line with ditches 7 and 9. Both 5 and 29 were shallow and had a deeper sub-rectangular pit or sump towards the N end, 51 in ditch 5, 52 in 29 (Figs. 3 and 17). These two ditches probably represent a trackway. Both ditches were filled with gleyed clay and gravel, overlaid at the N end of 5 by black loam clay with peaty patches and some charcoal. Continuous with the N end of 5 was an oval pit

54 with similar black fill. There were no finds, but the pit and ditch were probably contemporary.

Continuing the line of 29 c 50 m to the NW was ditch 155. This began within the main enclosure ditch, whose top fills it cut (Fig. 5), and was traced for 85 m, cutting across ditches 261, 260 and a short gully 263. 263 contained no dating evidence; for 260 and 261 see section on features outside the main enclosure entrance, above. Several bulges on the E side of 155, and varying dark and light gleyed clay and gravel fills, may indicate that lengths were recut on occasions.

155 and 29 are probably parts of one boundary. For much of the gap between them the main enclosure ditch runs along the same line, and possibly it or a hedge alongside it was still extant as a boundary. (The upper fills of the main enclosure ditch had been machined away here before excavation began, so this could not be confirmed.)

W of this line a succession of enclosures occupied part of the earlier enclosed area. Ditches 7 and 9 only survived intermittently, and their western continuation was numbered 31. Both were filled with very dark silty loam clays, the fill characteristic of these later Romano-British ditches (Fig. 14). Both cut ditch 4 and their continuation 31 also cut the Iron Age enclosure ditch 21. On the sketch plan made when only ploughsoil had been stripped (see Chapter 1: Aims and strategy) 31 is drawn turning northwards into 57, but when excavated after further stripping it petered out before this. The fill of 31 was darker than that of 57, and 57 continued S of 31, but little of either survived so possibly 31 did run into 57, perhaps recutting a pre-existing ditch.

Parallel to 31 and 25 m N of it was a long boundary ditch recut on several occasions. Its cuts were numbered variously 126, 160, 162 and 175, the most northerly, 162, being the latest (Fig. 15). At the E end it did not appear in the deeply stripped area, and may have been machined away. However, although the more southerly cuts were destroyed at this point by the post-medieval ditch, 162 ended just within the better-preserved area, and the earlier cuts as well may have ended here. 162 stopped in line with ditch 5, perhaps indicating that the trackway between 5 and 29 continued alongside the main enclosure ditch.

Ditches 126, 162, etc. continued westwards over ditches 450, 405 and 411, crossed the main enclosure ditch and ran on out of the stripped area.

126–162 cut most of the features with which they intersected (Fig.4). 450 appeared to run into 162, and gully 459 seemed to cut 126, but stopped short of 162, with which it may have been contemporary. Further E gully 107 cut across 175 but was apparently cut by 162.

162 and 126 also cut through 196, a gully curving westwards as it ran N (Fig. 4). 196 was not recognised when the section across 126 and 127 was dug, but may well be visible within the cut of 127 (Fig. 15 Section

126–162–127), since Romano-British pottery was found here but not elsewhere in 127. 196 did not appear N of the post-medieval ditch, so presumably ended within it.

Beneath 160 = 175 at the intersection with Iron Age ditch 151 was an oval sump 173 whose gleyed clay and gravel fills extended beyond the pit top along the bottom of 160. 173 cut a pit immediately N of it, 174, which had a similar U-profile (Fig. 15) and was cut by ditch 162. 174 had a shallow tail on the W side; originally its profile may have been like that of 492 (see Fig. 16). Adjacent to 174 on the NW was another pit, 128, truncated by the post-medieval ditch. It was of identical depth to 174 (though the sides of 128 were slightly undercut) and both features had silted up (Fig. 15). 128 produced a small group of 2nd century AD pottery, and there were early Romano-British sherds from 174 as well. These features were well below the top of peat in the main enclosure ditch, but did not contain any organic material.

Shallow gullies or animal burrows (Fig. A1)

A number of other features lay alongside ditches 126–162. These were probably all due to animal burrowing beneath the medieval headland. A description and plan of these will be found in the Technical appendix.

Later Romano-British enclosures
adjoining ditch 126–162 (Figs. 3, 4, 15, 35, 36)

Several successive ditches formed the W and N sides of enclosures abutting 155 and 126–162 or 31. The earliest of these was 415, which ran along the N edge of the main enclosure ditch, ending at the E on the edge of ditch 260 and c 3.0 m short of 155. At the W end there were two returns, 451 and 507, 6.0 m apart. 451 was cut by both 126 and 162, whereas 507 stopped just short of 162, so that 451 should be earlier; however, 507 appeared to be cut by the corner of 451–415. Both phases of 415 cut the main enclosure ditch 1 and ditches 411 and 405, though the latest silt down the middle of 1 overlay both 451 and 507, showing that it was still an appreciable hollow when they were dug through. At the S end 451 disappeared at the edge of the heavily stripped area.

At the intersection with 411, 451 cut a pit on its E side, 470. Its primary fill was dark silt and occupation debris (including a horse skull), but it was later infilled.

Halfway along, 415 and the main enclosure ditch adjacent were cut through by a large elliptical pit 412. This was very similar to another pit on the same N-S axis, 478, cut into the main enclosure ditch just E of 451 (Fig. 16). Both were deepest at the N end, with near-vertical sides on N, E and W and a more sloping side on the S. The bottom 0.5 m in both cases was waterlogged. 478 was partially backfilled, 412 silted up, and as in 478 there was a more loamy lighter-coloured

clay at the top. Neither pit produced much rubbish, and that only from the upper slow silting. These pits were probably wells like 492 (see section on other features inside the main enclosure, below).

Where 415 diverged from the main enclosure ditch at the E end it cut another large pit 491 (Fig. 16). The bottom clay silts of 491 contained charcoal, and these were overlaid by peat; there must have been c 0.3 m of standing water in this feature. Above the peat the pit was filled with mixed backfill. 491 was apparently cut by ditch 450 and so should be Romano-British, but early medieval pottery was found low down in the backfill, and how this contamination occurred is not clear, as there were no obvious signs of animal burrowing. 491 was presumably another well or waterhole.

Another phase of enclosure ditch 450 cut 415 just E of 491 and 507 just W of 451. 450 ran into 162 at the southern end, and was the latest enclosure. Just N of 162 it cut a similar length of ditch 501, which ran SW between it and 162. 501 was possibly an earlier phase of this enclosure ditch. At the E end 450 stopped just short of 262 (Figs. 3 and 4). Whereas the surviving fills of 415, 507 and 451 were generally mid-grey, 450 had dark clay silt with less gravel, like 162. The fills of all these successive enclosure ditches were darker towards the S.

Running parallel to 31 and 126–162 approximately midway between them was gully 96. It was traced for 17 m but its E end was cut away in the heavily stripped area. The gully had only one fill, which contained both 2nd century Roman and medieval pottery. Irregular hollows or channels adjacent to 96 were probably due to animal burrowing, which would explain the intrusive medieval sherds. Unless the alignment of 96 with 31 and 126–162 is coincidental, this gully belongs to the later phase of Romano-British occupation. It was cut by gully 138, which had the characteristic dark fill of the later Romano-British ditches (Fig. 14), and which ended 2.0 m short of 126 and c 5.0 m short of 31. 96 was also apparently cut by ditch 141–137, but since the fills of both were black and very similar, this relationship is not certain. 141 and 137 are described in the section on ditch circuits 4, 134, 411 and 57, above.

Other features inside the main enclosure (Fig.16)

Pit 492

This tadpole-shaped soilmark S of 126-162 and W of 451, with head to the W, was a pit whose bottom descended in steps to a deep circular hole at the head end. The sides were vertical on W, S and N. The bottom was c 0.4 m below the level of peat in the main enclosure ditch, but no peat had been allowed to form in it. Gravel erosion was followed by clean and gravelly clay silting, and the upper half of the pit filled with very dark silty loam, presumably eroding from the

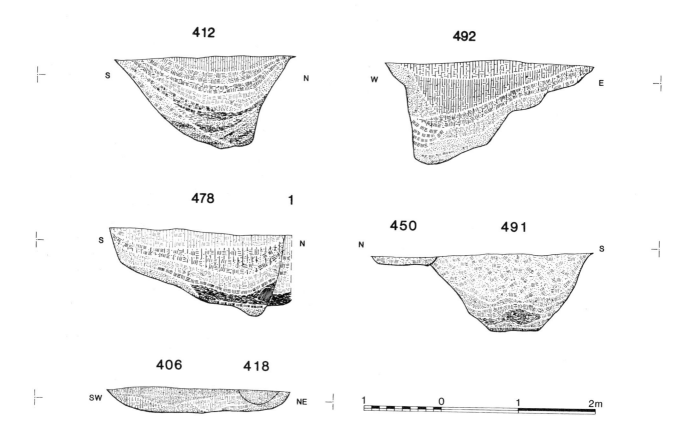

Figure 16 Sections of Romano-British 'wells' and other pits in the interior

surrounding topsoil. This was probably another well, and was the only such feature in which the characteristic 'tail' or shallower sloping side contained definite steps to facilitate access to the water.

Pits 406 and 518

Cut into 413 and 416 and N of 126-162 were two shallow, broad features. 406 was sub-rectangular with sloping sides and a flat bottom, filled with a series of clay and gravel silting layers containing occupation debris. Its NE corner was cut by a shallow oval hollow 418 (Fig. 16). 406 contained substantial parts of a samian 18–31 bowl, an intaglio of very simple type, usually dated to the 3rd century AD (Fig. 28 No. 1), and a fragment of a large and finely made glass beaker of the late 1st century AD. There were no finds in 418. Just SE of 406 was another smaller pit of similar depth, 518, with steep or near-vertical sides and an irregular bottom deeper on the S than the N. 518 was backfilled with a mixture of grey clean clay and dirty brown gravel and little clay. There was no pottery from this, but its similarity to 406 and its position adjacent suggests it may also have been Romano-British.

The area to the W of the main enclosure
(Figs. 13, 17)

Just outside the main enclosure ditch and aligned due W was ditch 27. This ditch ran into a D-shaped enclosure formed by ditches 28 and 50. By the time excavation began both 27 and the N side of 28 had been virtually obliterated by deep scraping, but both had been sketch planned when ploughsoil stripping first uncovered them. Both 28 and 50 were broad and flat-bottomed with steep sides, filled with peaty clay on the W and S, and a light gleyed gravelly clay on the N and E. Not all of the S side, feature 50, lay within the stripped area, and there may have been gaps on this side.

At the SE corner three phases were evident. Originally the E arm had ended at the SE corner, with a gap between it and the S side. Subsequently the southern ditch 50 was extended through this gap to the SE corner and up the E side, recutting 28. This was itself recut, the latest phase ending where the short arm projected E from the enclosure. The fill of the first phase was light-coloured clay and gravel, that of the last phase a dark peaty clay like that of ditch 50.

This enclosure was the northernmost of three. S of

28 on its E side were ditches 26 and 48. 26 formed one side of a second enclosure between 50 and a roughly parallel ditch 24; 48 was a steep-sided, much shorter feature, aligned upon the SE corner of the northern enclosure and upon the S end of 26. It had similar fills to 27.

Ditch 24, which divided the middle one of these three enclosures from the most southerly, had a bulbous terminal on the E, which extended northwards towards 26. 24 formed the N side of a circular enclosure with gullies 25 and 310.

There were wide gaps between 24 and 25 and between 25 and 310. At its W end 310 had been almost entirely scraped away, but there was clearly originally a gap between it and 24. From the middle of this gap another ditch ran off curving NW; this was probably the W side of the middle enclosure.

24 had one clay and gravel fill, but its bulbous eastern end was deeper, and was filled with black clayey peat and some gravel. The different fills may indicate that the E end was recut, possibly when the northern enclosure 28 was recut by 50.

Ditch 25 was of similar depth to 24, and had black peaty clay and burnt limestones at the N end, lighter clay with fewer limestones towards the S. 310 also contained burnt limestones.

S of 310 ditches 303 and 304 probably formed a trackway 4.0–5.0 m wide. 303 turned E after c 30 m parallel to 27, and ended in a confused soilmark opposite the E end of 27 and in line with the W side of the main enclosure (Fig. 13). It had several phases, the cuts moving progressively from E to W; very little was found in any of them. At the NW end 303 cut gully 311 at right angles and along its S side 303 cut across ditch 320, which was linked with Iron Age enclosure 17 etc. (see Chapter 1: The enclosure on the SW). Confused

soilmarks at the E end of 303 suggested that there may have been further ditches running NW or N.

Ditch 304 had two cuts of uncertain relationship (Fig. 17). It began further S than 303, opposite whose end was a small pit or posthole 312. At the S end 304 ran into a larger soilmark outside the corner of 303, apparently consisting of a short ditch running towards 303 and a second ditch continuing roughly S.

Only five sherds, all Iron Age, came from the enclosures, and none from 303 or 304. However, samian and other Roman sherds were found in 27, and from their layout 303 and 304 appear to belong with it. The Iron Age sherds presumably derive from activity in the vicinity of enclosure 17.

Some 30 m W of 304 and roughly parallel to it was a broad ditch 305. This contained a deeper sump with peat and gravel in the bottom overlaid by a thick layer of gravel (Fig. 17). Possibly 305 was a ditch with deeper pits along it, like ditch 202 on Site B (see Figs. 18 and 19). 305 contained a few sherds of Romano-British pottery.

Between 305 and 304 were pit 308 and a sinuous gully 309. 308 had 0.4 m of waterlogged peat in the bottom (Fig. 17). The pit then silted up, horizons of charcoal showing episodes of activity nearby. This pit produced a sherd of medieval 12th-century pottery from the upper silts (Fig. 27 No. 7), and may date from medieval use of the area as pasture before the appearance of ridge and furrow, but it is more likely that the pit is earlier, and this slow silting in the top accumulated as the organic fill at the pit bottom settled. 309 was very narrow and shallow, and contained no finds. It is reminiscent of gullies within Romano-British enclosures at Gravelly Guy, Stanton Harcourt (Lambrick 1985, Fig. 27).

W of 310 and 304 was another length of gully 317,

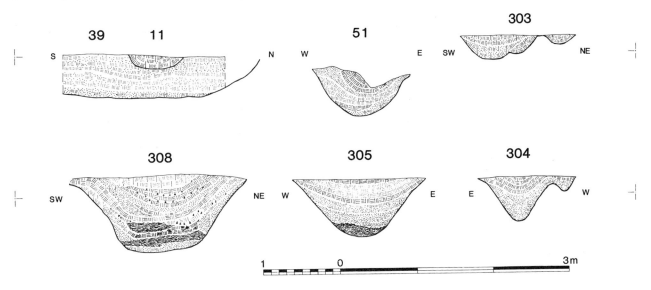

Figure 17 Sections of Romano-British ditches E and W of the main enclosure

possibly part of a fourth small enclosure. This was not planned or dug.

This series of small enclosures did not contain enough rubbish to suggest a domestic function, and with their multiple entrances are best seen as a series of paddocks for the handling and sorting of stock. The abundant burnt limestone, however, suggests that other activities were also carried out within them. 303 and 304 define a trackway leading off to the S, on either side of which were probably larger pasture fields, between 303, 27 and the main enclosure on the E, and between 304 and 305 on the W. Unfortunately only a short length of 305 was seen stripped.

SW of these features two intersecting ditches and a small group of shallow pits were salvaged (Fig. 13). 306 cut 313, but neither produced any dating evidence. 307 was a larger and deeper pit, whose lower half was filled with peat. It was probably another well similar to 60, 492, 412 etc. (see section on other features inside the main enclosure, above). None of these salvaged features produced any finds.

SITE B (Figs. 18 and 19)

Summary

This consisted of a strip of occupation bounded N and S by ditches on a WNW-ESE alignment. There were two phases of boundary ditches, the second pair being 10 m to the S of the first. In the first phase a smaller enclosure was attached to the N boundary; in the second phase the occupation zone was divided E from W by an intermittent ditch, the E part containing several wells and pits. W of this the N boundary ditch kinked and ran off NW, but was broken by an entrance where it crossed the former boundary line. Just inside this entrance, and attached to the S side of the boundary, was a group of small enclosures, one of them gated; the rest of the W part was empty, except for two rectangular hollows close to the S boundary. A probable house lay within the E part close to the S boundary, but it is not clear to which phase this belonged. The W part was cut across by a pair of long ditches on a NNW alignment, possibly forming a trackway.

Later, in the 11th or 12th century AD, a rectangular enclosure was dug S of the former occupation zone, and an intermittent boundary ran NNE across the E side of the Romano-British site just E of the line of wells.

The major ditched boundaries

Running E-W across the N end of the stripped area was ditch 36 (Fig. 18). The ditch filled by gradual silting; the pottery indicated a 2nd century date. Running off from 36 opposite the end of ditch 233 was ditch 609. No relationship was established, but it was probably a continuation of the boundary marked by 233. N of 36 the

only other feature was 37, which produced no finds. It was, however, similar to 235 (see below).

S of and roughly parallel to 36 were ditches 233 and 35. It was unclear which was earlier; for most of their depth they silted up together (Fig. 19). 35 was N of 233 on the E, but crossed and ran off to the S, probably becoming ditch 229, and forming the western side of an enclosure with ditches 228 and 209. 233 continued W across ditch 603, which produced late 1st/early 2nd-century pottery. The junction of 603 and 36 was not observed, but they were at right-angles, so were perhaps contemporary. What was probably a southerly continuation of 603, ditch 622, was seen but not planned or dug (Fig. 18).

Attached to the S side of 233 was an oval enclosure 601 with an entrance on the NW side. On either side of the entrance gap were stone-packed postholes (610–612), presumably for a gate. Along the E side of 601 was a darker oval of black soil, probably a later pit cut into the enclosure ditch. This oval enclosure also cut ditch 603.

Running W from 601 was a narrow gully 604 which formed a small rectangular annexe. At its N end it became indistinct, but may have continued up to feature 613, probably a well similar to 204 and 206 (see below). W of 604 were two narrow shallow gullies curving away to the W and SW, 614 and 615. Both were cut through by ditch 621, beyond which 614 disappeared; 615 continued and petered out only a few metres short of 606 (Fig. 18).

Ditch 35 split into several arms at the S end. Beyond these were short ditches 229 and 228, and continuing from these ditch 209. This had two cuts at the N end (Fig. 19). 209 intersected with ditches 222 and 223, both of which were very shallow; relationships were thus indistinct, but it appeared that 209 cut 223. 209 and 222 ended at their intersection in a slightly bulbous terminal. Continuing from 222 E of 209 were shorter ditches 221 a and b, one of which was cut across by 219. Probably all these separate lengths were originally part of one continuous boundary. Beyond 219 larger deeper ditches continued E, 203 S of 208. 223 also continued E of 209, and though it petered out, its line was continued by ditch 224.

Both 222 and 223 ran W out of the stripped area. During stripping another broad but very shallow ditch was observed between them, feature 620, which bottomed upon the surface of the gravel. It contained no finds.

Just N of 223 were two sub-rectangular soilmarks; 608 was shallow with sloping sides and a flattish bottom and 616 was not investigated. There were no finds from 608, but these features may have been Romano-British like 223 adjacent, perhaps similar to feature 406 on Site A.

Ditches 209 and 208 produced Romano-British pottery of late 1st- or 2nd-century date. 222, 221, 223

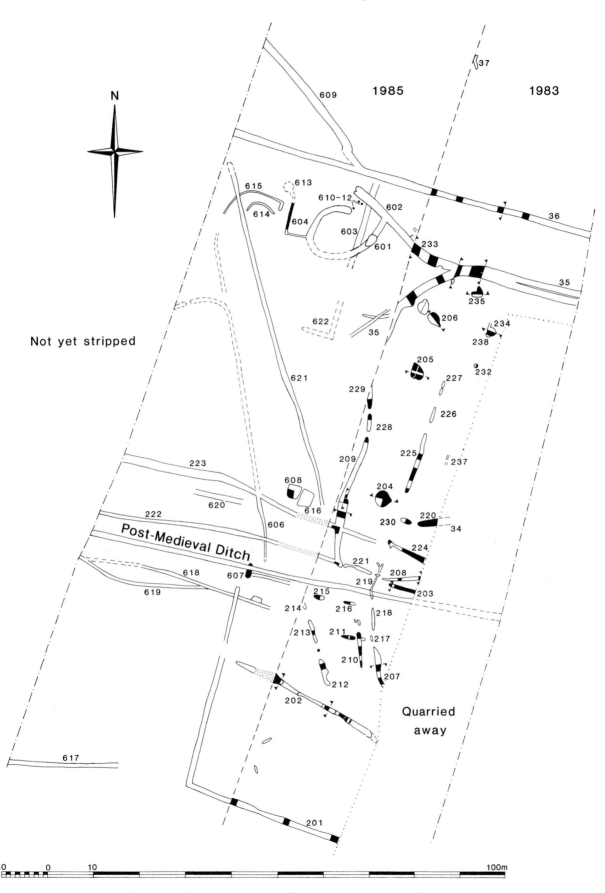

Figure 18 Plan of features in Site B showing excavated sections

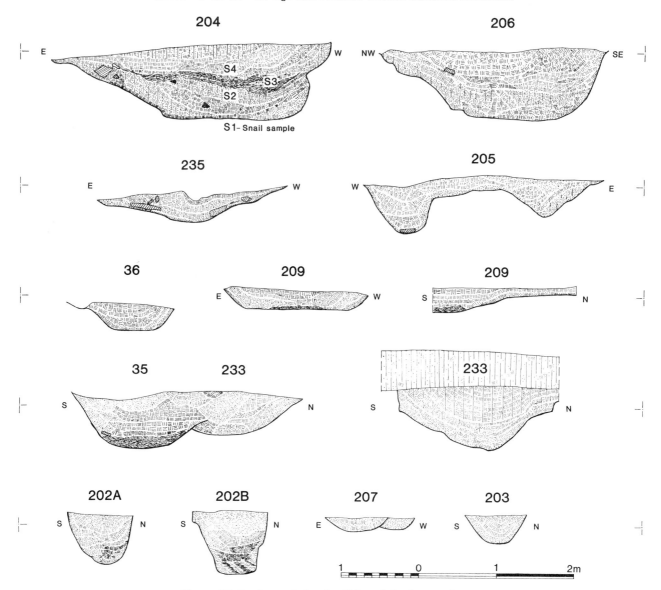

Figure 19 Sections of pits, 'wells' and ditches on Site B

and 224 were all undated, while 203 and a northern continuation of 219, ditch 225 (Fig. 18) contained medieval 11th- or 12th-century sherds as well as Romano-British pottery.

Ditches 35, 209 and 208 appear to delineate an enclosure within an E-W strip bounded by ditches 36 and 233 on the N and 222 and 223 on the S. Within this enclosure were several circular waterlogged features 204, 206 and 234, all probably wells, one or two smaller pits or postholes 232 and 238, an irregular hollow 205 and several lengths of gully, 230, 34 = 220 and 237.

Wells, pits and other features within the eastern enclosure

All the wells consisted of circular pits with vertical or near vertical sides and flat bottoms, with a small tail on the E side where the slope was less steep (Fig. 19). Unlike those on Site A, however, these tails were very short, and sloped quickly down to the pit bottom, without steps like those in 492. They cannot have provided a safe way down into the wells, so presumably had some other purpose than for access. A very large slab of gravel conglomerate was found in 204; such slabs were used as revetting in somewhat deeper wells excavated nearby at Eagle Farm, Standlake and Gravelly Guy, Stanton Harcourt, but may simply have been dumped in this instance (Allen 1986; Lambrick 1985).

Both 204 and 206 produced Romano-British pottery from fairly deep in their fills; 234 contained no finds. 234 appears to have cut a shallow pit 238, and running N from 234 was a narrow shallow gully, which soon petered out. There was another pit 232 c 7.0 m to the S. All these features are undated.

Close to 35 and 233 was a kidney-shaped feature, 235. This was very shallow and contained lumps of burnt limestone and burnt gravel conglomerate (Fig. 19). S of 206 was a larger triangular feature 205. This was generally shallow with an undulating bottom, but at the SW corner there was a deep pit with a slab of quern placed flat upon the bottom in the middle (Fig. 19). There was no post pipe to suggest that this feature had been a posthole, and no pottery to date it.

E of well 204 was a small oval pit 230 and a curving ditch, numbered 220 and 34. 230 was of similar proportions to 34 and was perhaps a continuation of it, but unlike 34 it did not contain any finds. 34 was broad with steeply sloping sides and a flattish bottom and was filled with stiff sticky clay over primary clay and gravel silting. There were large quantities of pottery in the ditch, and sherds of single vessels were scattered over several metres of ditch and from top to bottom, indicating that deposition had been rapid and that the clay had perhaps derived from a midden. The eastern part of 34 was salvaged before excavation proper began, and was not planned. It appeared to end where a band of concreted gravel ran N-S. E of this concreted area there were further patches of clay, but this area was badly damaged by machine stripping, and there were no finds from them.

No traces of any structure were seen, but the quantities of pottery suggest that a domestic building lay very close by. A short length of gully 237 which also contained Romano-British pottery was observed N of 34, but both ends had been removed by stripping.

The early medieval ditch system

Running N-S across the enclosure was an intermittent ditch numbered 225, 226 and 227. This was extremely shallow, and was probably originally one continuous feature. It lay directly in line with ditch 219, which was presumably also part of the same ditch. 225 produced both Romano-British and medieval pottery, like 203, and it is possible that the Roman sherds were residual, and that these ditches were part of a medieval enclosure system.

S of and parallel to 223 and 222 was another E-W ditch, 618, which split into two on the W, becoming 618 and 619. No finds were recovered from either, but they probably represent yet another boundary like 222 and 223. 618 was cut across by ditch 201, which appears to define the W and S sides of a large enclosure. In 201 the sequence of fills was ubiquitous; primary gravel spill and clay silting, then cleaner slow silting followed by a thick layer of homogeneous clay and gravel, probably backfill. A few sherds of Romano-British pottery were recovered, and in one section there were traces of a possible recut.

Ditch 202 seems to have been a boundary subdividing this enclosure, as it was aligned upon the only gap in the W side of 201. 202 consisted of a series of deep linear pits linked by much shallower lengths of flat-bottomed ditch. The pits were waterlogged (Fig. 19), and one of these contained part of a wooden bowl (Fig. 29). The shallow ditch exactly overlay the pits, and its clay fill dipped into their tops. It is not clear whether the ditch superseded a pit alignment, or was contemporary, the pits forming a series of sumps. The ditch fill did not cut horizontally across the pits, but the dip into the pits may have resulted from recent shrinkage of the peat layers beneath, rather than showing that the pits were still partly open when the ditch was dug. However, the exact correspondence of the pit and ditch widths suggests that both were contemporary. Ditch 305 at the S end of Site A was of similar character (Fig. 13 and Fig. 17).

Ditch 202 produced very little pottery, but this included both Romano-British and medieval sherds. Just beyond the N end of 201 was an oval pit, 607, cut through by the post-medieval field boundary ditch, and apparently at the terminal of a very slight E-W ditch (Fig. 18). The ditch was, however, so shallow that the relationship is uncertain. 607 had a black clayey fill containing much charcoal, burnt clay lumps and sherds of a medieval bowl (Fig. 27).

607 may have been an isolated pit, but the presence of medieval pottery in 203, 202 and 225 may indicate that there was a rectilinear ditch system of medieval date consisting of 201, 202, 607, 203, 219 and 225–7, overlying the Romano-British occupation. The character of the waterlogged remains from ditch 202 also supports a different date for these features (Chapter 4: The environment of Site B: disturbed ground).

Between 201 and 202 there was one possible man-made feature, a curving soilmark with silty clay fills but no finds. Between 202 and 203, however, were several lines of linear pits aligned S-E to N-W, and other pits aligned E-W. All of these were very shallow, and none produced any finds. 207 appeared to be a ditch rather than a pit, and had two cuts at its bulbous N end. It is possible that 212–4 was originally one ditch like 202, truncated so that only the deeper parts survived.

A possible trackway

Ditches 621 and 606 were on a similar alignment (Fig. 18). Both survived only as very shallow and narrow soilmarks. 606 was sketched but like 622 and several other features could not be plotted in the limited time available. It turned 90° to run SW shortly before the W edge of the site, and there was a gap for an entrance just W of this corner. 606 may have been linked to gully 615; if not, this pair of linear ditches may have formed a trackway running NNW. W and S of 606 were a number of irregular clay patches, some of which may have been features, but which had the characteristic very clean blue-grey or yellow-brown silty clay fills of natural hollows. These have not been planned.

Chapter 3

The finds

THE IRON AGE POTTERY *by T G Allen*

Summary

30.5 kg of pottery were found, comprising just over 1450 sherds; average sherd weight was 20.8 g. The assemblage is of a single period, later Middle Iron Age, and (like those from other valley settlements in the Thames Valley) consists largely of plain, coarse jars and bowls, with less than 3% decorated sherds. Almost all the forms and fabrics can be paralleled within a radius of 20 km, and suggest localised manufacture. However, several new decorative designs have come to light, and these have stylistic affinities with the southern fringes of the region in the area of Blewburton Hill.

The nature of the assemblage

Even in the best preserved areas the Iron Age ground surface was truncated, so that there was no vertical stratigraphy on the site, and due to the high water-table there were very few pits (see Chapter 1: Enclosure 496–512). Consequently, most of the pottery came from ditches, not from well-sealed contexts. Where ditches formed penannular small enclosures, one of which certainly, and others probably, surrounded houses, infilling with domestic refuse was continual and apparently rapid, providing assemblages that can be treated as single contemporary groups. However, the disturbance caused by later occupation and the differing states of preservation of these enclosures seriously hampers comparisons between them.

Much of the pottery comes from the successive ditches surrounding the central roundhouse, and from other ditches associated with it. This house lay in the best preserved area, and has provided the only substantial stratified sequence, all the forms from which are illustrated (Fig.s 20–23). Over 80% of each ditch associated with this roundhouse was emptied.

Many of the deeper features had clayey lower fills, and sherds from these had often lost their surfaces, while some fabrics tended to disintegrate upon excavation. This may have biased analysis of such aspects as surface treatment, but enough of the fabric survived to make fabric identification possible in all cases.

Methodology

The pottery was quantified by both sherd number and weight according to context, and the following attributes recorded upon Oxford Archaeological Unit forms:

Fabric
Form
Manufacture
Decoration
Surface Treatment
Firing
Function/Use

Fabric

Sherds were examined macroscopically and with the aid of x10 and x20 hand lenses. 17 fabrics were identified, full descriptions of which are given in the section on Iron Age pottery in the Technical appendix. These have been grouped into ten or more basic types, listed below.

List of main fabric groups

Group 1	Organic inclusions
Group 2	Sandy
Group 3	Coarse sand, and ferric and calcareous inclusions, flint, calcined bone etc.
Group 4	Ferrous inclusions
Group 5	Mixed sand and calcareous inclusions
Group 6	Calcareous
Group 7	Grog
Group 8	Flint
Group 9	Micaceous
Group 10	Shelly alluvium

Locally, Iron Age pottery fabrics tend to merge into one another, but most of the 10 types represent major differences in inclusions. Group 3 however, is separated on the basis of coarseness and its mixed inclusions. 3A fabrics are predominantly sandy, and when sandy fabrics are compared with others below 3A is counted together with Group 2. Group 3B was predominantly calcareous, but was too small to affect Group 6, and is omitted from calculations.

The nature of deposition of the pottery affects the reliability of estimating vessel numbers. For the central roundhouse complex in particular the absence of slow silting horizons in the ditch fills suggested that deposition was rapid, and sherds probably derived from inside the roundhouse soon after breakage. The results obtained from comparison of sherd count and estimated vessel numbers appear to support this; sherds are on average no

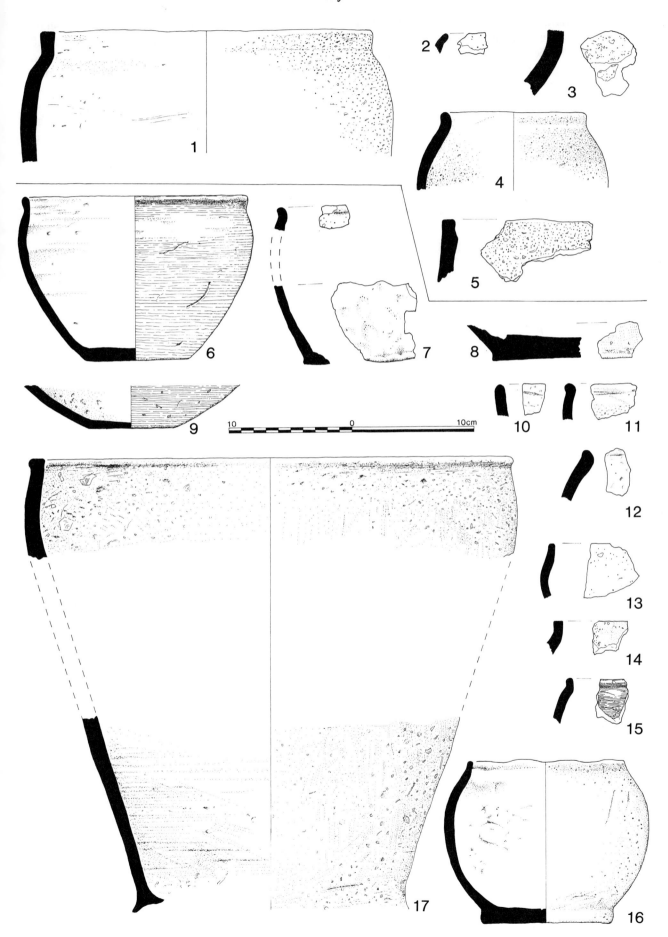

Figure 20 Iron Age pottery: central roundhouse enclosure phases 1 and 2

smaller than over the rest of the site, but over 20% of estimated vessels are represented by more than 5 sherds, and the ratio of sherds to estimated vessels for the house's enclosing ditches is 3:1, compared with 2:1 for the site as a whole.

Percentages of fabrics by weight, sherd count and estimated number of vessels are given in Table 1. The last of these categories was arrived at by counting as one sherds within single contexts which, though they did not join, appeared to belong to the same vessel. Although variations in fabric, form and firing were observed within a single pot, the range of fabrics present on this site and the variety of surface treatment, together with the evidence of texture and of surface accretions such as burnt residues, made it fairly easy to associate such sherds. This method of counting does attempt to counteract the bias of using sherd counts when numerous sherds of one vessel are present.

Table 1: Iron Age pottery: percentages of fabrics by weight, sherd count and estimated number of vessels

Fabric Group	Single Fabrics	Weight (%)		Sherd No.(%)		Estimated Vessel No.(%)	
		Single Fabrics	Fabric Groups	Single Fabrics	Fabric Groups	Single Fabrics	Fabric Groups
1	13	2.7	2.7	2	2	3.5	3.5
2	7	5.5		7.3		8.5	
	2	26.5	32.3	31	39.5	32.5	41.7
	16	-		-		-	
	8	0.3		1		0.3	
3a	2c	6.7		5		5	
	5	2	9	2	7.5	2	7.5
3b	21	0.3		0.5		0.5	
4	1	6.7	6.7	4	4	3.5	3.5
5	12	7		10		10.5	
	11	1	10	1.5	12.5	1.5	13
	10	2		1		1	
6	3a	17.5	35	12	26	11	22
	3b	17.5	14			11	
7	17	-	-	-	-	-	-
	19	-	-	-	-	-	-
8	20	0.3	0.3	0.5	0.5	0.5	0.5
9	14	0.5	0.5	1	1	1	1
10	9	1	1	1	1	2	2

Totals: Weight 30.200 kg Sherd No. 1446 Estimated vessels 702

Significant discrepancies between weight and sherd count occur in Fabric Groups 3, 4, 6 and 5. In Groups 3 and 6 this is due to large storage jars, confined to these fabrics, of which substantial proportions survived. Group 4 also tends to correspond to large vessels such as barrel jars; Group 5 shows the opposite trend. For the purposes of analysis estimated vessel and sherd counts rather than weight will be used; percentages and numerical proportions are generally calculated upon estimated vessel numbers, though sherd count is sometimes used, and is often given in brackets.

The largest fabric group was Group 2, sandy, followed by Group 6, calcareous. The mixed sand and calcareous Group 5, and the coarse sand and mixed inclusions Group 3 also formed significant proportions. Apart from Group 4, no other fabric occurred in more than a handful of instances.

Assemblages from the stratigraphic sequence were compared to see if there were any changes in fabric proportions over time.

Five phases were distinguished, corresponding to five of the six stratigraphic phases illustrated on Fig. 9.

Phase 1: 402, the first penannular enclosing ditch.
Phase 2: 477 and 401, the two arcs of the enlarged penannular ditch.
Phase 4: 433 and 425, the opposing terminals of a recut of 477.
Phase 5: 410, another recut of 477, 495, a ditch adjacent which also cut 477, and 488, a pit cutting 433, 495 cut not only 477 but also a small pit in its top, and so is probably later than 433. A number of vessels were common to both 495 and 410, so both of these features are phased later than 433 and 425, with 488.
Phase 6: Ditches 416 and 413, 416 cutting 488 and 413 being a recut of 416.

The trend throughout the region is for the proportion of sandy wares to increase with time (Lambrick 1984, 174). From their high Group 2 and 3A percentages enclosures 23 and 124 were perhaps still in use in Phases 4 and 5, while 496/512 may have gone out of use earlier. However, other factors such as preferences for different fabrics in different households may account for this.

In 23 the percentage for Group 4 fabric was unusually high, and there was a complete absence of Group 5 fabrics. In the central roundhouse sequence where Group 5 fabrics had the highest percentage in Phase 3, Group 4 comprised only 2.5%; possibly Groups 4 and 5 were alternatives used for vessels with the same functions.

The chronological variation of these fabric groups comprising more than 10% of the assemblages is illustrated below in Table 2. For a detailed breakdown of all fabrics see Technical appendix Table T1.

There appears to be a gradual increase in the proportions of Group 2 and 3A, that is, sandy fabrics. The drop in the proportion of Group 6 calcareous fabrics after Phase 1 is more difficult to assess, as the Phase 1 and 2 assemblages are so small, but Group 3 coarse sandy fabrics were absent from Phase 1, and the increase of Group 5 fabrics in Phases 2 and 4 may also indicate a falling off in Group 6 which Groups 3 and 5 made good. There is some evidence to suggest that Group 5 and 3 fabrics were preferred alternatives to Group 6 for certain types of vessel (see section on form and function, below).

Table 2: Iron Age pottery: proportions of fabric groups in successive phases of the central roundhouse enclosure (expressed as percentages of the total assemblage of each phase)

	Phase 1	Phase 2	Phase 4	Phase 5	Phase 6	
Context	402 401	477, 438 (+151) (& 430)	433, 425 & 488	410, 495	413/416	
Fabric groups 2 & 3a: sandy	28	30 (34)	38 (53)	51	61	
Fabric group 5: mixed sand & calcareous	7	18 (10)	24 (20)	15	-	
Fabric group 6: calcareous	43	24 (24)	26 (22)	19	22	
Estimated vessel no.	14	19 (29)	81 (133)	42	23	Total 178 (241)
Sherd count	58	106 (137)	276 (382)	91	38	Total 569 (706)

Other possibly significant indicators are the appearance of Group 7 and 8 sherds at the end of the sequence. Both grog and flint tempered fabrics are characteristic of Late Iron Age and Early Romano-British sites in the area, but not generally of Middle Iron Age assemblages. However, only one or two instances of these fabrics were present.

Proportions of major fabrics were also compared for assemblages from other enclosure groups (Table 3). However, as these assemblages represent at least two phases of ditch in every case, they cannot be placed securely within the stratigraphic sequence.

Table 3: Iron Age pottery: percentage of fabric groups in enclosures other than the central roundhouse

	Context				
	23	124	436/442	496-512/513	125
Fabric Groups 2 and 3A	66.5	64	54	42.5	56
Fabric Group 5	-	4	15	20	7.5
Fabric Group 6	22	28	18	28.5	23
(Fabric Group 4)	17	-	3	-	4

Sources of the fabrics

Most of the inclusions in the pottery were available close to the site. Fabric 9, which contained aquatic molluscs, probably came from alluvium (or channel silts) on the Windrush floodplain, and oolitic and shelly limestone particles were available in the gravels. Much of the sand probably also came from pockets in the gravel or from clays on the river's edge. The black shiny grains of Fabric 7 (part of Fabric Group 2) were probably limonite, which could have been obtained from pans precipitated in the gravel (De Roche in Parrington 1978, 69). Some of the quartz inclusions, however, seem to have come from the Upper and Lower Greensand, the nearest sources of which are 10 km to the S and 5 km to

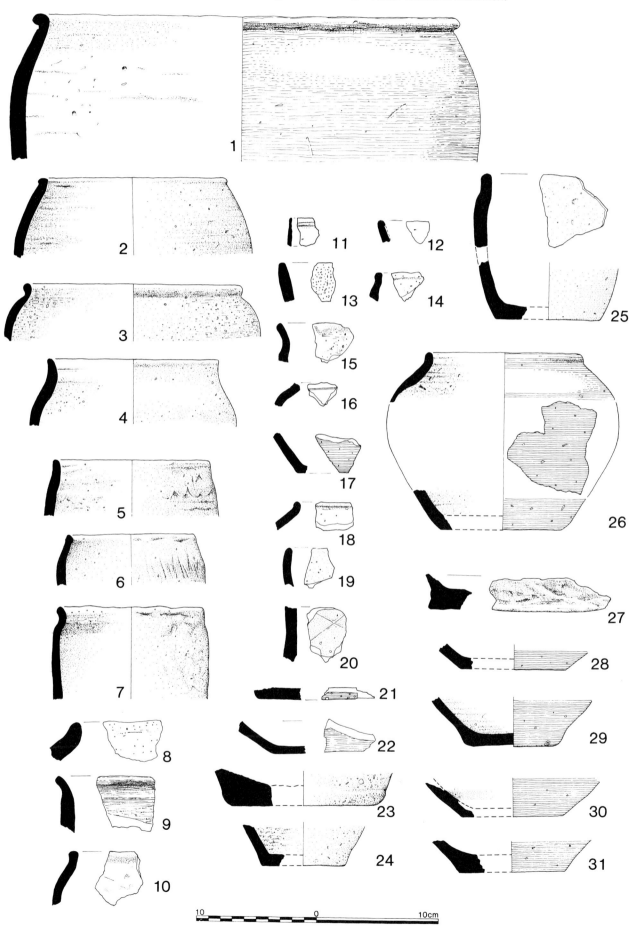

Figure 21 Iron Age pottery: central roundhouse enclosure phases 2–4

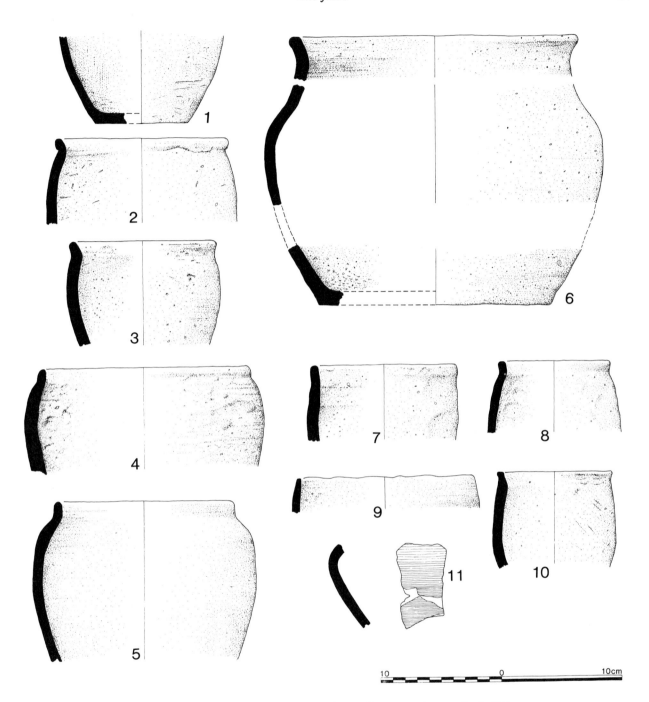

Figure 22 Iron Age pottery: central roundhouse enclosure ditch 425

the E respectively (see Fig. 1). Contact with this area is also suggested by some of the decorative motifs (see section on decoration, below).

Manufacture and surface treatment

All pots were hand-made; some were clearly pinched, for example Fig. 21 No. 7 and Fig. 22 No. 8, others coil built e.g. Fig. 23 No. 11 and Fig. 23 No. 24. 21% of the vessels were burnished, and another 14% smoothed inside and out. Table 4 shows proportions of burnished

vessels in comparison to proportions of the whole assemblage by fabric groups. A breakdown of burnishing giving numbers and percentages for all fabrics is given in Table T2 in the Technical appendix.

Vessels of Group 2, the finer sandy fabrics, and to a lesser extent Groups 1 and 10, the organic and alluvium fabrics, were clearly burnished much more often than vessels in other fabrics. A correlation between burnishing and certain vessel types, particularly globular bowls/jars, is evident (see also Forms). The proportion of burnished

Table 4: Iron Age pottery: percentage of burnished sherds by fabric groups

Fabrics	% of Burnished Vessels	% of Burnished & Smoothed Vessels	% of Whole Assemblage	
Group 1	5.3	4	3.5	(2)
2	68	60	41.7	(39.3)
3a	3.3	3	7.5	(7.5)
4	2	2.5	3.5	(4)
5	8.7	8	13	(12.5)
6	9	16.5	22	(26)
7	-	0.5	-	-
8	0.7	0.5	0.5	(0.5)
9	-	0.5	1	(1)
10	3.3	2.5	2	(1)

sherds in major context groups was also examined, but showed no clear differences; for details see Technical appendix Table T3.

Smoothing is not always a deliberate surface treatment; sometimes it results purely from pinching up the pots. It is, for instance, noticeable that there were very few instances of burnishing or external smoothing on vessels of fabric 3A, shelly limestone, but as many examples of internal smoothing as in any other fabric. Apart from this one fabric, however, instances of internal smoothing do not significantly alter the ratios of fabrics to burnishing and smoothing.

Exterior surfaces sometimes had a rough, vertically striated finish. This was due to the inclusions in the clay body being pulled over the surface in pinching up the sides, and was probably not a deliberate effect, though leaving the pot surface rough to improve grip is common in contemporary ethnic tradition (Blandino 1984, 66). There were no instances of deliberate 'wiping' with grass or other materials. One or two instances of knife trimming were noted.

Firing
Most pots varied in colour, indicating both oxidising and reducing conditions suggestive of open bonfire firing. For this reason colour was not recorded, except for burnished and/or decorated vessels, which from preliminary inspection seemed more uniform in colour and firing conditions. Previous reports have identified categories of

well-made vessels in which firing was apparently well-controlled (Harding 1972, 106–7; De Roche in Parrington 1978, 57 and 61). Of the burnished vessels in this assemblage only 25% were clearly the product of uncontrolled firing conditions, the majority being evenly reduced or oxidised. Both clamped firings and open fires that were smothered in the last stages are implied by the reduced surfaces, and the highly oxidised pots probably imply better draw and higher temperatures than is possible in open bonfires.

In line with findings at Mount Farm (Lambrick forthcoming), there is a high correlation between globular bowls and these deliberately reduced (or oxidised) vessels. 66% of vessels firmly identified as globular bowls were deliberately reduced black or dark brown, a percentage considerably higher than that for burnished vessels as a whole.

Form and function
There were 163 different rims and 75 bases, only 17 of which matched. The Middle Iron Age of the Upper Thames is characterised by a small range of vessel types with slack profiles and generally simple rim forms, so that it is almost impossible to separate fragmented assemblages into vessel form types. The rims and bases have been divided into two broad categories, jars/pots and bowls. A jar is defined as a vessel whose height is greater than its rim diameter, a bowl one whose height is less than this. Percentages of each for both rims and

bases are given below in Table 5. Actual numbers are given in brackets.

Table 5: Iron Age Pottery: rims and bases divided into jars/pots, bowls and uncertain form

	Jars/Pots		Bowls		Uncertain		Total
	%	No.	%	No.	%	No.	
Rims	44	(72)	18.5	(30)	37.5	(61)	(163)
Bases	52	(39)	36	(27)	12	(9)	(75)

Bases are more reliable than rims in estimating bowl form, as bowls are readily distinguishable by the obtuse angle of their bases. It is likely that a high proportion of the uncertain rims belong to bowls, which probably made up between 23% and 30% of the whole.

Almost all the sherds from the central roundhouse sequence which could be drawn and selected groups from other features are illustrated (Fig.s 20–25). Bowls include not only globular bowls (Fig. 20 No. 6, Fig. 23 Nos. 3, 4 and 18, Fig. 24 No. 1, Fig. 25 Nos. 15, 16 and 23) but also a group whose diameter is widest at the rim, for instance Fig. 24 No. 21 and Fig. 25 No. 17, and another with fairly straight sides rather like flower pots, e.g. Fig. 25 No. 19. The globular bowls include several with quite closed mouths and sharply upturned rims, Fig. 21 No. 26 and Fig. 25 No. 16, and two almost spherical profiles, Fig. 24 No. 11 and Fig. 25 No. 1. The last example well illustrates the problem of definition, as it is very close to one of Harding's barrel jars (Harding 1972, Plate 60 D). Fig. 20 No. 16 is unusual in having a distinct foot. In shape it lies on the border between bowl and jar. There were six or seven similar simple rims with slightly concave necks, and this form may have been quite common.

The term jar embraces an even wider variety of vessels. Barrel jars with incurving rims were common; in some cases the inturn was very pronounced (Fig. 23 Nos. 5 and 17). Globular jars were also present (Fig. 20 Nos. 4 and 7, Fig. 21 No. 2); a common variant had a high shoulder and slightly closed mouth (Fig. 22 Nos. 4 and 5, Fig. 21 Nos. 6 and 10, Fig. 24 No. 12), which also occurred in the storage jars (Fig. 20 No. 3 and Fig. 21 No. 1). Much more closed mouths were also represented (Fig. 21 Nos. 8, 18 and 26 and Fig. 24 No. 22). Fig. 24 No.2 was the most extreme example of this. It is uncertain whether this represents something akin to the bead rim jars of the latest Iron Age and early Romano-British period, or is an extreme development of the globular bowl. Fig. 22 No.6 seems to be a proto-necked jar.

Straight or slightly bow-sided vessels with simple rims, usually only roughly finished, were very common.

Most of these were small, like the group from 425, Fig. 22 Nos. 2, 3, 7, 8 and 10, and Fig. 23 No. 16 and Fig. 24 No. 4. These 'pots' seemed to form a discrete category, and were separated out. The following criteria were applied; the vessel profile had to be cylindrical or nearly so, without sharp shoulders or distinctive rim-types, and bases also with vertical or near-vertical sides. Some short slightly everted or inverted rims were included (e.g. Fig. 21 Nos. 6 and 9) and one or two vessels with slightly bulging sides (e.g. Fig. 25 No. 29). Of a total of 220 separate vessels represented by rim and base sherds, 55 appear to belong to this 'pot' form. Table 6 shows that in comparison to overall fabric proportions for the whole site Fabric Group 5 represents a very high proportion of this type of vessel, and Group 6 slightly more so than overall.

Proportions of bowls and jars/pots were compared by fabric and fabric groups (Technical appendix, Table T4). Most bowls occurred in fabric 2, and fabric 3 was used largely for jars. Group 2 fabrics were also popular for other types of vessel than bowls, but sandy fabrics were clearly deliberately chosen when making bowls. This accords with the evidence for greater burnishing of Group 2 vessels; over 40% of the externally burnished vessels and just under 40% of all burnished vessels were attributable to bowl forms.

Burnt residues and limescale

Instances of limescale were very few, but 102 vessels had burnt residues inside and 21 more had burnt residues outside, altogether 14% of the whole assemblage. A breakdown of the fabrics in which this occurred is shown in Table 7.

Compared with overall fabric proportions for the site Group 6 vessels have a very high incidence of burnt residues, and Group 5 vessels as well. The proportion of 'pots' that had burnt residues on them was 65%, in comparison to 26.5% of all vessels represented by rims and bases, suggesting a strong correlation between this form and cooking.

The very high percentage of Group 6 vessels with burnt residues is not fully accounted for by the 'pots' in this fabric group. There were also burnt residues on all of the closed-necked jars like Fig. 20 No. 4 and Fig. 24 No. 22 and on bowls like Fig. 20 No.16, though similar rim forms in Group 2 and 3 fabrics were not so affected. 'Storage' jars were predominantly made in Group 6 fabrics, and several of these were burnt on the inside. Some potters have suggested that as an 'opener' limestone provides a stronger bond and is better able to resist thermal shock than sand, which may explain the preference for cooking vessels in these fabrics, but alternatively these fabrics may have been those most readily available locally, and hence used for the utilitarian vessels.

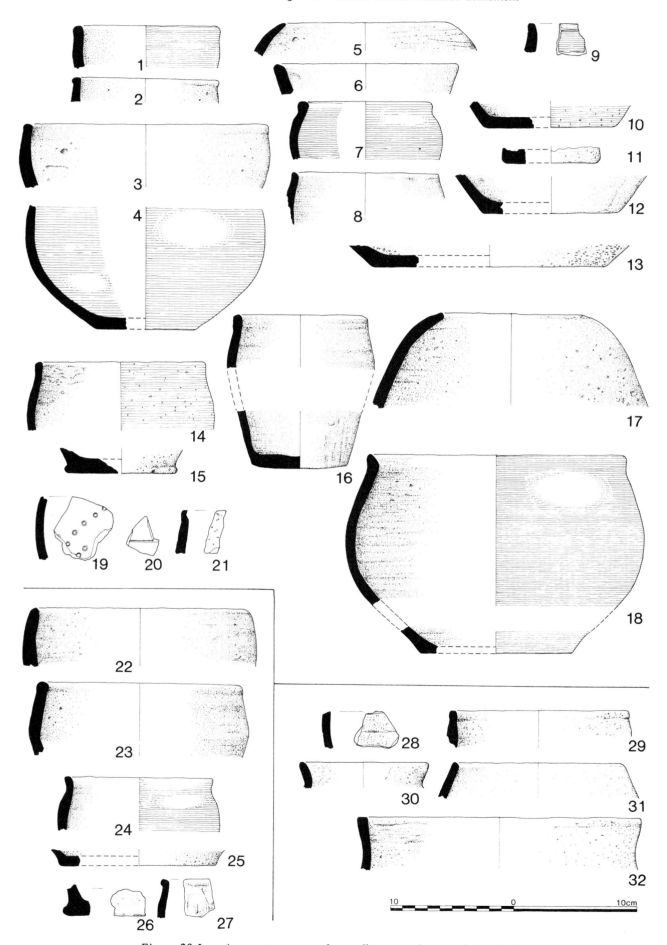

Figure 23 Iron Age pottery: central roundhouse enclosure phases 4–6

Table 6: Iron Age pottery: fabric proportions of 'pots' compared to those of all vessels

Fabric group	Fabric	Instances of pots by fabric		by fabric group		% of whole assemblage of EVs	
		No.	%	No.	%	Fabrics %	Fabric groups %
1	13	2	3.5	2	3.5	3.5	3.5
2	7	2	3.5			8.5	
	2	20	36			32.5	
	16	-	-	22	40		41.7
	8	-	-			0.7	
3	2c	1	1.5	1	1.5	5	
	5	-	-			2	7.5
	21	-	-			0.5	
4	1	1	1.5	1	1.5	3.5	3.5
5	12	12	22			10.5	
	11	2	3.5	14	25.5	1.5	13
	10	-	-			1	
6	3a	3	5.5	14	25.5	11	22
	3b	11	20			11	
7	17	-	-		-	-	
	19	-	-		-	-	
8	20	-	-			0.5	0.5
9	14	-	-			1	1
10	9	1	1.5	1	1.5	2	2

Total 55

Table 7: Iron Age pottery: incidence of burnt residues by fabric and fabric groups

Fabrics	Residue on Interior		Residue on Exterior		All residues Combined Totals	
	No.	%	No.	%	No.	%
Group 1	1	1	-	1	1	
Group 2	38	37.5	4	20 (48)	42 (39)	34
Group 3	5	5	2	10	7	5.5
Group 4	4	4	-	-	4	3
Group 5	17	17	6	29	23	19
Group 6	35	34.5	9	43	44	36
Group 7						
Group 8						
Group 9						
Group 10	1	1	-	-	1	<1
Total Number	101		21		122	(128)

One or two instances of both limescale and burnt residues on the same vessel were found on globular bowls, showing that vessels could be used for a variety of purposes. In common with other sites, however, the evidence suggests that this was the exception rather than the rule; analysis at Mount Farm showed that limescale occurred almost equally on fineware and coarseware vessels, whereas burnt residues were almost confined to coarsewares (Lambrick in Cunliffe and Miles 1984, 169).

Vessel size

Rims were divided into open and closed forms, and the open forms measured, in order to assess the range and frequency of vessel sizes. Straight sided 'pots' were classified with the open forms. 84 rims were measurable to within 20 or 30 m; a histogram of the percentages according to diameter is given (Fig. A2). Over 50% are small vessels with diameters of 140 mm or less, and over half of these are 'pots'. These proportions were compared with those from a similarly sized assemblage from a Middle Iron Age settlement at Claydon Pike, Fairford (Fig. A3: S Palmer, pers. comm.). There was clearly a difference of emphasis between the two assemblages; possibly the smaller proportion of large vessels at Watkins Farm indicates that other materials or methods were being used for storage, or perhaps a different diet is reflected. Alternatively, the prevalence of small cooking pots at Watkins Farm could imply individual rather than communal cooking, or preparation of a variety of small dishes instead of one large stew.

Decoration

Twenty-three definite and three possible instances of decoration were found, comprising 34 and 37 sherds and representing 3.0–3.5% of the total estimated vessel number and 2.2% of the sherds. Of these, 15 instances were simply of grooves or incised lines, some just below the rim (Fig. 25 No. 22), one forming a cross on a base sherd, and the others parallel or single lines on body sherds. All the uncertain examples were of single incised lines. There was also one instance of an irregular criss-cross of lines scratched onto a burnished surface after firing.

More complicated designs included rows of impressed dots on either side of grooves (Fig. 25 Nos. 4, 5 and 31) and impressed circles, probably made with a sawn tibia (Fig. 23 No. 19, Fig. 25 No. 16). Fig. 25 No. 27 incorporated both of these motifs, and it also had a row of short slashes alongside a further incised line. There was also one possible example of finger impressions along a slight shoulder.

Fig. 25 No. 31 and Fig. 24 No. 9 were of uncommon fabric, form and decoration. The sandy fabric of both vessels was of a distinctive sub-type. The bag-shaped jar

Fig. 25 No. 31 had an unusual variant of the 'pendant swag' design, in which the lines hanging from the dimple form a complete spiral surrounding it. The closest parallel is that illustrated from Yarnton, Oxon. (Harding 1972, Plate 68 F), which is also from a large vessel. Fig. 24 No. 9 also used incised lines and dots in a criss-cross diagonal design, and the decoration is like that on saucepan pots and globular bowls from Blewburton Hill (Harding 1972, Plate 66 E and Plate 68 H). Despite its slightly inturned mouth this vessel may have been of this for m, and thus perhaps an import from the S.

Another design was a line of crescent-shaped impressions between two narrow grooves, the crescents formed by a circular-ended tool pressed in at an angle (Fig. 25 No. 28). This decorative motif is relatively uncommon N of the Thames, but is characteristic of the globular bowls and jars from Frilford (Lambrick 1984, 170–172). Above the upper groove were faint traces of a parallel line of small circular dots.

One further design was pairs of parallel horizontal grooves defining narrow bands infilled with a continuous zig-zag of three parallel grooves, on the upper body and shoulder of a closed vessel (Fig. 25 No. 21). The decoration is extremely regular and the fabric is slightly unusual for an Iron Age sandy fabric; just possibly this vessel, which comes from a Roman context, was wheel-made. The incurving shoulder implies either a necked bowl form or a narrow-mouthed jar, both of which are Late Iron Age or early Roman forms. The decoration is closely paralleled on a necked bowl in a Late Iron Age assemblage from the big enclosure ditch at Cassington, Oxon. (Young in Case and Whittle 1982, Fig. 76 No. 1).

Discussion

The range of forms places this assemblage firmly in the Middle Iron Age tradition, similar to groups from Cassington (Harding 1972, Plates 61–4), City Farm W, Hanborough (Harding in Case et al. 1964, 79–87) and Stanton Harcourt (Hamlin 1966, 12–21). More recent work on assemblages from Ashville (De Roche in Parrington 1978, 40–74) and Farmoor (Lambrick and Robinson 1979, 35–46) has suggested an increase in the proportion of sandy fabrics throughout the Iron Age, and Watkins Farm would fit late in this sequence. Fabric proportions, forms and proportions of burnished pottery were also similar to those of the Phase II occupation at Farmoor, where radiocarbon dates of the later 3rd and mid 2nd century BC were obtained (Lambrick and Robinson 1979, 37–38).

Many of the forms can be paralleled at any stage in the Middle to Late Iron Age sequence from Ashville, Phases 2 and 3 (Parrington 1978, 50–74), but some suggest that the occupation continued into Phase 3. The incurving body and sharply upright rim of globular bowls

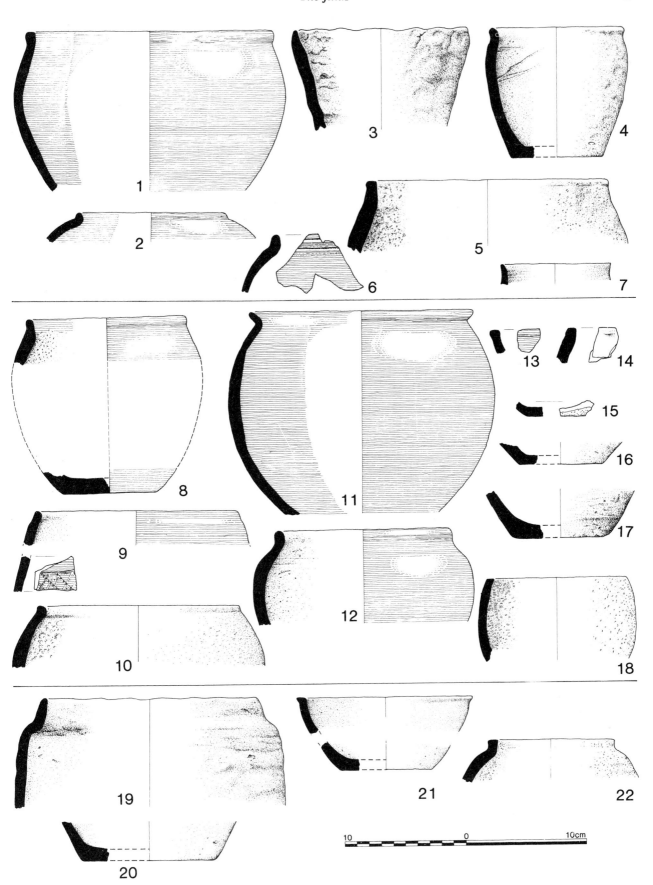

Figure 24 Iron Age pottery: enclosures 124/163, 496/512 and miscellaneous

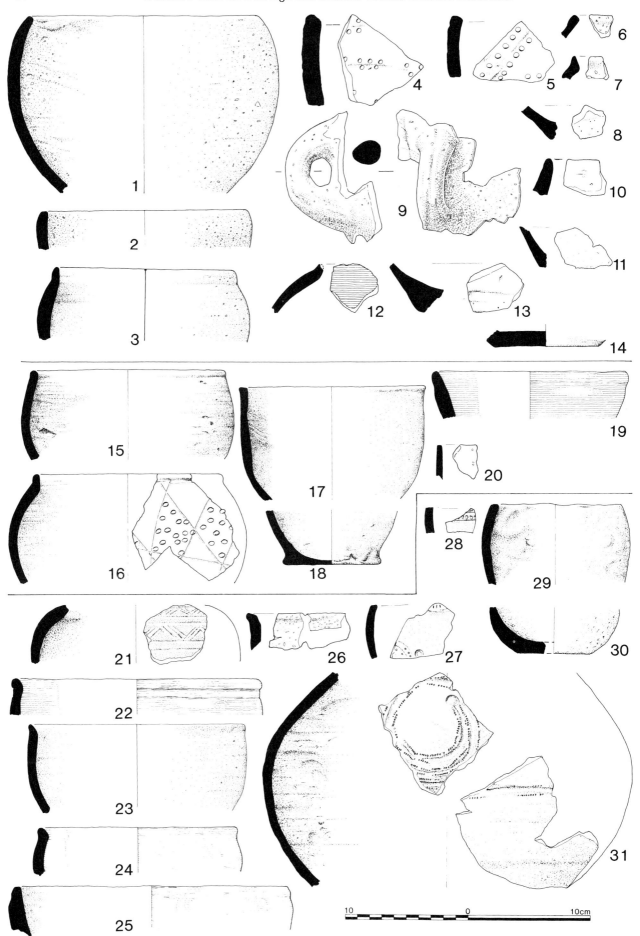

Figure 25 Iron Age pottery: enclosures 23/32, ditch 125 and miscellaneous

Fig. 24 No. 6 and Fig. 25 No. 16 are not common features elsewhere, but are paralleled at Ashville (Parrington 1978, Fig. 51 No. 317), where they are dated to the Late Iron Age. Similarly, the steeply incurved mouths of several vessels like Fig. 24 No. 2 are most akin to the bead rim jars or bowls of Phase 3 at Ashville (Parrington 1978, Fig. 50 No. 297 and Fig. 52 Nos. 348 and 349).

Fig. 25 No. 21 has already been mentioned as a likely bead rim jar or necked bowl form, and closed forms like Fig. 21 No. 26 are also likely to be late. The proto-necked jar, Fig. 22 No. 6, is also paralleled most closely in Phase 3 at Ashville, as is the Frilford-type decoration. Bead or proto-bead rims as on Fig. 21 No. 3 are also a late development at Ashville (Parrington 1978, Fig. 50 No. 286 (proto-necked jar); Fig. 52 No. 357 (Frilford-type decoration); Fig. 49 No. 275 and Fig. 50 No. 302 (Bead or proto-bead rims)).

Radiocarbon dates have been obtained from contexts representing the full date range of occupation at Watkins Farm (see Table 8). These broadly agree with the suggested pottery dating.

Table 8: Radiocarbon dates from the Iron Age site

Context	Harwell ref.	Type	Description	Phase	Date	Calibrated Ranges (R.L.Otlet program, data Stuiver and Reimer 1986)	
404/4	7051	Bone	Main enclosure	1	2340 ± 90 bp	68% 580 BC to 330 BC	95% 780 BC to 200 BC
487	7047	Bone	Pit (below central roundhouse enclosure ditch)	1-2	2210 ± 90 bp	68% 420 BC to 170 BC	95% 460 BC to 30 BC
60	7053	Wood	Well		2160 ± 70 bp	68% 310 BC to 130 BC	95% 390 BC to 30 BC
151	8254	Charcoal	Hearth (trackway ditch in main enclosure)	4-6	2190 ± 70 bp	68% 350 BC to 160 BC	95% 400 BC to 50 BC
553/1	8255	Charcoal	Hearth (external enclosure ditch)		2060 ± 80 bp	68% 200 BC to O AD	95% 360 BC to AD 10
498	8253	Wood	Pit burial		3060 ± 60 bp	68% 1400 BC to 1250 BC	95% 1490 BC to 1130 BC

The results, expressed as DC13, AGE BP and Cal RANGES, are given in accordance with the method outlined in Harwell Notes Sheet NS/2/88. The calibrated age ranges were computed using a Harwell Isotope Measurements Laboratory program with the data files provided by Washington University, USA compiled by them from the recommended data of Stuiver and Reimer (1986), Pearson and Stuiver (1986) and Pearson et al. (1986).

Catalogue of illustrated Iron Age sherds
F = fabric

Figure 20
Context 402: 1–F 3b; 2–F11; 3–F3b; 4–F3b; 5–F3b
Context 477: 6–F13; 7–F12; 8–F3b; 9–F2a; 10–F7; 11–F2; 12–F1b; 16–F3b; 17–F3a
Context 438: 13–F12
Context 424: 14–F12c; 15–F12c

Figure 21
Context 477: 1–F2c; 2–F3c
Context 433: 3–F3b; 4–F3b; 5–F2; 6–F2; 7–F11; 8–F10; 9–F12; 10–F3c; 11–F2; 12–F7; 13–F3b; 15–F10; 17–F3b; 18–F2; 19–F11; 20–F3c; 21–F3b; 22–F12; 24–F3b; 25–F2; 26–F7; 27–F2; 29–F2
Context 425: 14–F3b; 16–F2; 23–F3b; 28–F2; 30–F7; 31–F2c

Figure 22
Context 425: 1–F1b; 2–F12; 3–F12; 4–F1a; 5–F2; 6–F10; 7–F12; 8–F12; 9–F12; 10–F12; 11–F2

Figure 23
Context 503: 1–F2b; 2–F2; 9–F3b
Context 410: 3–F2c; 4–F2; 5–F1a; 6–F2; 7–F2b; 8–F2; 10–F3b
Context 410: 11–F12; 13–F3; 17–F2
Context 495: 12–F2; 14–F3b; 15–F3b; 16–F2; 17–F2c; 18–F2; 20–F7; 21–F3a
Context 488: 22–F12; 23–F2; 24–F2; 25–F3b; 26–F13; 27–F2
Context 413: 28–F3b; 29–F3b; 30–F3b; 31–F2; 32–F3b

Figure 24
Context 151: 1–F2a; 2–F1b; 3–F11; 6–F2b
Context 430: 4–F1a; 5–F3b; 7–F7

Context 124: 8–F3b; 9–F2; 10–F3; 11–F2; 12–F3b; 16–F2; 17–F2c
Context 141: 18–F3a
Context 124: 13–F2b; 14–F2b; 15–F3b

Figure 25
Context 496/512: 19–F2; 20–F2c; 21–F2c; 22–F3b
Context 23/32: 1–F1a; 2–F3a; 3–F1b; 4 and 5–F2; 6–F3a; 7–F1a; 8–F2; 9–F1b; 10–F8; 11–F7; 12–F2a; 13–F2; 14–F1b
Context 125: 15–F2; 16–F13; 17–F2; 18–F2; 19–F7; 20–F17
Context 5: 21–F2
Context 160: 22–F7
Context 4: 23–F7
Context 126: 24–F2a
Context 34: 25–F12b
Context 136: 26–F3a
Context 1: 27–F2
Context 127: 28–F7
Context 8: 29–F2
Context 134: 30–F13
Context 137: 31–F7

THE ROMANO-BRITISH POTTERY *by Sheila Raven*

Introduction
The pottery assemblage consists of 3,393 sherds weighing 34 kilos. 2,255 sherds came from Site B and 1,138 sherds came from Site A.

The fabric analysis included a sample of the Iron Age pottery and 57 medieval and post-medieval sherds for comparison with the local Roman fabrics. The Iron Age and the medieval pottery are the subjects of separate reports.

The nature of the assemblage
Most features were ditches or gullies and were poorly sealed. In some cases the deposition of the pottery may have occurred over a long period of time, with a problem of residuality in such features. Distinctive fabrics and forms also provide an indication of the degree of dispersal in this assemblage; only single sherds from Oxfordshire colour-coat vessels and one sherd from an amphora were recovered.

Since no Romano-British structures or other settlement foci were found, the pottery can only provide a broad indication of the date and duration of Romano-British occupation on the site. The excavated features appear to represent peripheral areas of occupation, and only part of those.

Features on both sites continued beyond the limits of the excavation, and over much of the excavated area they were badly truncated or destroyed by stripping. Few inferences can therefore be drawn from the pottery. A

number of sherds have also suffered from waterlogging and erosion, which may well have removed burnishing or lightly incised decoration.

Method of study and extent of archive
The following attributes of the pottery were recorded and analysed:

Fabric
Manufacture
Firing (considered with fabric)
Form
Decoration and surface treatment

The assemblages from Site A (contexts 1–33, 37–199, 260–518) and Site B (contexts 34, 35, 36, 200–260) were analysed separately. Unstratified sherds have been quantified, but have not been included in the main calculations for fabric and form percentages.

No detailed form classification has been attempted. Fine wares were few, as is usual on such native sites, and assemblages from individual features were generally small. It has not therefore been possible to examine the chronological development of the pottery within the site, and the aim has been to provide a broad chronology for the settlement and a general picture of the assemblage.

A cross-section of the local Romano-British fabric types was selected for analysis by thin section and atomic absorbtion. The results and discussion by Ian Whithead and Helen Hatcher will be found in the archive.

Fabrics
Seventeen major fabric groups were distinguished with the aid of a x10 binocular microscope. These are:

1. Amphorae
2. Mortaria
3. Samian
4. Fine Ware - colour-coat
5. Fine Ware - decorated
6. White Wares
7. Oxidised (R, M, PM)
8. Reduced - grey
9. Reduced - black and brown/orange
10. Mixed sandy wheel-made
11. Coarse mixed sandy (I/A, R)
12. Mica inclusions
13. Flint gritted (M)
14. 'Grog' inclusions
15. Calcareous inclusions (I/A, R, M)
16. Miscellaneous
17. Salt-glazed (PM)

I/A= Iron Age, R=Roman, M=Medieval, PM= post-medieval

In the recording most of the categories were further

divided; for the full fabric series see the technical appendix on the Romano-British pottery. In order to obtain large enough groups for fabric percentages the 17 major fabric types were condensed into six broader fabric groups such as 'White wares', 'reduced wares' etc.

The proportions of these broad fabric groups on Sites A and B are compared below in Table 9.

Table 9: Roman pottery: percentages of broad fabric types by sherd count and sherd weight

		Site A	Site B
Total sherd number		1077	2255
Total sherd weight		15,421 grams	18,104 grams
Average sherd weight		c 15 grams	c 8 grams
		% of Total	% of Total
White wares	Number	13	25
	Weight	16	11
Oxidised wares	Number	9.6	10
	Weight	6	9.8
Samian and	Number	2	1
Colour-Coated ware	Weight	1	1
'Grog' wares	Number	11	3
	Weight	17	5
Reduced wares	Number	64	60
	Weight	58	80
Calcareous wares	Number	3.5	2
	Weight	3	1.5
All fine wares (Categories 3, 4, 5, 6.1, 7.1, 8.1, 12.1)	Number	13	30
	Weight	9	16

The very high percentage for fine wares on Site B as calculated by sherd number can be explained by the very large number of small, fine, white ware fabric 6.1 sherds — most of which probably come from one vessel. The figure for fine ware percentage by sherd weight is therefore more reliable. The white wares percentage should be viewed in the same light.

Using sherd weight as the more reliable indicator, fabric proportions between the two sites are generally similar. There is, however, a noticeably higher percentage of 'grog' wares on Site A, which is perhaps made up for in the Site B assemblage by the higher proportion of reduced wares. Even discounting the fragmented vessel, there is also a significantly higher percentage of fine wares on Site B.

Eight major vessel forms, running from closed to open vessels, were defined (the proportions of these are listed in Table 10). These form types were defined following criteria used in the Rough Ground Farm pottery report (Green forthcoming). Subdivisions were

made within the two categories containing the widest range of examples — namely Category 3 Jars, and Category 6 Bowls — and a simple division was made between Tankards and Cups in Category 5. Further subdivision was not thought profitable because there were so few complete profiles and because many of the basic form groups contained so few examples (for instance only three incomplete lids were present). A rim series is illustrated (Fig. A3) and this shows how little of the profiles was generally present.

Table 10: Roman pottery: percentages of major vessel types on sites A and B

	% of total	
Roman pottery	Site A	Site B
Flagons/Jugs	0	2
Jars	79	72
Beakers	2	2
Cups/Tankards	1	4
Bowls/Dishes	16	18
Lids	1	0
Mortaria (Bowls)	1	1
Amphora)	0	1
Total of vessel rims	121	98

Site B assemblage shows a slightly greater diversity of forms and a higher proportion of 'fine ware' vessels.

Even among the jars and bowls the paucity of substantially complete profiles makes accurate distinctions between variants very difficult. For this reason bowls and dishes have been assessed as one category in the major vessel forms. It appears from the more complete examples, however, that bowls were more numerous than dishes on both sites.

Imported pottery

Samian

The site produced only a small quantity of continental wares. Apart from one Dressel 20 amphora sherd (see below) 35 samian sherds represent the only foreign imports.

The majority of the datable sherds are 2nd century AD, but both Sites A and B produced a few small sherds of 1st century date and South Gaulish manufacture. A tiny plain rim from feature 131 may come from a small, cylindrical decorated bowl of Knorr 78 type, dated AD 60–80 (Oswald and Pryce 1920). Some of these early samian pieces may be residual, as many of the sherds are very abraded. Longevity of use is also an important factor to consider when using samian for dating. The section of a Dr. 18/31 dish from context 406/A/2, which has a rivet hole on the shoulder, demonstrates that at

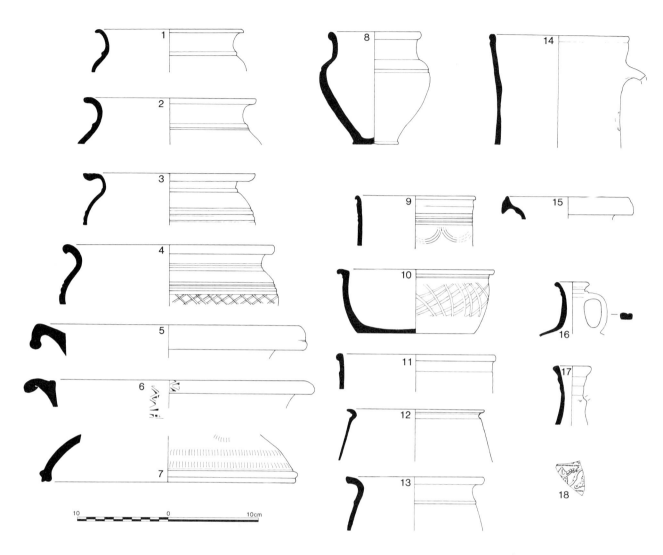

Fig. 26 Romano-British Pottery

least one vessel on this site was kept beyond its normal lifespan. It was associated with a 3rd-century intaglio (see Fig. 28).

Apart from the possible Knorr 78 bowl, the forms represented are Dr. 33 cups, Dr. 37 bowls, and Dr. 18 and 18/31 dishes. The fabric types consist of more or less equal proportions of South Gaulish and Central Gaulish ware (from Sites A and B) and a small number of sherds which may be East Gaulish. Of the two decorated relief-moulded pieces one (Fig. 26 No. 18) is certainly from the Central Gaulish factory of Les-Mortres-De-Veyre, its motifs corresponding to those of Drusus I. This comes from gully 96. The other piece, which comes from ditch 34/Cut 2, may also come from the same factory, but is very abraded.

Many thanks to Dr Grace Simpson for her assessment of the collection, and to Catriona Turner for further comments.

Amphorae *by David Williams*

Watkins Farm has yielded only one sherd of amphora. This is from a Dressel 20 type — the commonest form found in Roman Britain. These amphora were made in the Guadalquivir region of Spain (between Seville and Cordoba) and were used for the transportation of olive oil.

The date range for this form of amphora ranges from the pre-Roman period 1 levels at Camulodunum to the 3rd century AD (Williams and Peacock 1983, 263–260).

Mortaria

There are only eight sherds of mortaria from Sites A and B together, and all are of the hard, sandy, off-white fabric typical of the Oxfordshire mortaria industry (Young 1977, 56). Of the two rims found, one is from Site A, context 89 (with joining sherd from 126, Fig. 26

No. 5) and corresponds to Young's Oxfordshire category M2, dated to AD 100–170; the other, Fig. 26 No. 6, comes from Site B, context 206/2, and is closest to Young's Oxfordshire type M1, dated loosely to the first half of the 2nd century. The rim bears a maker's stamp for which no exact parallels have been found.

Discussion

Date

The assemblage consisted mostly of late 1st and 2nd century types. The majority of the BBI forms such as simple everted rim jars and bowls with lattice decoration (Fig. 26 No. 10) are indicative of this date. The samian is largely 2nd century and of Central Gaulish origin (Fig. 26 No. 18). Other fine wares such as the poppy head beakers and the compass-decorated 'London Ware' bowl (Fig. 26 No. 9) also belong to this period, as do the ring-neck flagons (Fig. 26 Nos. 16 and 17) and the M1 and M2 Oxford mortaria (Fig. 26 Nos. 5 and 6).

First century occupation is probably indicated by sherds of South Gaulish samian, the grog fabric, e.g. fabrics 14.2, 14.3, and the 'Savernake type' wares. Fabric 11 is a coarse sandy ware of local origin akin to Iron Age fabrics found on the site and does not often occur in this area after the end of the 1st century AD. Nevertheless, the very small quantity of hand-made pottery and preponderance of fully Romanised sandy fabrics suggest that occupation began very late in the 1st century AD. Other 1st-century local assemblages contain a higher proportion of calcareous coarse fabrics and other 'native' wares e.g. Hardwick, Smithsfield and Stanton Harcourt, Gravelly Guy (Allen forthcoming; L S Green, pers. comm.).

Diagnostic 3rd- and 4th-century types are limited to a BBI flanged bowl, an Oxfordshire colour-coated flanged bowl and other sherds of colour-coat, all of which come from Site B. Some of the common jars from Site A, datable only to a broad 1st-4th century AD range, may of course have been 3rd- or 4th-century, but alternatively occupation on Site A may not have continued into the 4th century.

Proportions of forms and fabrics were otherwise generally similar on Sites A and B. Predictably, the largest fabric group on both sites was reduced grey wares. The next largest was white wares (see Table 9), composed mostly of the coarser fabric 6.4, which is quite distinct from the finer wares of the main Oxfordshire kilns. Some of the forms in Fabric 6.4 also vary from the standard Oxfordshire white ware products (Fig. 26 Nos. 1, 2 and 17). Grog fabrics 14.2 and 14.3 and the coarse 'native' style fabric 11 were restricted to Site A. These are characteristically early, and their apparent replacement by reduced sandy wares on Site B could indicate that Romano-British occupation began earlier on

Site A. Site B, however, produced a number of early fine wares such as the 'London Ware' bowl (Fig. 26 No. 9), the poppy head beakers and the flagons (Fig. 26 Nos. 16 and 17). There was a higher proportion of fine wares on Site B and the difference between Sites A and B may therefore have been of function and status rather than chronology.

Trade

Most of the pottery consisted of coarse wares of a wide variety of fabrics derived from the local clay belts and calcareous gravels. This could have derived from any of a number of kiln sites. The mortaria and colour-coat vessels were all Oxford products. BBI and possible Savernake wares show contacts with the SW and W, and the tankard (Fig. 26 No. 14), which is uncommon in this area, possibly came from Swindon (L S Green, pers. comm.). As on other sites in the area, BBI imports clearly inspired imitations in local fabrics, particularly the BBI dog-bowl form (Fig. 26 No. 10).

The thin section analysis has shown that the 'Savernake type' wares contain a distinctive mudstone/siltstone: this may be a fruitful line of study for distinguishing between the commoner coarse wares. Further analysis of other assemblages is now under way.

The scarcity of continental imports and the local origin of the fine wares suggest that, like other early Romano-British sites in this area, this site was of a low status, and involved for the most part only in local trade.

Catalogue of illustrated Roman pottery

Site A

Context 41: Figure 26 No. 1
Jar 3.1/25
Narrow-necked, everted rim, one narrow cordon at neck. Fabric 6.4: hard, coarse fabric, abundant quartz inclusions, cream colour. Sooty on rim and outer neck — perhaps deliberate burning as in Young's finer burnt White Ware from Churchill Hospital kiln site. AD 1st to 3rd century (Young 1977, No. W32).

Context 43: Figure 26 No. 2
Jar 3.1/33
Form and fabric as above. Similar sooty area. Reeded cordon on neck. AD 1st to 3rd century (Young 1977, No. R24).

Context 51: Figure 26 No. 14
Tankard 5.2/44
Large, single-handled vessel. Fabric 8.2: coarse grey sandy fabric, common quartz inclusions, occasional mica. Such tankards tend to be early Roman at sites such as Cirencester and Shakenoak (Wacher and McWhirr, 1982). The fabric is not identical to the

Severn Valley or Wiltshire fabrics of probable 1st century date and resembles more the coarse grey mugs from Shakenoak dated mid to late 2nd century.

Context 96: Figure 26 No. 18
Samian bowl Dr. 37 or Dr. 30.
Relief-moulded acanthus motif, trifide, beads segmenting compartments. Product of Drusus I at Les Martres-De-Veyre factory in Central Gaul (Terisse 1968, No. 186). c AD 100–120.

Context 126: Figure 26 No. 5
Mortarium 6*/28
Roll rim and internal bead. Fabric 6.1: hard, off-white, small quartz inclusions, large pink, grey, transparent and white trituration grits. Product of Oxfordshire kiln group (Young 1977, No. M2). c AD 100–170?

Context 131: Figure 26 No. 8
Jar 3.2/34
Necked wide mouthed jar with shoulder groove. Fabric 8.2: moderate hard, grey, sandy ware, common mixed quartz inclusions. This form has a wide date range but this example was associated with 2nd century BBI pottery. c AD 1st-4th century.

Context 134: Figure 26 No. 7
Lid 8/84
External and internal rounded flange. Horizontal zones of rouletting below flange, fine vertical lines. Fabric 15.2: hard, calcareous, fine oolitic limestone, grey core, grey and orange/brown surface. No exact parallels found. Probably early Roman because of the fabric. c AD 1st or 2nd century?

Context 162: Figure 26 No. 11
Bowl 6.4/3
Copy of D. 37 form with slightly recessed zone below rim. Fabric 6.1: fine, hard, cream ware, no visible inclusions. Product of main Oxford kiln group (Young 1977, No. W54). c AD 150–300.

Context 450/F/1: Figure 26 No. 3
Jar 3.1/39
Necked jar with large everted rim reeded on upper face. Cordon at neck and three grooves on body. Fabric 6.4: hard, coarse granulated cream ware with abundant quartz inclusions. A very unusual form. No close parallels in Oxford types. A grooved necked bowl from an Oxfordshire kiln group (Young 1977, No. R38) is similar but lacks the reeded rim. AD 1st-3rd century.

Site B
Context 34/Cut 1: Figure 26 No. 9

Bowl 6.4/49
'London Ware' type copy of Dr. 37 form with three wide shallow grooves above compass-incised triple avis. Fabric 502: fairly hard, buff, sandy ware, small quartz inclusions, and black-brown ?iron ore. Pale grey core, buff exterior. Most likely to be local version of the 'London Wares' (Young 1977, No. R68). c AD 2nd century.

Figure 26 No. 16
Flagon 1/8
Ring-neck flagon, single handle. Fabric 6.1: fine, hard, cream ware, small quartz inclusions. An Oxfordshire type, generally of 2nd century date (Young 1977, No. W2). AD 100–240.

Figure 26 No. 15
Flagon 1/6
Large pendant wall-sided rim, one cordon on neck. Fabric 6.1: fine, hard, cream ware. Few visible inclusions, Oxfordshire White Ware (Young 1977, No. W7). c AD 150–240.

Figure 26 No. 12
Beaker 4/19
Bag beaker with small moulded, out-turned rim. Fabric 7.1: hard, fairly fine red-orange ware, small quartz and occasional red iron ore. Probably not a product of the main Oxfordshire kilns, but a local variant. Represents the most common of Young's oxidised beaker forms with limited production in second half of the 3rd century (Young 1977, No. O20); occurs earlier elsewhere. c AD 2nd or 3rd century.

Figure 26 No. 13
Butt-beaker 4/38
Wide-mouthed, everted rim, slight cordon on shoulder. Fabric 9.4: coarse granulated brown black, common quartz inclusions, occasional red iron ore and grog. A coarse local version of Gallo-Belgic forms (Young 1977, No. R29). c AD 50–200.

Context 34/220: Figure 26 No. 10
Bowl 6.5/37
Curved sides, out-turned rim, wide band of acute burnished lattice on body. Fabric 9.4: hard, coarse, granulated black-brown ware, common quartz inclusions, occasional iron ore and grog. A local version of the popular BBI lattice-decorated bowls (Gillam 1968, 31 and 71, Fig. 31, Nos. 307–8). c AD 130–200.

Context 35/E/4: Figure 26 No. 17
Flagon 1/8
Ring-neck flagon with expanded bead rim and two

widely-spaced grooves. Fabric 6.4: hard, coarse, granulated cream ware, common mixed quartz inclusions. Clearly a local version of the finer Oxfordshire white-ware flagons and probably early in date. c AD 1st or 2nd century.

Context 204: Figure 26 No. 4
Jar 3.2/34
> Wide-mouthed, necked jar, everted rim, grooving on shoulder and burnished regular on acute lattice beneath. Fabric 8.1: fine, hard, sandy dark grey ware, small quartz inclusions, some mica. Probably an early Roman form of local manufacture (Brodribb 1971, 68). c AD 1st or 2nd century.

Context 206/2: Figure 26 No. 6
Mortarium 6*/29
> Short roll-rim, turned under at tip, internal bead. Fabric 2 which is Oxfordshire white-ware mortaria and Young's type M1 in form (Young 1977, 68). The maker's stamp on the rim bears some resemblance to one found at Dorchester, Allens Pit (Young 1977, Mortaria stamp No. 14). c AD 100–150.

MEDIEVAL POTTERY *by Sheila Raven* (Fig. 27)
57 sherds of early medieval pottery weighing 1.26 kilos were found, of which 47 came from Site A. They occur as intrusions in Iron Age or Romano-British ditches and gullies, and there are no obvious medieval features; they probably derive from the overlying ridge and furrow. On Site B one medieval pit was found, feature 607. Ditches 201, 202, 203 and 225 contained both Roman and medieval sherds, and it is possible that the Roman material was residual rather than that the medieval pottery was intrusive (see Chapter 2: Site B). Only three basic fabric types were present, namely fabric 7.4, (a granulated, pale orange ware with abundant quartz inclusions; only one sherd was found); fabric 13, (a coarse heavily flint-gritted buff/grey ware) and fabric 15.8 (an oolitic limestone tempered ware of orange and brown/grey colour with smooth soapy feel). For fabric list see Technical appendix, section 2, Romano-British pottery.

Twelve rim sherds and one 'sagging' base sherd were found, none of them glazed or decorated. These are illustrated and described below (Fig. 27). No complete profiles were present, but cooking pots and storage jars would seem to be the commonest forms. No. 9, Rim 103, from ditch 96/4M may be a deep-sided dish, and Nos. 1 and 2 may be straight-sided cooking pots with clubbed rims.

The predominance of calcareous fabric 15.8, which corresponds closely to fabric AC, 'Oxford early medieval ware' from the St Aldate's excavations in Oxford (Durham 1977, 115) suggests a date range from the 11th to the 13th centuries for this collection. Since the collection is so limited, only a broad date range can be given. The flint-tempered fabrics at 'The Hamel', Oxford (Mellor 1980, 160–182) are imports from the S from the late 12th century onwards. The forms of the Northmoor flint-tempered pieces fit into the broad 11th to 13th century date range of the rest of the medieval pottery from the site.

Catalogue of illustrated medieval sherds
'R' refers to Rim number, 'B' to Base number and 'F' to fabric code.
Site A
Context 96 (surface): Figure 27 No. 8
R106/F15.8:
> Bowl with flattened internally beaded rim

Context 96/4M: Figure 27 No. 9
R103/F15.8:
> Deep-sided dish or cooking pot/storage jar with thickened rim. Shallow groove below rim.

Context 126 (Top): Figure 27 No. 10
R101/F7.4:
> Storage jar in pale orange fabric, densely gritted with quartz inclusions. Thumb-impressed rim, wheel-made.

Context 136/1: Figure 27 No. 5
R104/F15.8:
> Cooking pot/storage jar with clubbed rim.

Context 138/1: Figure 27 No. 6
R108/F13:
> Cooking pot/storage jar with beaded rim. Straight-sided vessel or straight-necked? Coarse flint-tempered fabric.

Context 138/1/6M: Figure 27 No. 2
R105/F15.8:
> Cooking pot. Rounded everted rim., flattened on top.

Context 162/1: Figure 27 No. 4
R111/F15.8:
> Cooking pot/storage jar with thick rounded rim. Straight-sided.

Context 162/2M: Figure 27 No. 3
R107/F15.8:
> Cooking pot/storage jar with sloping clubbed rim.

Context 308/2: Figure 27 No. 7
R112/F15.8:
> Cooking pot/storage jar with T-shaped rim.

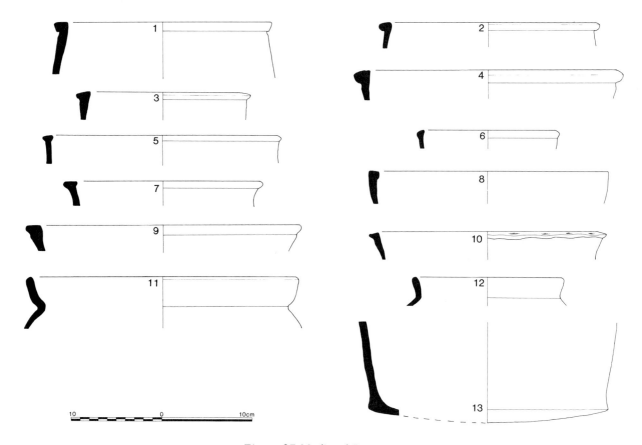

Figure 27 Medieval Pottery

Site B
Context 410/D/1: Figure 27 No. 1
R109/F15.8:
> Cooking pot/storage jar, with clubbed rim, straight-sided.

Context 492/3: Figure 27 No. 11
R110/F13:
> Large cooking pot/storage jar, with simple everted rim. Coarse flint, tempered, buff-brown ware.

Context 202/D/3: Figure 27 No. 12
R102/F13:
> Cooking pot/storage jar with simple everted rim. Coarse flint tempered, buff-grey/brown ware.

Context 202/D/3: Figure 27 No.13
B1/F13:
> Sagging base of large cooking pot/storage jar.

BRIQUETAGE *by T G Allen*
(With help in identification from Elaine Morris)
47 sherds from Droitwich salt containers were found, weighing 986 g in all. For a full breakdown of quantities by context see Technical appendix Table T6. The fabrics were identified following Morris's classification (Morris 1985, 336–379); the majority were of Fabric Type 2, and all of this came from Site A. 110 g were of Fabric Type 1 or 1a, which occurred on both Sites A and B. Type 2 is generally found in Later Iron Age contexts, dated 1st century BC or AD. Type 1 is also in use at this time, but is found in earlier contexts as well, from c 300 BC onwards.

The index of briquetage in relation to Iron Age pottery on the site is 0.032. This is considerably higher than that for other sites in the region for which it has been quantified, 0.01 at Claydon Pike, Fairford and 0.004 at Mingies Ditch, Hardwick (Morris in Miles and Palmer forthcoming), but this is probably not an indication of a much greater consumption of or trade in salt at Watkins Farm. Only five or six containers need be represented on Site A and one on Site B; as with the pottery, rapid filling of the deep enclosure ditches around houses, into which rubbish was deliberately thrown, probably ensured high survival of sherds. Excavations at Gravelly Guy nearby (see Fig. 1) have recovered similar proportions of briquetage to those at Watkins Farm (G Lambrick, pers. comm.). At present sites in the Stanton Harcourt area represent the most south-easterly distribution of Droitwich salt.

Briquetage came from four of the small enclosures on Site A; the central roundhouse, 485, 124–163 and 442–436. It occurred only very rarely in features that were not associated with, or that did not cut, these enclosures. The presence of Fabric Type 1 on Site B ought to imply Iron Age or very early Romano-British occupation, but there is no other evidence of this. Just possibly the Droitwich salt industry was still operating at the end of the 1st century AD, as these sherds are unlikely to have derived from Site A, some 250 m away.

FIRED CLAY *by T G Allen*

6769 g of fired clay were found in Iron Age contexts. For a table of fired clay by context, fabric and type and full fabric descriptions see Technical appendix Section 2 and Table T7. Most of the clay, however, was of three main fabrics:

A - calcareous, abundant fine limestone.
F - mixed sand and calcareous inclusions and red ferrous lumps.
C - fine quartz and sparse organic inclusions.

Identifiable types of object were loomweights (six identifiable and six possible) and spindle whorls (one definite and one possible), and there were six groups of fragments from wattle and daub walling, plus three other possible instances. The walling occurred in Fabrics F and A, the loomweights (see Fig. 28 No. 13) mainly in Fabrics C and A, and the spindle whorls only in Fabric C. Some correlation between fabric and function is evident, the hard Fabric C being preferred for clay objects. The walling may have derived either from buildings or from ovens; its distribution is confined to the central roundhouse, enclosure 23 and external enclosure 485 etc.

Insufficient fired clay was recovered from Romano-British contexts to make breakdown of fabrics useful. Parts of two flat clay slabs were found, both of Fabric K, with abundant organic grass/straw impressions and coarse limestone gravel. Similar slabs have been found on other local Romano-British sites, e.g. Smithsfield, Hardwick with Yelford (Allen forthcoming), but their function is uncertain. Possibly they were heated and used as hotplates to keep food warm.

COPPER ALLOY OBJECTS *by T G Allen*
(*with contributions by Martin Henig* and *Cathy King*)
There were four finds, two from Iron Age and two from Romano-British contexts, all on Site A. These were:

Iron Age
151/1
Fragment of bronze strip.

Figure 28 No. 2 301/2
Bronze strip. This had one bulbous end pierced with a hole. At the other end the metal was folding round, and had snapped off at the fold. Possibly a decorative strip attached to a garment or leather object.

Romano-British
Figure 28 No. 1 406
Ring of copper alloy, diameter 20 mm.
There is a band across each shoulder demarcating the hoop from the bezel. Ovoid bezel, 10 x 8 mm., containing a setting of sky-blue glass imitative of sapphire impressed with a simple human figure.

The ring is of a trinket type which would normally date to the third century and the intaglio can be classed amongst the Romano-British imitations characteristic of this time and largely confined to southern Britain, demonstrating the spread of the practice of wearing rings capable of serving as signets down to the peasantry (Robinson 1978, 249–51; Henig 1978, 132–3 and 255–7 Nos. 539–78, XVII-XVIII).

162/2
Coin
Dupondius of Trajan, c AD 116–117. RIC 676.
Obverse: IMP CAES NER TRAIANO GER DAC [PARTHICO PM TRP COS VI PP].
Reverse: SENATUS POPULUSQUE ROMANUS SC.
Emperor standing between two trophies.

I am indebted to Dr Martin Henig for the report on the ring with intaglio, and to Dr Cathy King for identification of the coin.

IRON OBJECTS *by T G Allen* (Figure 28)
Seven complete or fragmentary iron objects were found, all from Site A. Four of these were from Romano-British contexts, and three from the upper fills of the central roundhouse enclosure ditches, 410/D/2 and 433/1. The Iron Age fills were, however, contaminated by animal burrowing and contained intrusive Roman and medieval pottery, so it is possible that these iron finds were Romano-British or later. None of the objects was X-rayed. Three are illustrated:

Figure 28 No. 3 96
Knife with narrow blade.

Figure 28 No. 4 433/1
Ring-headed pin or key

Figure 28 No. 5 433/1
Latch lifter. This is an unusually solid and heavy example, but a similar one was found at Barton Court Farm (Miles 1986, Fiche 5: G2).

The others are:

8	Knife blade fragment
96	Iron strip with hole at one end.
410/D/2	Large sheet iron fragment. Possibly from a spade?
162/1	Rod fragment, circular cross-section

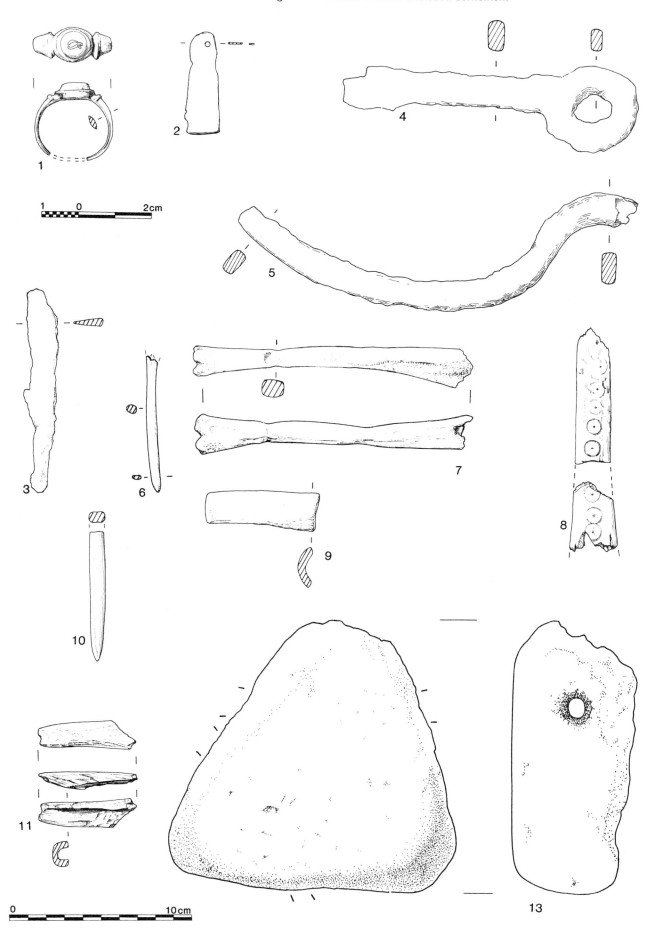

Figure 28 Copper alloy, iron, bone and fired clay finds

There were also seven nails, ranging from 50 to 100 mm in length. Six came from Site A, one from Site B. Two of the six were from secure Iron Age contexts, four from Romano-British or contaminated contexts. A length of iron strip and a piece of horse-harness were also found unstratified. Both were probably modern.

ROMAN GLASS by John Shepherd
Only two pieces of glass were found. These were:

Site A 406
Fragment of the rim of a large bowl, flattened hollow tubular section. Coloured glass, dull blue metal. Manufactured in the mid-late 1st century AD.

Site B 36/D/1
Fragment of the lower part of an unguentariu m, (Isings 1957, Type 28a or 82a1). Free blown. Thick naturally coloured glass, greenish-blue metal. Manufactured from the mid 1st to the 3rd centuries AD.

The date of both pieces agrees with the pottery evidence for occupation on Sites A and B. However, the presence of 1st century glass in pit 406, along with a Central Gaulish samian bowl and a 3rd century intaglio, suggests that this glass bowl was a treasured heirloom.

WORKED BONE by T G Allen (Fig. 28)
Six objects were found, four from Iron Age enclosure ditches, one from a Romano-British ditch and one from a posthole of uncertain date. They comprise:

Figure 28 No. 6 442/A/1
Narrow needle with eye, highly polished. Top of eye missing. From pig fibula

Figure 28 No. 7
Sheep tibia with polished shaft and grooves worn in four places across the shaft towards either end. Similar bones have been found at Farmoor and Mount Farm (Lambrick and Robinson 1979, 55–6, Fig. 29 No. 3). They were perhaps spacers used in weaving.

Figure 28 No. 8 413/C/1
'Weaving comb' with inscribed dots and circles. Head and teeth missing. From long bone of cow or horse. Very similar decoration to a comb from Ashville, dated to Period 3, Late Iron Age (Parrington 1978, 80, Fig. 59 No. 26).

Figure 28 No. 9, 23
Cylindrical handle, polished. Antler tine.
Figure 28 No. 10, 85
Large thick pin or needle, head missing. ?Antler. Possibly a dress-pin.

Figure 28 No. 11 13/1
Gouge or awl, point and head missing. Sheep tibia. Similar implements made from sheep tibias or metatarsals were found at Ashville in early Iron Age contexts (Parrington 1978, 82, Fig. 60 Nos. 35–7). There are traces of polish on the broken end, suggesting that this was a gouge rather than an awl, or that it was re-used.

There was also a sawn and polished fragment of horn, possibly goat.

The bone implements show that, apart from bone-working itself (see Chapter 4: Carcass butchery), the Iron Age inhabitants were carrying out weaving and probably leather working.

FLINTS by T G Allen
Two flakes and one blade were found, in features 498/3, 496/3 and 96 respectively. The flakes were both of a mottled dark grey and cream flint with traces of white thin cortex, and probably derive from the same nodule. The blade is an orange-brown flint with milky patches and some patination and a little white cortex at the distal end. The bulbar end is missing. All three were probably made using local pebble flint from the Unbedded Glacial Drift.

WOOD by T G Allen
Three objects were found, part of a plank in feature 60, a board of some sort with burial 498, and part of a wooden bowl on Site B in feature 202.

60/3
Ash plank. This was 0.46 m long, 0.18 m wide and 5 mm thick, of trapezoidal cross-section. There were 31 rings to the bark, which had been removed, but bark beetle damage was visible on one edge of the plank. The plank had flat surfaces top and bottom and sloping sides. The unbroken end was convex.

498/6
Board, probably of alder. This consisted of a thin flat rectangular board 0.38 m long, 0.28 m wide and 5 mm thick. The grain ran longitudinally, and one or two small knots protruded slightly from the otherwise flat surface. Across one end was a thicker lump of wood, segment-shaped, the inner side straight and at 90° to the grain of the board, the outer convex, making the object rounded at this end (see Fig. 7). The convex side appeared to be chamfered or bevelled down from the top to the bottom, not of uniform thickness right to the edge. This segment was 50 mm wide and 18–20 mm thick.

When first uncovered the whole object appeared to be made from one piece of wood. However, the thicker piece separated when the object was lifted, and on close inspection the grain was seen to be running across at 90°

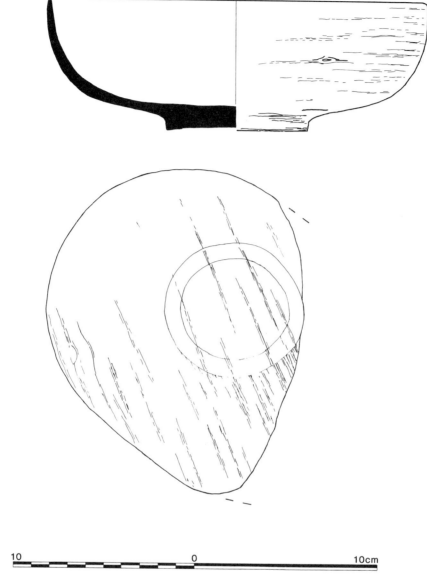

10   0   10cm

Figure 29 Wooden lathe-turned bowl from 202

to that of the board. No pegs or other indications of how the two pieces were joined were found, but the wood was highly decayed, and there is no doubt that both were part of one object. Possibly it was glued together.

202/C/4 (Fig. 29)
Alder or hazel bowl. Two-thirds of a lathe-turned bowl, 210 mm in diameter and 57 mm deep internally, with a simple tapered rim and a small footring.

LEATHER *by T G Allen*
Fragments of leather were found in pit 498 adjacent to and covering the board and other pieces of wood. They perhaps came from a bag or skin containing these objects.

A pair of Roman leather shoes was found in the bottom of ditch 35 on Site B. Both were fragmented; the better-preserved one was approximately 275 mm long, 73 mm wide at the heel and 80 mm wide at the base of the toes. The upper and sole had been nailed along the edge of the sole, the holes being very close at the toe end, and the soles were studded with hobnails up to 10 mm across. The sole was made up of three layers, sole, middle-sole and insole; part of the middle-sole and the stitching which attached it to the insole was preserved. Small fragments of the upper part of the shoe at the toe and heel also survived. Not illustrated.

Chapter 4

The Iron Age and Roman Environment

THE HUMAN BONES by Mary Harman

Several groups of human bones were found, in features 12, 23, 405, 410, 495 and 498. All were well preserved but badly broken and incomplete, and all but those in 405 were attributable to the Iron Age.

Feature 498, a waterlogged pit, yielded a very fragmentary skeleton. Most of the vertebrae and the hand and foot bones are missing. The size of the bones and the shape of the ilium suggest that this was a female. Half of the maxilla and part of the mandible are missing; enough remains to show that two of the lower right molars were lost before death. Only one molar tooth was found, showing light wear, but the occlusal surface of this and some other teeth are covered with calculus. The age at death is difficult to assess but was probably over 30 years. In Feature 12, an antenna ditch just outside the entrance to the main enclosure, there were skull vault fragments comprising the occipital, parts of the parietals and temporals of an adult, or possibly a late adolescent, of unknown sex.

In the ditch 495, in different levels of two different sections 2.0 m apart, there were several skull vault fragments comprising the occipital, both parietals and several frontal fragments from an adult. A supraorbital ridge and a moderate roughness for the attachment of the nuchal muscles suggest that this is the skull of a male. There were several wormian bones in the lambdoid suture and the metopic suture was open, an unusual but not rare feature. This skull is remarkable in the number of cuts on the vault surface. On the frontal, a little above the right orbit, is a cut 30 mm long, delivered at an oblique angle from the right side of the man. There are three cuts on the right parietal; two near the sagittal suture, and one nearer the middle of the bone. The length of cut varies from 35–39 mm; all were inflicted from the left side, two at a fairly steep angle, breaking off a long narrow wedge of bone, one at a more shallow angle, causing an oval area of bone to flake off. The vertical depth of all the cuts from the surface of the skull varies from 1–2 mm. None penetrated to the brain. There is no sign of infection or of healing; the person may have died from loss of blood from these and possibly other injuries, or immediately from a more serious injury inflicted at the same time. It is possible that the blows result from *post mortem* mutilation but unlikely that they were inflicted on dry bone. This skull and the tibia in 410 (see below) may be derived from a nearby burial disturbed in antiquity though in view of the injuries it is possible that the skull had been detached from a body and retained for

a time as some sort of trophy before becoming incorporated in the ditch filling.

Feature 410 contained the shaft of a left tibia from an adult. It does not belong to the skeleton in 498, but it could belong, stratigraphically and spatially, to the skull in Feature 495, and this is not impossible osteologically.

Feature 23, probably a house enclosure, contained part of a right humerus from an adult. It is not part of the skeleton in 498.

405, a ditch of early Romano-British date, contained a fragment of the distal end of a tibia from an adult, probably a residual bone from an earlier burial disturbed in antiquity. There was also another inhumation on Site A, just inside the main enclosure ditch on the N side, but there was not time to excavate this. It lay within a grave-shaped feature on a N-S alignment, and was probably Romano-British.

THE ANIMAL AND FISH BONES
by R Wilson with Enid Allison

Summary and introduction

Over 8,200 bones and fragments were collected from the Iron Age and Roman occupations on Site A and nearly 1,000 from the Roman features on Site B. Many fragments are newly broken and the preservation of the bones is not good. The Romano-British assemblages are small and, unlike the Iron Age bones, cannot be associated with obvious domestic foci; consequently this report concentrates on the Iron Age bones.

The general conclusions drawn from the bones are typical of Iron Age sites elsewhere in the region. However, this enclosed site provided the opportunity to study the spatial distribution of Iron Age bones within the settlement. The results reinforce previous ideas about human and natural processes in the deposition of bones at different periods (Wilson in Page et al. forthcoming; Wilson in Allen and Robinson forthcoming).

Spatial configuration of bones and centres of domestic activity

The spatial differentiation of bones around centres of household activity is held to be the key to intrasite analysis. The Iron Age house sites, identified by their surrounding penannular ditches and by concentrations of pottery, lay within the main enclosure ditch. As expected most debris was associated with the features in this area, particularly the central and southern groups of penannular gullies; large stretches of the main enclosure ditch were excavated (Fig. 3) but produced few bones. Predictably (Wilson 1985, 81–93), the medium-sized remains, typified by those of sheep and pig, and also burnt and worked bones, were most abundant in the Iron Age penannular gullies and are deemed indicators of household or domestic activity. Larger bones, those of cattle and horse, were relatively more abundant at the site periphery: in the main enclosure ditch, in the external entrance way antennae ditches, 12 and 13 etc., and further away in the south-western enclosure 17–20 etc. Burnt bones were few in these features. These Iron Age trends do not appear to be affected by recutting of the main enclosure ditch in the Romano-British period and problems of distinguishing Iron Age from Romano-British deposits within it.

Some other Iron Age feature groups contained sufficient sheep, pig, burnt and worked bones to suggest households or domestic activity adjacent. These were the small enclosure gullies 124–163 and 496–513, and the small north-western enclosure gullies 485 etc. outside and abutting the main enclosure ditch.

Early Romano-British deposits fitted into this general central to peripheral trend of site debris. For example ditches 405 and 411, inside and parallel to the main enclosure ditch on the northern side, were intermediate or peripheral in character. Another feature group in the eastern area, consisting of 96, 136 etc., was also intermediate in character.

Later Romano-British deposition is more difficult to assess. Evidence of specific domestic activity is scanty or ambiguous with a problem in the central area from redeposited Iron Age material. According to the interpretative model the abundant cattle and horse bones, noticeably in the northern area (for example in the waterholes or wells), would indicate coarse debris deposited away from the main centre(s) of occupation.

Bone preservation,
bone retrieval and the spread of bones
An index of bone degradation among the skeletal elements of sheep showed that most groups of bones were considerably degraded (73–82%) though preservation appeared better in the main enclosure ditch group (36%). Some bones from the deeper features, for example the dog skeletons, were visibly better preserved.

Although bone degradation markedly affects the presence of skeletal elements, it does not appear to bias the percentage representation of species bones unduly providing that there is good retrieval of loose teeth and other elements (Wilson 1983, 81–93). The percentages of small elements of sheep retrieved are not as high as at some other sites, but this is probably due to bone degradation of many of the small elements of the joints and foot.

Spatial differentiation
of bones outward from household sources
On the basis of Iron Age evidence from another contemporary enclosed settlement at Mingies Ditch, Hardwick with Yelford, Oxon. (Wilson in Allen and Robinson forthcoming), an explanatory model for the spatial differentiation of bone debris is proposed as follows. Three main interactive causes are postulated. The first two, scavenging and rubbish clearance from inside houses and from some outside areas, for example external hearths, tend to disperse larger bones and fragments from central areas of intensive human activity. Small and fine refuse may be thrown or scattered outwards too but some will tend to be left behind.

The third factor is that coarse and fine debris from carcass butchery accumulates at or near slaughtering and butchery places, which are located at increasing distances from houses and hearths relative to the size of species carcasses. Small carcasses can be butchered and cooked with a minimum of mess and other inconvenience in or near houses. Butchery of large carcasses is more disruptive of household activity and ought to take place further away. Increase in the size of carcass is also thought to alter the type of butchery. Joints of medium sized animals may be carried to the fire to be cooked and eaten and their bones tend to accumulate near there. Butchery of meat from the carcasses of large animals, however, probably cut out many bones prior to cooking and left them at the periphery of the occupation area.

The quantitative contribution of each cause to the spatial spread of bones is not yet known but the majority of surviving bones remain within 15 m of houses, although it seems certain that scavenging scatters some bones much further.

Bones at Watkins Farm were probably well chewed and scattered by scavengers — articulated bones were uncommon and horse bones in the house gullies often lacked epiphyses, as if scavenging had destroyed them.

Debris in the house gullies at Watkins Farm was coarser in character than refuse around the houses at Mingies Ditch. This difference is, however, largely due to the high representation of sheep and pig in spreads of bones on the Iron Age ground surface at Mingies Ditch; the Iron Age ground surface was not preserved at Watkins Farm, and the character of debris in the house gullies on both sites is similar. The overall impression from both sites is that rubbish was not thrown far, often accumulating just outside houses, whence coarser material was scattered into deeper features. Some of the coarse debris occurred near houses due to selection of horse and cattle bones for the manufacture of implements.

Three dog skeletons were uncovered in the main enclosure ditch and two in the south-western enclosure. Although dog bones were found in the central area, this appears to indicate the disposal of dead dogs at the site periphery — those, that is, that were not eaten (see below).

Carcass butchery

Informative instances of butchery were recorded. Skinning, meat removal (and bone working) are evident from horse bones, and skin or meat removal from a proximal tibia of a dog. The general impression of other butchery marks is that butchery even in the Roman period conforms to the Iron Age or Celtic pattern at sites such as Ashville, Abingdon (Wilson in Parrington 1978, 126-8), and not to that at the Roman site of Claydon Pike, Lechlade (Levitan and Wilson in Miles and Palmer, forthcoming).

During both periods at rural sites, however, the butchery of large carcasses at least was probably carried out on the ground. A cattle sacrum from 137 was chopped through the side from the anterior, Romano-British evidence that carcasses were not hung by the back legs and then cut down the middle from the 'posterior' end of the animal (Mingies Ditch: Wilson in Allen and Robinson forthcoming).

Skeletal element distributions of sheep, cattle and horse did not suggest any differences between central and peripheral areas. They suggested little about the type of butchery or location of slaughtering places, and perhaps confirm the impact of natural agencies destroying bones with concurrent activity of scavengers leaving most others scattered randomly, apart, that is, from the outward drift of the large bones.

Two sets of articulated cattle vertebrae did, however, survive in the northern and western part of the main enclosure ditch, 404, and in a Romano-British parallel ditch, 405. These could indicate nearby slaughtering places, the backbones being left there after the removal of the meat. Possibly scavengers dragged the vertebrae there though a large backbone might not be easily managed.

Articulated limb bones, notably of horse, were occasionally found at the site periphery including pit 499 and the entrance-way ditches. Moderately complete crania were spread more widely. Some of this material may reflect only the better survival of bones in the peripheral features and it is difficult to say whether scavenging or place of butchery was the predominant factor.

Skeletons of late or uncertain date

An undated burial of a horse, which died aged about 15 years, lay most intriguingly in the middle of the central house in feature 464. Robust bones and an estimated shoulder height of 1.36 m indicate that it was taller than most Iron Age horses and a later date, perhaps in the Roman period, is conceivable.

Other articulated debris includes the bones of a large foal, dated by pottery to the 18th century or later, from 55. A juvenile pig skeleton from 49 has large bones, a broad cranium, and suspiciously fresh, unstained, internal cortical bone and indicates a post-medieval burial.

The dog skeletons in the main enclosure ditch may be Iron Age or Romano-British.

Species abundance

Wild species were represented by occasional bones of red deer, hare, cat (?wild), water vole, field vole and frog. A group of pike bones occurred in an Iron Age well, feature 60. Enid Allison identified single bones of mallard and heron from the central house gullies, one of buzzard from the main enclosure ditch, and two of greylag or domestic goose in Romano-British ditch 162. Although uncommon, these wild species show that

Table 11: Fragment frequency in major groups of bone

	Main Site Iron Age	Early R-B	R-B	R-B	Site B Sieving (a) IA (main site)
	F	F	F	F	
Cattle	405	278	123	107	1
Sheep/goat (b)	429	100	42	21	10
Pig	87	24	27	8	-
Horse (c)	237	138	53	55	-
Dog	34	40	1	15	-
Cat (d)	2	-	-	-	-
Hare	-	2	-	-	-
Red deer	2A	2+A	A	-	-
Unidentified	2409	1796	688	786	333
TOTAL	3605	2385	935	992	344
Burnt	34	4	8	10	13
Bird	2	1	1	-	-

A = Antler R-B fragment may be from roe deer

a = Sieving also recovered 2 bones of water vole *Arvicola* sp. and 3 of frog. One of field vole *Microtus arvalis* occurred among a small amount of Roman sieved debris. Field vole was also recovered from an Iron Age well 60 along with bones of a pike.

b = Probable goat tooth p4 identified among sieved bones.

c = Dog and horse may be over-represented due to presence of articulated or cranial debris.

d = Cat bones are of large individuals and could be of wild cat.

fishing and hunting were part of the Iron Age economy; evidence for this has been absent from previous excavations in the area including Mingies Ditch.

Domestic species predominated (see Table 11). In comparison with other Iron Age assemblages fragment frequencies of horse were unusually high at or above 20% of the identified bones. The relative abundance of Iron Age cattle is also high but not especially unusual. As at other sites, sheep bones were still the commonest among the Iron Age bones and cattle commonest among the Romano-British.

Estimates of the Minimum Number of Individuals (MNI) from the mandibles, however, show a greater representation of the medium and small sized species. Since bones of robust and mature individuals, especially horses, survive best and are recovered more readily, fragment frequencies are less reliable than MNI in estimating the relative abundance of animals at this type of site. This argument is reinforced by the evidence of considerable bone degradation.

Results from MNI still confirm a relative decline into the Roman period of the representation of sheep and increases of cattle, pig and horse, though sheep and pig may be under-represented in the later group due to depositional differences noted earlier. Even then the method of calculating MNI appears to under-represent sheep. Actual MNI indicate that 48% of individual

mammals (excluding rodents) were sheep, but the percentage could be argued to be as high as 60%.

Since spatial and depositional variability have been demonstrated within single settlements, strict comparability between results from different sites is difficult, in that most excavations have been partial and different types and quantities of site deposits have been excavated. In broad terms, however, cattle and horse appear better represented than usual in Iron Age features. In rank order, the abundance by percentages of MNI of these two species at Upper Thames Valley gravel sites is: Farmoor, Appleford, Barton Court Farm, Watkins Farm, City Farm, Mingies Ditch, Mount Farm and Ashville. If Watkins Farm is late in the Iron Age then the results may be affected by the declining representation of sheep into the Roman period.

Animal size and breed

Typically, the size of the Iron Age animals was small but size increased during the Roman period. An Iron Age polled cranial fragment of cattle was found but horn cores were more numerous.

Mortality patterns

The patterns of the mandible and tooth age stages of cattle, sheep and pigs (Fig. 30) are typical of those at other Iron Age settlements and less Romanised settlements of the early Roman period. Those of sheep

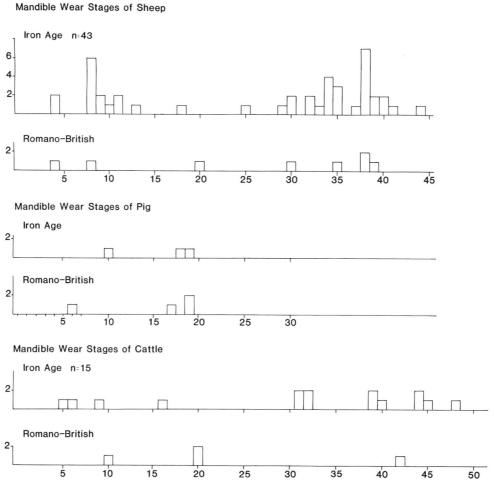

Figure 30 Histograms showing mandible wear stages of sheep, pig and cattle

show strong peaks in the mortality pattern in the first year and in old age, and the cattle mandibles also group in the same age stages. This is generally interpreted as reflecting an emphasis on dairying for cattle and uponewes for wool and for breeding in sheep, killing off male calves and lambs before their first winter. The kill-off pattern of sheep may, however, also have been dependent upon the amount of available grazing and fodder left after the cattle had been provided for. Pigs, as is usual, did not live beyond adulthood. Age data from horses also confirm that most horses died as mature or old individuals though both epiphyses and mandibles indicate that the percentage of immature horses was greater than at some other sites.

Females appear best represented among the metapodials and pelves of cattle and horse.

Three unexceptional instances of pathology were recorded: two of horse indicating the tendency of bones in the hock joint to fuse, perhaps as a result of packhorse or riding stress or injury. No evidence indicative of the keeping of draught oxen was found.

Culture and economy

There is little to suggest major differences in culture and economy from other regional sites. The animal husbandry was probably part of a relatively self-contained subsistence pattern and concentrated on animal rearing and dairying, with sheep playing a secondary role for meat and wool.

An anomalous representation of horse bones has largely been accounted for in terms of bone taphonomy. Nevertheless cattle and horse still appear better represented than usual. A case might be made for specialised breeding and training of horses, some of which died immature. Though some husbandry and economic changes are indicated by the species representation, the butchery evidence suggests Romano-British continuity with the Iron Age or Celtic pattern.

Bones from Site B

Only 206 bones could be identified to species. This Romano-British debris is similar in composition to that at the main site with cattle and then horse best represented. The proportion of sheep and pig is even lower than in the Roman period on Site A, but dog is well represented (see Table 11). Neither excavation area has an obvious centre of domestic activity, but some focus or foci might be expected in the vicinity.

THE CHARRED PLANT REMAINS *by Lisa Moffett*

Samples for charred plant remains were taken from both the Iron Age and Romano-British phases of the site (see Figs. 31 and 32). One objective of the sampling programme was to see if there was any change between these phases. Greater emphasis was placed on the Iron Age, and a further objective was to see if there were differences between the small enclosures within the main Iron Age enclosure, which might perhaps have been related to the activities carried out within them. However, the number of items recovered in most of the samples was too low for this. A number of the examples, particularly the Romano-British ones, contained no charred plant remains except for wood charcoal. Those samples which did contain charred plant remains appear to reflect a concentration of activity in one area of the Iron Age site, as discussed below.

The cereal remains consisted of spelt (*Triticum spelta*), a possible club wheat grain (*Triticum* cf. *aestivo-compactum*) and six-row hulled barley (*Hordeum vulgare*). The spelt was identified by its obtuse-angled and strongly veined glume bases (the bases of the protective enclosing chaff parts). Only a few glume bases were well preserved enough to be identified; the rest had to be referred to the emmer/spelt (*Triticum dicoccum/spelta*) indeterminate category. The presence of emmer cannot be ruled out, although there is no direct evidence for it. The barley was identified as the six-row type from one rachis fragment and from one grain which was well preserved enough to show the asymmetric 'twist' characteristic of the lateral florets of six-row barley. This evidence does not exclude the presence also of two-row barley, but the six-row variety is the kind generally known from prehistoric and Roman period sites in Britain.

Many of the non-cultivated species present are plants of both disturbed and arable habitats. A few, such as stinging nettle (*Urtica dioica*), elder (*Sambucus nigra*) and henbane (*Hyoscyamus niger*), do not grow as crop weeds and prefer nitrogen-rich habitats and disturbed ground. Hawthorn (*Crataegus* cf. *monogyna*) may have been growing either as clumps of scrub or, possibly, as hedges (M Robinson, pers. comm.). Spikerush (*Eleocharis palustris/uniglumis*) is a wet ground plant. It appears in more of the samples than any of the other non-cultivated plants and may have grown in the waterlogged enclosure ditches. All of these plants could have been growing around the site in the disturbed habitats provided by human occupation, and the surrounding grass and scrub. Some undoubtedly were introduced onto the site as weeds in the cereals.

The distribution of the plant remains seems to locate clearly the primary area where crop products were coming into contact with fire and being disposed of, at least in the Iron Age phase (Fig. 31). This area appears to be the NW side of the central house enclosure in the area of feature 487. Other features within the main enclosure contain a thin scatter of charred remains, but no charred remains (except a few fragments of wood charcoal) were recovered from the ditch itself or from outside it, except for hearth 553. As expected, the cereal

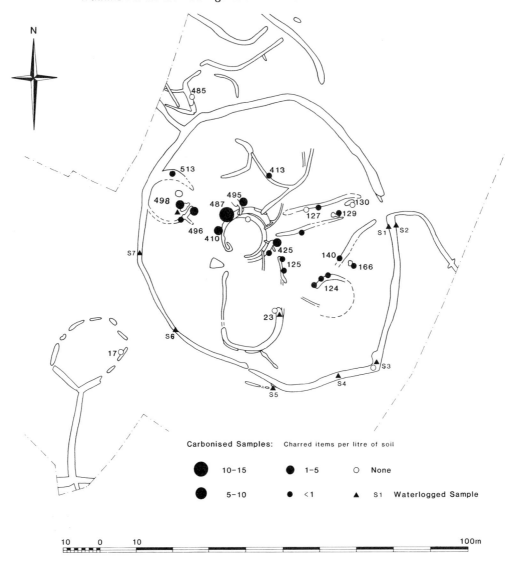

*Figure 31 Site A: Plan of Iron Age features showing
position of environmental samples and density of carbonised remains*

remains thus reflect the disposal pattern of other domestic rubbish.

This pattern of distribution and the general paucity of remains suggest small-scale processing of cereals for immediate domestic use. Glume wheats such as spelt need to be parched and pounded to release the grain, and the most effective way of removing the waste product — the chaff and weeds — is by winnowing to remove the lighter chaff and weed seeds and then sieving to remove the denser chaff items (such as glume bases and spikelet forks), small dense weed seeds and small tail grains. When this grain processing is done on a large scale, it generates a large amount of the chaff/weed by-product which may be stored and used as tinder (Hillman 1984a). If the processing is done on a small scale from day to day, the chaff may go straight back into the hearth or oven used for parching (Hillman 1984b). Both chaff and

grains may also become charred as a result of accidents during parching.

The numbers of items in these samples are, in the main, too low to attempt to recognise whether they originate from chaff by- products or prime grain products (a minor amount of mixing between crop-processing products is inevitable). Layer 4 in well 498, burnt debris overlying a burial in the pit, contained mainly emmer/spelt chaff, perhaps used to start the fire, but the total amount of chaff present is small. A sample from house enclosure ditch 496-512 adjacent contained mainly grain (chiefly barley) and weeds. These deposits may simply represent two separate incidents of rubbish disposal. The one feature which did contain substantial amounts of charred plant remains, pit 487, appears to be a mixed deposit. A quarter of the items in this sample are prime cereal grains (barley and wheat) with some

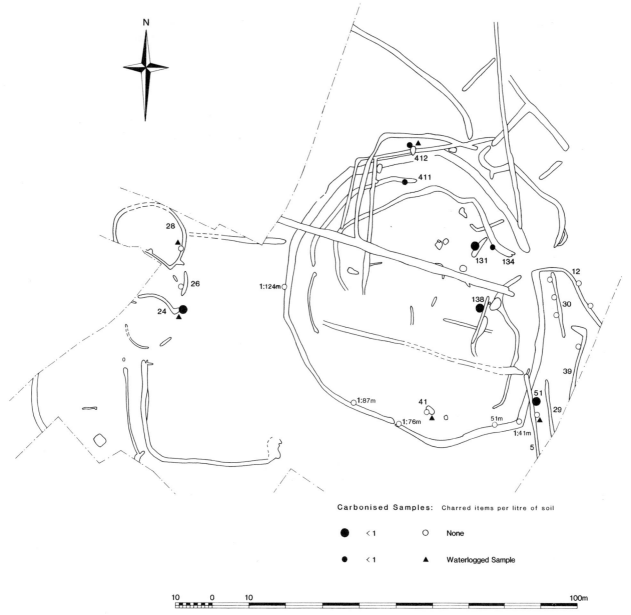

N

Carbonised Samples: Charred items per litre of soil

● < 1   ○ None

● < 1   ▲ Waterlogged Sample

10   0   10   100m

Figure 32 Site A: Plan of Romano-British features showing position of environmental samples and density of carbonised remains

(mainly spelt) chaff. More than half of the sample was composed of weed seeds, but not all of them were from arable weed species, as henbane and elder were present as well. This suggests that the material was originally derived from several sources, although it could all have become charred at the same time.

There is little difference between the Iron Age and the Romano-British material except that there is less overall from the Romano-British phase (Fig. 32). The charred remains are still confined within the main enclosure ditch and there is no visible concentration within the enclosure area. However, there are probably not enough samples to detect a concentration if one existed; most of the Romano-British samples come from

the main enclosure ditch and features outside it, which could also account for the reduced amount of material.

It is not possible to determine from the plant remains if this site was a 'producer' or if it was exclusively a 'consumer' of crops. The presence of cereals on the site is not necessarily an indication of arable agriculture. In theory a 'producer' site would be expected to have the remains of crop-processing activities such as the straw remains from the threshing and first winnowing stage (Hillman 1981). There is no assemblage at Watkins Farm identifiable as any of the types of products that would be generated only at a 'producer' site. In practice, however, these products are often not found even on clearly arable farm sites because the circumstances under which these products are exposed to fire and thus preserved by charring are relatively rare.

Martin Jones has attempted to reconstruct the economy of Iron Age gravel terrace sites by plotting the percentages of grains, weeds and chaff on triangle scattergrams and noting how the assemblages cluster (Jones 1985). He contrasts the weed-dominated assemblages of two First Terrace sites which he interprets as 'consumer' sites (Smithsfield and Claydon Pike) with the more grain-dominated assemblages of two sites on the Second Terrace which he interprets as 'producer' sites (Ashville and Mount Farm). His argument (possibly a contentious one) is that prime grains are more likely to become charred at the site of production. If this theory is correct, then Watkins Farm ought to be roughly comparable to Smithsfield and Claydon Pike. In fact, the triangle scattergram (Fig. 33) for the Iron Age samples at Watkins Farm does not compare very convincingly with either pair of sites. Perhaps it would be more useful to work from the empirical evidence and to concentrate on determining which types of charred remains we can expect to find on sites where the subsistence base can be deduced by independent means.

To sum up, the relative scarcity and distribution of charred cereal items suggests cereal use and processing on a small or domestic scale. The depositional pattern suggests that the rubbish generated (which may also have included grains accidentally charred in a cooking process) was being disposed of on the NW side of the central round house, probably near where these processes were taking place. This pattern of activity might have continued into the Romano-British period, but there are too few samples to be able to say. It is not possible to tell from the charred plant remains whether the crops were grown at the site or whether this was strictly a 'consumer' site.

THE WATERLOGGED SEEDS, INSECTS, MOLLUSCS AND OTHER BIOLOGICAL EVIDENCE
by Mark Robinson

Introduction
The Iron Age and Romano-British settlement at Watkins Farm, Northmoor, was situated on the First Gravel Terrace of the river Thames. The site was low lying with the permanent water table only about 1.2 m below the modern ground surface, although the free draining nature of the gravels would have prevented the soil from remaining waterlogged for long. The site was above the usual flood level of the Thames in recent years but it was on the margin of the great flood of 1947 (information from Lt Col D Williams). Prior to excavation the site was a barley field, but in a few places a stone-free non-calcareous brown silty clay had survived beneath the modern ploughsoil, sealing the

Pleistocene gravels. Mollusc shells were absent from this truncated ancient soil and its interface with the gravel. The surface of the gravel, which largely comprised oolitic limestone, showed some evidence of leaching.

Waterlogged organic sediments occurred in the deeper Iron Age and Romano-British archaeological features, which were extensively sampled for macroscopic plant and invertebrate remains. Some non-waterlogged sediments were also sampled for molluscs. Bones were picked out by hand during the excavation with some wet sieving being done to check that recovery rates were adequate. Site A was sampled for carbonised plant remains.

Full details of the samples and the results are given in the Technical appendix section 3.

The environment of Site A, Iron Age

Conditions in the waterlogged features
Seven waterlogged samples were examined from along the length of ditch 1, the main enclosure ditch around the Iron Age settlement (Figs. 31 and 32). The macroscopic plant remains suggest that the ditch had been colonised by a range of aquatic plants. Seeds of the submerged aquatic plant *Ranunculus* S. *Batrachium* sp. (water crowfoot) were present in most of the samples. There was evidence both from the seeds and the phytophagous weevil *Tanysphyrus lemnae* that *Lemna* sp. (duckweed) covered the water's surface. Other water plants represented by macroscopic remains in a few of the samples include *Montia fontana* (blinks), *Apium nodiflorum* (fool's watercress), *Zannichellia palustris* (horned pondweed) and *Chara* sp. (stonewort). *Lycopus europaeus* (gypsy wort) apparently grew along the side of the ditch.

Aquatic Coleoptera, especially *Helophorus brevipalpis* gp. and Hydraenidae, for example *Hydraena testacea*, occurred in the ditches, but they were all taxa that can live in small bodies of stagnant water. The aquatic molluscs from the ditch can tolerate similar conditions, the presence of *Armiger crista* probably reflecting well-vegetated conditions while the occurrence of *Planorbis planorbis* would suggest that the ditch did not dry up seasonally.

A sample was also examined from sump 23, at the end of a gully forming a small enclosure within the main Iron Age enclosure. A single *Chara* oospore comprised the only remains of aquatic plants. Shells of aquatic molluscs were absent, although a few small water beetles such as *Helophorus brevipalpis* gp. were present.

The non-aquatic plant and invertebrate remains seem mostly to have entered the deposits through a variety of natural agencies. There is no evidence for much dumping of rubbish from the sediments. Although the main enclosure ditch had been colonised by a full flora and

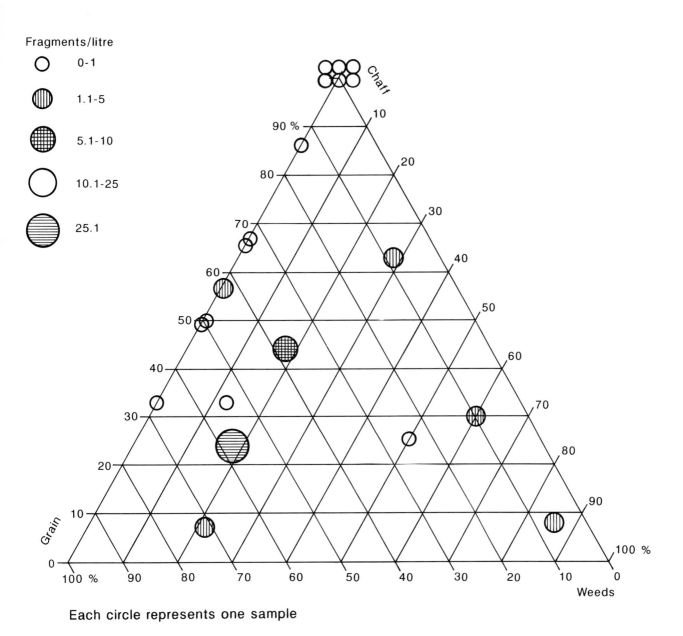

Each circle represents one sample

Figure 33 Diagram showing the relative proportions of cereals, chaff and weeds

invertebrate fauna appropriate to a small stagnant ditch, there is no evidence to suggest that the site experienced flooding during the Iron Age.

The general environment
The results from insect remains, which give more wide-ranging information than the other lines of evidence examined from Watkins Farm, suggest a relatively open although not entirely treeless landscape in which pasture was important. The more local information from the waterlogged seeds gives little hint of grassland, the seeds mostly being from plants of various sorts of disturbed

ground and scrub. The terrestrial molluscs were species of open habitats.

Grassland
There was a relatively strong presence of Scarabaeidae and Elateridae that feed on roots in grassland (Table 12: 11). The chafer *Phyllopertha horticola* and the click beetle *Agrypnus murinus* were the most abundant species. They are common species of permanent grassland. Scarabaeoid dung beetles, especially *Aphodius* spp., comprised 14% of the terrestrial Coleoptera. This suggests that there was a significant presence of domestic

Table 12: Percentages of terrestial coleoptera in Iron Age and Roman contexts

Species Grouping	Mingies Ditch Iron Age	Watkins Farm Iron Age	Roman Site A	Roman Site B
1. Aquatic	59.9	11.9	40.0	63.9
2. Pasture/Dung	13.5	14.3	15.2	5.0
3. ?Meadowland	4.3	3.7	2.9	9.5
4. Wood and Trees	1.8	1.6	0.8	1.7
5. Marsh/Aquatic Plants	0.9	2.2	0.3	3.1
6a. General Disturbed Ground/Arable	0	0	0	0.6
6b. Sandy Disturbed Ground/Arable	0	0	0.3	0.3
7. Dung/Foul Organic Material	10.3	10.8	8.5	6.4
8. Lathridiidae	2.2	2.7	1.9	5.9
9. Synanthropic	0.1	0.2	0.8	0
10. Esp. Structural Timbers	0.7	0.8	0.5	0.6
11. On Roots in Grassland	5.7	7.0	5.6	6.4
Total number of terrestrial individuals	2126	511	375	357

Species in groupings: 1, water beetles, defined as species that can spend a significant part of their adult life under water; 2, dung beetles from the genera Geotrupes, Colobopterus, Aphodius, and Onthophagus; 3, weevils of the genera Apion (excluding the identified mallow, nettle and willow feeding species) and Sitona (excluding the shrub feeding species); 4, wood and tree feeding Coleoptera plus fungus feeders and predators that are strictly associated with wood. Anobium punctatum and Lyctus sp. have been excluded; 5, Chrysomelidae and Curculionoidea that feed on marsh or aquatic plants; 6, Amara apricaria, A. bifrons, and A. tibialis, Agonum dorsale and Harpalus rufipes; 7, Cercyon spp., Megasternum sp., Cryptopleurum spp., Anotylus rugosus, A. sculpturatus and Platystethus arenarius; 8, Lathridiidae; 9, Stegobium paniceum, Ptinus fur etc. (Robinson in Jones and Dimbleby 1981, 265 and 268); 10, Anobium punctatum and Lyctus spp.; 11, various Elateridae and Scarabaeidae (Robinson in Jones 1983, 34).

animals grazing the grassland. The macroscopic plant remains do not provide much evidence of the grassland flora. Seeds of *Juncus* spp. (rushes), which due to their small size tend to have a greater dispersive range than the seeds of many other grassland plants, were relatively scarce from Watkins Farm compared with the results from Iron Age sites in the region on the Thames floodplain. The phytophagous Coleoptera included *Mecinus pyraster* and *Gymnetron labile*, which feed on *Plantago lanceolata* and *P. media* (plantains). Clover- and vetch-feeding weevils of the genera *Apion* and *Sitona* were present, although not in sufficient numbers to suggest meadowland conditions.

Disturbed ground

Seeds of annual and plough-tolerant weeds of the class Stellarietea occurred in sump 23 and some of the enclosure ditch samples. They included *Chenopodium polyspermum* (all seed), *Polygonum persicaria* (red shank), and *Urtica urens* (small nettle), all character or differential species of the Polygono-Chenopodietalia (Silverside 1977, 240–5). The Polygono-Chenopodietalia is an order of root crops, spring-sown cereals, gardens

and nitrogen-rich disturbed grounds, such as occur around settlements. The presence of *Chenopodium ficifolium* (goosefoot) and *Polygonum lapathifolium* (pale persicaria) suggests that its basophilus alliance, the Fumario-Euphorbion, occurred at Watkins Farm. Members of the Centauretalia cyani, an order which is more closely tied to arable agriculture, were absent or poorly represented; for example there was a single seed of *Valerianella dentata* (lamb's lettuce) (Silverside 1977, 317–21). There was no evidence from the insect remains to suggest arable and it seems likely that the seeds of annual weeds were mostly from plants growing on disturbed ground within the enclosure. Waterlogged remains of definite crop species were absent from these samples.

Seeds from ruderals which tend to occur around settlements such as *Papaver somniferum* (opium poppy), *Hyoscyamus niger* (henbane) and *Ballota nigra* (black horehound) were present. Seeds of *Urtica dioica* (stinging nettle) and *Sambucus nigra* (elder) were numerous both from sump 23 and the main enclosure ditch. Nettle-feeding insects included the beetle *Brachypterus* sp. and the bug *Heterogaster urticae*. These two plants probably grew on neglected ground in the enclosure.

Scrub or hedges

There was much evidence of scrub from the macroscopic plant remains, especially from the main enclosure ditch. The following taxa were represented:

Rhamnus catharticus	(purging buckthorn)
Rubus fruticosus agg.	(blackberry)
Prunus spinosa	(sloe)
Crataegus monogyna	(hawthorn)
Salix sp.	(sallow)
Sambucus nigra	(elder)
Thelycrania sanguinea	(dogwood)

The relatively low proportion of tree-dependent insects would suggest that the scrub was localised to the vicinity of the enclosure ditch. The tree leaf-feeding beetles were mostly species restricted to *Salix* and *Populus*, for example *Phyllodecta vulgatissima*, *Chalcoides* sp. and *Ramphus pulicarius*. There were even fewer beetles of dead wood, but the boring weevil *Acales turbatus*, which favours dead wood such as *Crataegus* in hedges was identified from two samples. A fertile female and 15 workers of the ant *Lasius fuliginosus* suggest the proximity of a nest. *L. fuliginosus* often nests in stumps or hedges, tending aphids on shrubs.

The most plausible explanation for the localised scrub is that there was a mixed hedge around the settlement, running adjacent to the main enclosure ditch. In view of the time it takes for a single species hedge to become quite as mixed as the range of taxa from the enclosure ditch might suggest (Hooper 1971, 6–13), it would seem likely either that a mixed hedge was planted or a hedge created by the selective clearance of scrub.

Accumulated organic material

A range of the beetles identified, especially Staphylinidae, occurs in various types of decaying organic material. However, they were not particularly abundant for a settlement site. One beetle of note from Sample 1-S6 from the main enclosure ditch was *Cetonia urata*, the rose chafer, a large bright metallic green creature. Its larvae live in compost while the adults tend to be attracted to flowering shrubs (Britton 1956, xi, 26; Paulian 1959, 269).

The woodworm beetle *Anobium punctatum*, was identified as was *Ptinus fur*, a synanthropic beetle that often lives indoors but also occurs in birds' nests. The presence of these two beetles was slight (Table 12: 9 and 10).

Iron Age burial

The discovery of a partly articulated human skeleton in an Iron Age waterlogged context, well 498 (see Fig. 7), raised the possibility that insect remains associated with the inhumation could be recovered. The forensic entomology of corpses has been thoroughly studied, and insect evidence has the potential to give much information on conditions at the time of burial.

Preserved organic remains were absent in samples from immediately under and adjacent to the skeleton, but a pocket of organic sediment survived beneath a badly decayed board, possibly of alder, at a similar level in the pit to the skeleton, and it proved productive of biological remains.

The presence of cladoceran (water flea) ephippia suggests that the pit contained water at the time of the burial, but there was not the range of aquatic plant and invertebrate remains that was discovered from most of the other waterlogged contexts. For the most part, the assemblage of plant remains from 498 was similar to that from sump 23, with seeds of *Urtica dioica* and members of the Polygono-Chenopodietalia being abundant. One interesting addition was *Onopordum acanthium* (cotton thistle), a ruderal of waste ground. Remains of flax and bracken were also present.

The insect results from 498 also showed a similarity to the results from sump 23, although there was perhaps a higher proportion of beetles which occur in decaying organic material. However, the most numerous beetle, although only represented by three individuals, was *Omosita discoidea*, a carrion feeder. *O. discoidea* does indeed feed on corpses, but it is a late colonist in the stages of faunal succession. It occurs under old bones, in dry carcasses and on similar material (Fowler 1889, 238; Harde 1984, 190). *O. discoidea* was one of the most numerous beetles recovered over the course of a year from a dead fox on Bookham Common, Surrey, during a study of the succession of Coleoptera on carrion (Easton 1966, 205 and 208). It was not recorded until five months after the corpse had been exposed, but it remained an important member of the community until the end of the seventh month.

The sample from well 498 did not contain puparia of the flies, especially from the families Calliphoridae and Muscidae, which render an exposed corpse a seething mass of maggots during the early stages of decay (Easton and Smith 1970, 209–10; Smith 1973, 484–5). Neither was there the more restricted dipterous fauna of a buried corpse, although the anaerobic conditions that would result from burial beneath the water table would probably prove hostile to such a fauna. For example the insects found in association with Lindow Man, an Iron Age or Roman body found in a Cheshire bog, did not include any species that were definitely dependent on the corpse (Girling 1986). In contrast, *Rhizophagus parallelocollis*, the graveyard beetle, has been recorded from several non-waterlogged medieval burials sealed in coffins (Girling in Detsicas 1981, 82–4).

Unfortunately, it is uncertain whether the three individuals of *O. discoidea* from well 498 were related to the human remains. This concentration of *O. discoidea* is higher than in any other archaeological sample from the region. If these beetles were from the corpse, it would imply that the body had been allowed to decompose for some months before being placed in the pit. If not, all the plant and invertebrate evidence from well 498 shows is that conditions on the site at the time of the burial were similar to those suggested by the other waterlogged Iron Age deposits.

Environmental
change during the occupation of the site
The results do not suggest that there were any major changes in environmental conditions during the Iron Age occupation of the enclosure. The earliest samples were Sample 1-S5, which was from an early cut of the main enclosure ditch, and Sample 1-S1, which was from the earliest organic sediments where the enclosure ditch was at its deepest, near the main entrance. These two samples had a better representation of annual weed seeds, both in terms of seed numbers and the range of species, than Samples 1-S3, 1-S4, 1-S6 and 1-S7, which possibly accumulated later in the life of the site. This was perhaps the result of an enclosure hedge becoming a more substantial barrier with time, preventing debris from the enclosure reaching the ditch. Sample 1-S2, which was from the later organic sediments in the main enclosure ditch near the main entrance, above Sample 1-S1, gave results similar to Samples 1-S1 and 1-S5. This suggests that part of the site remained frequently disturbed ground.

Evidence from waterlogged plant remains
and charcoal for activities at Site A, Iron Age
A waterlogged seed and capsule fragment of *Linum usitatissimum* (flax) were discovered in the sample from well 498, adding a further crop species to the list of cereal crops obtained from the carbonised evidence (Tables T20-T22). The First Gravel Terrace would have been suitable for the cultivation of flax (and cereals), but it is uncertain whether the occupants of the site cultivated crops nearby or imported oilseeds and cereals from elsewhere.

Frond fragments of *Pteridium aquilinum* (bracken) were present in well 498 and it is most likely that the bracken had been collected from an area of acidic soil. The nearest source would probably have been on the sands of the Lower Corallian, across the river Thames. It had perhaps been imported for use as bedding.

There were a few fragments of waterlogged *Quercus* (oak) from the main enclosure ditch, a worked plank of *Fraxinus* (ash) was discovered in well 60 and a board, possibly of *Alnus* (alder), was discovered in well 498. The charcoal was mostly from 'hedgerow' species, *Rhamnus catharticus* (purging buckthorn) charcoal being conspicuous in some contexts, but *Quercus* charcoal was also present. Since the evidence from the Coleoptera is for an open landscape, this would suggest that the site

was exploiting a small or distant piece of woodland for its large structural timbers. Most of the firewood, however, seems to have been from thorny scrub which was probably cut locally.

The environment of Site A, Romano-British

Conditions in the waterlogged features
Waterlogged samples were examined from gullies 28 and 51. The macroscopic plant remains suggest that they had aquatic floras of *Chara* sp. (stonewort), *Ranunculus S. Batrachium* sp. (water crowfoot) and *Callitriche* sp. (starwort). Their faunas of aquatic insects mostly comprised small water beetles of the families Hydrophilidae and Hydraenidae, and larvae of Trichoptera. Aquatic molluscs were present in both samples, but those from gully 28 included *Valvata cristata*, a species of flowing ditches, streams and rivers. It is possible that gully 28 drained into the stream system of the area.

The other waterlogged samples, from sump 24 and wells 41 and 412/5 (Fig. 32), contained a few water beetles and cladoceran ephippia.

As for the Iron Age waterlogged deposits, the non-aquatic plant and invertebrate remains seem mostly to have entered these features through a variety of natural agencies. There was no evidence for the flooding of this part of the site during the Roman period.

The general environment
The coleopteran evidence suggests the landscape of the Romano-British site to have been very open, wood and tree dependent beetles having decreased in abundance by half compared with the Iron Age results. The waterlogged seeds of terrestrial plants were mostly from plants of grassland and various sorts of disturbed ground.

Grassland
There was a close similarity between the Iron Age and Romano-British results from Site A for Coleoptera indicative of grassland. The same species of scarabaeoid chafers, grassland elaterids and scarabaeoid dung beetles were present and they comprised similar percentages of the terrestrial Coleoptera (Table 12: 2 and 11). Similar pastureland conditions probably prevailed.

A strong grassland element was present amongst the seeds from gully 28:

Ranunculus cf. *repens*	(buttercup)
Linum catharticum	
Potentilla anserina	(silverweed)
P. reptans	(creeping cinquefoil)
Prunella vulgaris	(self heal)
Leontodon sp.	(hawkbit)
Cirsium sp.	(thistle)

Seeds of *Juncus articulatus* gp. (rushes) were present in all the Romano-British samples from Site A but otherwise there were few grassland seeds in them apart from Sample 28. The phytophagus Coleoptera again included a few clover-feeding weevils, for example *Hypera punctata*, and the plantain-feeding weevil *Mecinus pyraster*. The results from the Coleoptera, together with the macroscopic plant remains from gully 28, suggest a flora of rather damp circumneutral pasture, as might indeed be expected to occur on a low-lying part of the First Gravel Terrace.

Disturbed ground
A similar range of seeds from annual and plough-tolerant weeds belonging to the Polygono-Chenopodietalia occurred in the Iron Age and Romano-British waterlogged deposits at Site A. It is possible that there was arable land in the vicinity of the settlement, but the weed flora and the few waterlogged flax remains from gully 51 are insufficient to confirm the proximity of arable. Most of the weeds probably grew on disturbed ground around the settlement

Seeds of the almost ubiquitous *Urtica dioica* (stinging nettle) and *Sambucus nigra* (elder) were again present. These two species were probably joined by *Chaerophyllum temulentum* (rough chervil) growing in neglected or shady corners of the settlement.

Scrub
Unlike the Iron Age phase of the site, macroscopic remains of woody taxa were not abundant in most of the waterlogged deposits. Apart from remains of *Rubus fruticosus* (blackberry) in gully 28, seeds of thorny hedgerow species were almost absent. There is no evidence to suggest that gullies 28 and 51 were lined by hedges. However, leaves, buds and capsules of *Salix* sp. (willow) occurred in gully 51. Whereas the *Salix* leaves from the Iron Age deposits were from a broad-leaved member of the section *Vimen* (sallows) with a glandular margin, such as *S. caprea* or *S. cinerea*, the leaves from gully 51 were very elongate and had revolute margins. This indicates that they were from *S. viminalis* (common osier) or *S. viminalis* x (hybrid osier). The sample from gully 51 was the only one to contain willow-feeding leaf beetles (the Chrysomelidae *Phyllodecta vulgatissima* and *Chalcoides* sp.). Perhaps osiers grew alongside the gully.

Accumulated organic material
There was not much difference between the Iron Age and Romano-British faunas of accumulated organic material and decaying plant remains from the site. A range of Staphylinidae, Lathridiidae etc. of such habitats was present although none was abundant. A few specimens of *Anobium punctatum*, the woodworm beetle, were again recorded. Perhaps the only difference of any

significance was the occurrence in the Romano-British samples of a slightly greater range of synanthropic beetles. *Ptinus fur* was joined by *Typhaea stercorea* which feeds on fungal spores, especially on straw and hay waste indoors, and *Stegobium paniceum*, a minor pest of stored grain and other farinaceous material.

Evidence from waterlogged plant remains and charcoal for activities at Site A, Romano-British
The couple of flax capsule fragments are insufficient to establish that flax was processed at the site rather than that linseed was imported. The find of a stone of *Prunus domestica* (plum) from well 41 gave the only evidence of horticultural crops from the site. The discovery of osier remains from gully 51 is interesting for it is possible that the osiers had been planted and their pliant rods cut for wickerwork.

Most of the more substantial pieces of waterlogged wood from the Romano-British deposits were oak, and oak charcoal was identified. However, a brief inspection of the Roman period charcoal showed that most of the firewood was small diameter roundwood from a variety of shrubs.

The environment of Site B, Romano-British

Conditions in the contexts investigated
Sample 206/8 was from a waterhole (Figs. 18 and 19). The seeds suggest that the surface of the stagnant water it held was covered with *Lemna* sp. (duckweed). The fauna of the waterhole comprised the slum aquatic molluscs *Aplexa hypnorum* and *Anisus leucostoma*, trichopteran (caddis fly) larvae, and a few small water beetles, particularly *Hydraena testacea*. *Mentha* cf. *aquatica* (water mint), *Iris pseudacorus* (yellow flag) and rushes of the *Juncus articulatus* group apparently grew in the shallow water and on the marshy ground around the edge of the waterhole.

Feature 204 was a pond with a full stagnant water flora and fauna, rather than a waterhole. Samples 204S1, 204S2 and 205S3 were from the sediments which accumulated during its life as a pond. The macroscopic plants remains from them suggest a submerged aquatic flora of *Chara* sp. (stonewort), *Ranunculus* S. *Batrachium* sp. (water crowfoot), with *Apium nodiflorum* (fool's parsley), *Mentha* cf. *aquatica* (water mint), *Alisma* sp. (water plantain) and *Juncus articulatus* gp. (rushes) growing around the margin. The aquatic molluscs included *Armiger crista*, which favours well vegetated habitats, and *Planorbis planorbis*, which can tolerate neither foul water nor its habitat drying out. The aquatic insects included *Sialis* sp., the alder fly of fishermen, which breeds in lakes, ponds and rivers where there is an abundance of silt (Kimmings 1962). There was a wide range of beetles of stagnant water including *Hydroporus* sp., *Agabus bipustulatus*, *Helophorus* spp, *Hyrobius fuscipes*, *Ochthebius minimus* and *Limnebius papposus*. Although seeds of *Lemna* sp. (duckweed) were absent, the weevil *Tanysphyrus lemnae*, which is restricted to feeding on duckweed, was well represented. Beetles which would have lived around the edge of the pond would have included the amphibious *Dryops* sp. and *Lesteva longoelytrata*, which occurs amongst moist vegetation and litter near water.

In complete contrast only Cladocera (water fleas) seem to have lived in Ditch 202, remains of aquatic plants being entirely absent.

The non-aquatic plant and invertebrate remains seem mostly to have entered these features through a variety of natural agencies. There was no evidence for flooding from any of the samples mentioned so far. However, shells of *Valvata cristata* and opercula of *Bithynia* sp. occurred in a molluscan assemblage from the upper fill of pond 204 which accumulated after it had ceased to function as a pond, Sample 204/S4. These are flowing water species which would not have been able to survive in a water-filled hollow on the site of the former pond. It is possible that these shells had been introduced by flooding, but the deposit was not pure alluvium as it also contained gravel. Reworked fragments of flowing water molluscs were present amongst gravel used to backfill the main Iron Age enclosure ditch (Technical appendix section 3, Mollusca) and it is possible that some of the shells in Sample 204 S4 had been reworked.

The general environment

The evidence from the Coleoptera would suggest that the general landscape was open, although the macroscopic plant remains included a significant woodland or scrub component. The remaining seeds of terrestrial plants were from species of grassland.

Grassland and coarse herbage

Scarabaeidae and Elateridae that feed on roots in grassland were as abundant as from Site A, but the percentage of Scarabaeoidae that feed on animal droppings on pastureland, such as *Aphodius* spp, was very much reduced (Table 12: 11, 2). However, the percentage of clover- and vetch-feeding weevils of the genera *Apion* and *Sitona* was particularly high in comparison with other sites in the Thames Valley (Table 12: 3; Robinson in Jones 1983, 39). These weevils tend to be abundant in meadowland.

The Coleopteran assemblage from Site B predominantly comprised specimens from pond 204. These results suggest that although grassland was

important, there was not a strong presence of domestic herbivores in the vicinity, and it seems unlikely that the pond could have been used for the watering of cattle during the period when it was silting. It is possible that the grassland took the form of meadowland. Seeds of two meadowland herbs, *Silaum silaus* (pepper saxifrage) and *Centaurea* cf. *nigra* (knapweed), were identified from the pond but remains of the full range of meadowland plants were absent. It seems more likely that there was an area of neglected grassland, perhaps transitional to scrub, in the vicinity of the pond, where the vegetation also included such plants as *Epilobium* sp. (willow herb) and *Rumex conglomeratus* (clustered dock), both of which were well represented by seed.

There were few remains of grassland plants from Samples 206/8 and 202/3.

Disturbed ground

Waterhole 206, pond 204 and ditch 202 each gave rather different evidence from macroscopic plant remains about the presence of disturbed ground at Site B. The results from Sample 206/8 suggest the presence of nitrogen-rich, frequently disturbed ground on which grew weeds of the Polygono-Chenopodietalia, including *Thlaspi arvense* (field penny-cress). Waterlogged remains of arable crops were absent. The seeds also included *Conium maculatum* (hemlock) and *Urtica dioica* (stinging nettle), characteristic weeds of the nutrient-rich waste ground that tends to be associated with human settlements, agricultural buildings etc.

Remains of plants of disturbed ground were rather sparse from pond 204 apart from species which often occur in hedgerows or at the edge of scrub, such as *Torilis* sp. (hedge parsley) and *Galium aparine* (goose grass). However, remains of *Papaver somniferum* (opium poppy) and *Linum usitatissimum* (flax) were recovered.

In contrast, the seeds from Sample 202/3 were almost all from annual weeds. The most abundant seeds were from *Anthemis cotula* (stinking mayweed), a plant that is now very much an arable weed but formerly grew in abundance around settlements. It is possible that the seed assemblage from Sample 202/3 was derived from arable land. Indeed, the assemblage was so different in character from the other waterlogged assemblages from Site B that it is possible that ditch 202 belonged to a different phase of use of the site.

Scrub and woodland

Waterlogged macroscopic remains of woody taxa were much in evidence in pond 204, rather less so in waterhole 206 and absent from ditch 202. Seeds, buds or leaves of the following trees and shrubs were identified from pond 204:

Rubus fruticosus agg.	(blackberry)
Crataegus monogyna	(hawthorn)
Salix viminalis or *viminalis* x	(osier)
Populus sp.	(poplar)
Fraxinus excelsior	(ash)
Sambucus nigra	(elder)

Populus sp. was identified from buds, but it is uncertain which species was represented. The two native species, *P. tremula* (aspen) and *P. nigra* (black poplar) grow in a very few localities on the First Terrace of the Thames, but *P. alba* (white poplar) and *P. canescens* (grey poplar), whose status in the British flora is uncertain (Rackham 1986, 206–8), are more widespread. The seeds of herbaceous plants included species which occur in hedgerows and around the edge of woodland on moist ground, such as *Barbarea vulgaris* (winter cress) and *Chaerophyllum temulentum* (rough chervil), but there was not a full woodland flora. The percentage of tree and wood-dependent Coleoptera was very similar to the percentage from Site A Iron Age (Table 12: 4). The species present were again willow- and poplar-feeding *Chrysomelidae* (leaf beetles) and the wood-boring weevil *Acalles turbatus*. The lace bug *Physatocheila dumetorum*, which is associated with lichen-covered rosaceous shrubs, was an interesting addition to the fauna and it serves as a reminder that prior to modern air pollution, branches would have had a more luxuriant covering of lichen.

It is clear from the results that the landscape around pond 204 was not predominantly woodland. Although *Crataegus* sp. (hawthorn) was present, the list of trees and shrubs does not comprise the normal range of thorny scrub species, neither is it obviously a hedgerow assemblage. It is possible that a clump of poplars, osiers and ash had been planted next to the pond.

Other habitats

There was similar evidence to that from Site A for the presence of decaying organic material but synanthropic beetles other than the woodworm beetle were absent.

Discussion

The results from the investigation of waterlogged biological remains from Watkins Farm, Northmoor, were very similar to those from an enclosed Iron Age settlement about 4 km to the NW, on the floodplain of the river Windrush at Mingies Ditch, Hardwick (Allen and Robinson forthcoming). In both cases, the landscapes were predominantly pasture but the settlements were apparently surrounded by mixed hedges. A remarkable similarity was shown between the Coleoptera of these two Iron Age sites (Table 12). The only major difference was in the much higher percentage of aquatic Coleoptera from Mingies Ditch, which is readily explained by the enclosure ditches on that site extending further below the

water table. The environment of these two Iron Age sites contrasted with the environment of the open Iron Age pastoral settlement at Farmoor, which seems to have been set in a landscape almost devoid of trees and shrubs (Robinson 1981, 260). The Iron Age sites at Mingies Ditch and Watkins Farm are perhaps best seen as pioneering settlements, bringing a landscape which has not been fully cleared and which is without well defined boundaries into more intensive use.

The Iron Age settlement at Watkins Farm was largely or entirely pastoral, whereas a large contemporaneous settlement at Gravelly Guy, about 2.5 km to the NW on the Second Thames Terrace, (Fig. 1) had a considerable involvement in arable agriculture. The importance of arable land on the higher gravel terraces of the Thames and grassland in the valley bottom during the Iron Age has already been noted (Robinson in Cunliffe and Miles 1984, 7). The soil at Watkins Farm, however, could have been cultivated even though it would not have made such good arable as the soil at Gravelly Guy. Flax seeds and capsule fragments were discovered in small quantities from the Iron Age site and both Romano-British sites at Watkins Farm. While flax is commonly found on Romano-British sites it is an unusual find for an Iron Age site in the region. None of the finds need indicate flax cultivation at Watkins Farm but the occurrence of capsule fragments might suggest that the crop was being processed at the site rather than that linseed was being imported.

There were some other interesting species records from the waterlogged deposits of the Iron Age enclosure ditch. A specimen of the dung beetle *Onthophagus nutans*, which is now extinct in Britain, was identified from Sample 1S6. This beetle has already been recorded from Iron Age deposits at Mingies Ditch, 4 km to the NW and Blackditch, 2.5 km to the N (Allen and Robinson forthcoming). There must have been a thriving population of *O. nutans* in the Stanton Harcourt area during the Iron Age.

Seeds of *Conium maculatum* (hemlock) were present in Samples 1S4 and 1S7, from the later organic sediments of the Iron Age enclosure ditch. There are no other pre-Romano-British finds of hemlock from the region. Hemlock seeds have, however, been identified from sediments in an Iron Age ditch at Fisherwick, Staffs., dated to 180 ± 100 bc (Greig in Smith 1979, 185–6).

The Romano-British environment of Site A seems to have been similar to that of other Romano-British sites on the First Gravel Terrace, with a strong presence of pastureland and an uncertain presence of arable (Robinson 1983, 37–40). However, there was no evidence for hedged boundaries. The occurrence of beetles which tend to be associated with settlements and agricultural buildings was at a low level, comparable to Iron Age settlements of the valley bottom rather than suggesting the 'intensity of occupation' shown by most Romano-British sites (Table 12: 8 and 10) (Robinson 1981, 280–1).

The results from Site B, Romano-British were unusual, in that there was evidence neither for pasture nor arable. The finds of *Populus sp.* (poplar) buds from pond 204 provide the first evidence for a tree that had not previously been suspected of growing on the Thames terraces during the Roman period. The discovery of leaves of *Salix viminalis* or *viminalis* x (osier) from both the Roman sites is interesting because they comprise the only archaeological evidence so far from the region for the shrub which became the willow most commonly planted for wickerwork and basketry. It is probable that *S. viminalis* was so used in the Roman period.

The evidence from Watkins Farm has served to show that the nature of Iron Age settlement at Mingies Ditch was not unique and to give new details about the Romano-British environment of the First Gravel Terrace.

Acknowledgements

This work was done in the University Museum, Oxford, and funded by the Historic Buildings and Monuments Commission (Oxford). I am grateful to Lt Col D Williams of the Thames Conservancy for information on flooding.

Chapter 5

Discussion

INTRODUCTION

This site is of interest because it is one of a group of contemporary sites in the Stanton Harcourt area. In this discussion much reference will be made to the double-ditched Iron Age enclosure at Mingies Ditch, Hardwick, 3.5 km up the Windrush Valley (Fig. 1, Allen and Robinson forthcoming), and in order to facilitate comparison between the two sites a simplified plan of Mingies Ditch is provided (Fig. 34).

THE IRON AGE

Date and length of occupation

The longest stratigraphic sequence, the development of the central roundhouse, need not have occupied more than 70 or 80 years; penannular ditches filling with occupation debris, as these did, may have needed recutting every ten years, or even more frequently. The pottery is purely Middle Iron Age, and the radiocarbon dates do not indicate early Iron Age occupation, or continued Iron Age occupation after the late 1st century BC. This site, like Mingies Ditch, appears to represent colonisation of low-lying areas in the Middle Iron Age, with a relatively short period of occupation before abandonment.

The main enclosure

The main enclosure appears to have been laid out between marker posts, judging from the slight corners at intervals around it joining straighter lengths of ditch. Some degree of symmetry is also evident N and S of a line from the E entrance to the corner mid-way up the western side, the southern part being slightly larger. A similar use of marker posts has been suggested at Mingies Ditch, and there too a roughly symmetrical layout about an E-W axis is evident for both the enclosure ditch circuits.

The middle of the central roundhouse enclosure lies upon the axis of symmetry, and also upon a line at 90° to it joining the western ends of the straight N and S sides of the main enclosure (Fig. 34). This siting is unlikely to be coincidental, and suggests that the central enclosure was an original part of the layout.

The evidence for a bank or hedge inside the main enclosure ditch is equivocal. Enclosure 496–512 was dug right up to, and then running into, the ditch, and the entrance between 22 and 23 on the S suggests that there was no barrier at this point either. There was no evidence in the main enclosure ditch of bank erosion on the inside

or outside during the Iron Age, except possibly on the NE, where clay and gravel spill down the inside was particularly heavy. Romano-British cleaning out of the ditch, however, may have removed such evidence elsewhere. Silting early in the Romano-British occupation may include bank material (see section on early Romano-British occupation below) which could have derived from erosion of an Iron Age bank, but could equally have spilled in from a recently constructed one.

The waterlogged environmental evidence suggests that there was a hedge alongside the ditch, whether created by selective scrub clearance or planted (see Chapter 4: The environment of Site A Iron Age: scrub or hedges). Except for the two enclosures mentioned above, there were no Iron Age features within 2.0–3.0 m of the main enclosure ditch, so in general there may have been a band of upcast inside the ditch upon or through which a hedge was growing, as at Mingies Ditch.

Over 70% of the main enclosure ditch was excavated, but no concentration of finds or other evidence was found to suggest that the ditch was used for rubbish dumping. Even adjacent to enclosures 22–23 and 496–513 there was no greater density of finds, which were concentrated towards the interior around the house enclosure ditches. Gaps in the hedge other than these are therefore unlikely, though it is possible that much Iron Age material was cleaned out in the Romano-British period. A similarly low and even density of finds was recovered from the inner enclosure ditch at Mingies Ditch, strengthening the belief that the hedge acted as a barrier, but there only 25% of the ditch was excavated.

There may have been another bank or hedge outside the main enclosure ditch, but ditches 485–490 and 261 come very close to it, and it is difficult to envisage a barrier outside still existing when ditch 415 was dug close alongside on the N. Romano-British developments are discussed more fully below (see also Fig. 36).

The interior: preservation

At the contemporary enclosed settlement at Mingies Ditch the Iron Age ground surface had survived, allowing the recovery of structures which had left only slight traces in the ground, in one case a stake wall, in another mostly thin layers (Fig. 34, Houses 5 and 4). In contrast, most of the site at Watkins Farm was heavily truncated, and similar evidence here would have been destroyed. It would therefore appear that the plan recovered from Watkins Farm is very incomplete, and

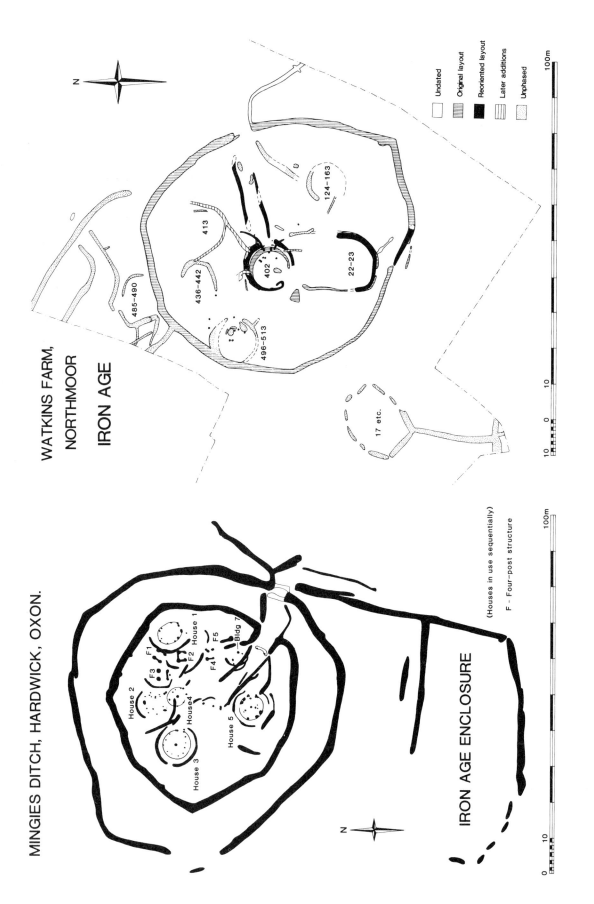

Figure 34 Phase plan of Iron Age features and comparative plan of the Iron Age enclosure at Mingies Ditch, Hardwick, Oxon.

that attempts to interpret the size of the settlement or its internal organisation are pointless. However, differences in the character of features at the two sites suggest that the loss of the Iron Age ground surface might not be as significant at Watkins Farm as it would have been at Mingies Ditch. Only four of the five roundhouses identified at Mingies Ditch had surrounding gullies, and the deepest of these was only 0.55 m deep from the ground surface, except at a sump; other house gullies were up to 0.40 m deep. In contrast, the penannular and other enclosure ditches at Watkins Farm were from 0.55 to 1.10 m deep from the surviving surface, to which at least 0.1 m must be added for depth from the original Iron Age ground surface, showing that small enclosures were more strongly defined there.

The difference cannot be explained simply in terms of the water table. Features deeper than the gullies at Mingies Ditch remained virtually dry; the house gullies appear to have been dug just deep enough to penetrate gravel and so drain. Conversely, the ditches at Watkins Farm were dug well into the gravel, but not always down to the level of the water table. Chronological difference cannot be invoked as these sites were contemporary; either social or other functional considerations were probably involved. Enclosure sizes at Watkins Farm are compared to the house enclosures at Mingies Ditch in Table 13.

Table 13: House-enclosures and their dimensions in comparison with those from Mingies Ditch

Watkins Farm		Mingies Ditch	
Context Nos	Dimensions	Context	Dimensions
402	10.0 m x 9.0 m	House 1	10.0 m x 8.5 m
496-512	11.5 m x 11.5 m	House 2	10.2 m x 9.2 m
477-438-401	12.0 m x 12.0 m	House 3	11.0 m x 11.0 m
22-23	14.0 m x 10.0 m min.		
124-163	?10.5 m x 10.5 m	House 5	10.0 m x 10.0 m
436-442	9.0 m x 5.0 m min.	Bldg. 7	6.5 m x 6.5 m

The Watkins Farm enclosures are generally slightly larger, which might imply some difference in status. The centrally placed enclosure at Watkins Farm may also indicate a greater concern with status, but there were no Wessex-type large roundhouses here, and any difference is a slight one of degree, not of kind.

Alternatively, the substantial ditches around small enclosures at Watkins Farm may reflect different uses of the interiors of the two enclosed settlements. At Mingies Ditch it was shown that the area between the double ditches was used regularly to pen animals, and it was suggested that only parts of the interior were used for animals, and probably not continuously. Lacking a double ditch, the interior of the enclosure at Watkins Farm was probably used much more for animals, with a correspondingly greater need to protect the houses, especially the thatch, and hence deep ditches around the

buildings. Waterlogged samples at Watkins Farm contained a higher percentage of dung beetles than those at Mingies Ditch, which may provide corroborative evidence for this interpretation.

A combination of factors therefore suggests that houses or other important structures at Watkins Farm would have been surrounded by substantial ditches and so would not have disappeared without trace. Since even the southern part of the enclosure was seen and sketch planned when shallow enclosure ditches and gullies still survived, the plan of the interior is believed to represent fairly accurately what originally existed, and its organisation is discussed below.

Linked penannular enclosures

The close association between the central penannular enclosure and the southern U-shaped one, 22–23 etc., is shown by linking ditches 21, 125, 424 and possibly 32. 424 cuts 401, showing that this link existed while the central enclosure was surrounding a house facing the E entrance, and the orientation of 402 and of 22–23 suggests that it probably existed earlier on. The blocking of the southern entrance in the main enclosure ditch may well have been contemporary with the blocking of the southern entrance in 22–23 and consequently with the reorientation of the central enclosure to face the E entrance.

The quantities of pottery and animal bone from 23 demonstrate domestic activity close by (Table 14), but since this enclosure was stripped very deeply before its interior was planned no features survived which might have shown whether it surrounded a house. Fills and finds around the central roundhouse, in the trackway ditches and other associated features, suggest that refuse was concentrated in a scatter up to 6.0 m from the house, mostly around the front. The rubbish in enclosure 23 appears to be too far away to belong to this distribution. It could have derived from enclosure 124–163, though 23 is over 8.0 m from the entrance to 124–163. Significantly, however, there is a complete absence of Group 4 fabric in the pottery from 124 and of Group 5 fabric in that from 23, though in other respects fabric proportions are similar. If these two assemblages belonged to one house, this implies selective clearance of these particular fabrics. However, there was a wide variety of other types of domestic debris present in 22–23, greater than that in 124–163, and it is more likely that the assemblages from 124 and from 23 are distinct, and reflect a preference for these fabrics in different households or for different activities. It is therefore likely that enclosure 23 surrounded a house.

Comparative linked enclosures

Pairs of associated enclosures are known in the Upper Thames from Ashville, Farmoor, Claydon Pike and

Salmondsbury (Allen, Miles and Palmer 1984, 89–101). At Salmondsbury the enclosing ditches surrounded two round buildings turned partly towards one another, and both parts of the enclosure were of equal size. At Ashville and Claydon Pike a penannular gully was joined by a ditch to a smaller sub-circular enclosure, and again their entrances were turned slightly towards one another. At Claydon Pike the larger enclosure may have contained the only house, but domestic refuse in quantity came from both enclosures, and buildings small enough to have stood within the U-shaped enclosure have been excavated at Mingies Ditch (see Fig. 34). The sub-circular enclosure at Claydon Pike is also similar to enclosure 436–442 at Watkins Farm, wider across than from front to back, and 436–442 also contained enough rubbish to be considered a possible focus of domestic activity. The Salmondsbury houses quoted above were oval, not circular, and wider than deep, and the southern one was 7.5 m across but only just over 6.0 m deep. This shape of building would fit such U-shaped enclosures.

At Ashville a circular enclosure was attached by a ditch to another slightly smaller one. At a later stage the smaller enclosure became U-shaped. In the earlier phase the larger enclosure contained a roundhouse, but its ditch was continuous and it is uncertain which way it faced; in the later phase both enclosures faced E. A concentration of domestic rubbish was noticed in the terminals of both later phase enclosures, but not in the early ones. Postholes enclosed by the smaller enclosure are interpreted as a circular structure replaced by rectangular ones, attributed respectively to the first and second phases, but as all these lie within the second phase enclosure there may only have been structures in its later phase (Parrington 1978, 11–15 and Fig. 12).

A pair of penannular enclosures of equal size, facing one another in close proximity, was also found at Claydon Pike (Hingley and Miles 1984, 61–3 and Fig. 4.6). These were not actually linked by gullies but may have been contemporary, analogous to the paired structures suggested at Glastonbury (Clarke 1972).

At Farmoor paired enclosures were not seen as representing two houses (Lambrick and Robinson 1979, 138); in every case one enclosure was ancillary to the other although there was no difference in size between them. No good structural evidence was recovered from these enclosures, and refuse distributions are not recorded.

Enclosure 22–23 at Watkins Farm is if anything larger than the central roundhouse enclosure, and the area enclosing it and the central roundhouse is 32 m long, with probably 8.0 or 9.0 m between any structures. The greatest length of any other paired enclosure in the region is 27 m, and most are much closer than this, with structures set only 3.0–5.0 m apart. This perhaps suggests that 22–23 was not ancillary to the central roundhouse, and that both houses were semi-independent.

The relative importance of these two enclosures may have changed, as the central enclosure was enlarged (from 402 to 477 and 401), whereas 22–23 was recut at the same size. Table 14 compares the range of artefacts

Table 14: Comparison of the range of finds from small Iron Age enclosures

	Central roundhouse								
	402	401-477	425-433-451	410-495-488-416	22-23	124	496-512	442-436	485
High % of sheep and pig bones	x	x	x	x	x	x	?	?	?
Querns			x		x	(x in 166)			
Decorated pottery				x	x	x			
Briquetage	x	x	x			x		x	x
Weaving/ spinning			x loomweights	x comb spindle whorl? loomweight?	x spindle whorl loomweight	x ?spacer	loomweights (+ 499)		
Metalworking			x		x				x
Human bones				x	x		(x in 498)		
Wattle	x	x			x				x
Other					knife handle			needle	

It appears that the central roundhouse performs a wider range of functions in its later phases. Almost all the activities are represented in the central roundhouse and in 22-23. 124 has all the more domestic activities, including what was probably a spacer for a loom, but there is no metalworking debris or human bones, which may have had some ritual or status significance. The evidence for domestic occupation in 496-512 and 436-442 is more equivocal, but much less of 496 survived for excavation.

found in each of the small enclosures on the site. Both 23 and the central roundhouse produced finds indicating a wide range of activities, but evidence of these was only present in the enlarged central roundhouse enclosure, not in 402. Some division of function and status between 23 and 402 and between the first and subsequent phases of the central roundhouse is therefore likely, but since the terminals of 402 were truncated this suggestion must be treated with caution.

The limited but similar range of finds from both 496 and from 436–442, together with an almost identical percentage of sheep and pig bones (low in relation to the other 'house' enclosures), strengthens the possibility that these enclosures too were linked like those at Claydon Pike, but the limited survival of 496–512 makes any such conclusions only tentative.

Settlement layout and population

In contrast to the slight and single-phased house gullies at Mingies Ditch, which seem to reflect a frequently shifting (though organised) layout, the house sites at Watkins Farm indicate a fairly static settlement. The central enclosure appears to persist throughout, and all the other three larger enclosures have two phases or more. This may have been due partly to the number of inhabitants, as two or more households were probably present contemporaneously at Watkins Farm (occupying 23, 402 and 496), whereas only one (or possibly two) houses were used at a time at Mingies Ditch, any second house being small (Allen and Robinson forthcoming). A population of from four to 12 adults is indicated, perhaps an extended family group. It is also possible that occupation at Mingies Ditch was interrupted or sporadic, as blocking ditches were found across the entrance; there were no such ditches at Watkins Farm, and occupation was probably continuous.

The orientation of the penannular enclosures at Watkins Farm is very varied, and seems to reflect their relationships to one another and to the position of the main enclosure entrances. Their entrances do not conform to the predominantly E- or SE-facing pattern seen at sites such a Claydon Pike, Fairford (Hingley and Miles 1984, 59 Fig. 4.4) or Gravelly Guy (Lambrick 1986, 112-4 and Fig. 30). It has been suggested (Hingley and Miles 1984, 63) that this general orientation is due to the prevailing wind direction, which blows from the NW; possibly hedges or banks around enclosed sites provided substantial protection from the wind, allowing other factors to determine entrance orientation. The position of well 60 may have influenced the orientation of the entrance of 124–163.

The trackway in the interior

Parallel ditches 151 and 127 divide the interior N from S between the main enclosure entrance and the central roundhouse enclosure. They need not have been contemporary. From its black occupation-rich fill and from pottery links with vessels in 477 and 425, 151 was clearly contemporary with one or more phases of the enlarged central enclosure. The occupation material within it, however, fell off dramatically 5.0–6.0 m from the central enclosure, and beyond this finds were few and fills were light in colour. Unfortunately 127 was almost completely obliterated by Romano-British and later ditches within a radius of 5.0–6.0 m from the central enclosure, and hardly any pottery was recovered. A small surviving length (Fig. 15) was lighter in colour than 151, but while 151 lay directly in front of the central enclosure entrance, 127 lay to one side, and so may not have received as much rubbish.

127 stopped well short of the main enclosure ditch, and there may have been an entrance to the N half of the enclosure between them. There was also a gap between 127 and the central enclosure, though if 127 and 430 were contemporary this was blocked off at that time. 151 stopped further from the main entrance than 127, midway between it and the line of 140–172. In the absence of conclusive evidence they can be interpreted either as contemporary roadside boundaries to a track leading up to the central house, or successive internal divisions. On analogy with the internal ditches and trackway at Mingies Ditch, 127 and 151 are seen as contemporary. This arrangement would have provided two entrances, either between 127 and 151 up to the central enclosure, or between 151 and 140 into the southern half of the site. There may have been another gap between the end of 140–172 and the main enclosure. Perhaps the fact that 151 stops so far short of the main enclosure ditch indicates that it was contemporary with 127. At its W end 151 stopped short of 425, 401 and 424, presumably leaving access from the central enclosure to the S. 151's position midway between 127 and 140 allows for a gate or hurdle that could be swung either way as required. At Mount Farm, Dorchester, Oxon. up to three or four enclosures for stock control had interconnecting entrances which were of standard width, suggesting that gates or hurdles could be hung between them and closed either way (G Lambrick pers. comm.).

The trackways at Mingies Ditch and that at Watkins Farm had different functions; at the former the trackway channelled traffic up to gates at the centre of the interior, at the latter it separated the approach to the central house from the rest of the enclosure's interior. The dominant central position of the house facing onto the entrance will have been reinforced by the digging of the trackway. This layout has a similarity to the 'homestead' sites of NE England (Jobey 1970, 51–96; Jobey 1973, 11–54).

It is not known for how long the roadside ditches remained effective barriers, but fills rich in Iron Age occupation debris in the very top of 151 suggest that it was completely silted up before occupation ceased.

The external enclosures

Enclosure 485 on the NW contained daub and other domestic material, suggesting that it had at some stage surrounded a structure. It perhaps had the same use as the similarly placed enclosure at Mingies Ditch (Fig. 34), which also had domestic debris adjacent to it; possibly these were watchmen's shelters for guarding animals sleeping outside the main enclosure. The southern enclosure 17 etc. contained very little rubbish, and was probably agricultural.

The environment and economy (Fig. 2)

The evidence of the environmental samples, admittedly few in number, indicates that the site was surrounded by scrubby grassland with wetter areas. There is no conclusive evidence of earlier occupation, but that some clearance is likely to have occurred earlier to create this partly open environment is indicated by the Late Bronze Age evidence at Mingies Ditch nearby (Allen and Robinson forthcoming). A relict stream course only 100 m S of the main enclosure, which appears to be overlain by medieval ridge and furrow, may have provided a source of water close by, and this, together with the slight rise on which the settlement sits, perhaps influenced the choice of site. During the Iron Age and Romano-British occupations the site apparently did not flood; alluvial clay in the main enclosure ditch dating to the 1st century AD is seen as redeposited material from elsewhere (see Early Romano-British occupation below) and it was not until after the abandonment of Site B that alluvium was deposited there. Nevertheless, the site was low-lying and wet.

Although arable agriculture has been practised on the site since the medieval period, the area was apparently not sufficiently well drained for this in the Iron Age and Romano-British periods. Waterlogging in the ditches shows that the water table was less than 1.0 m below ground surface. There were only two pits, 166 and 499, in the settlement, neither over 1.0 m deep, and grain storage below ground in the usual Iron Age manner would clearly not have been possible. The environmental samples do not indicate crop processing on any scale in either period (Figs. 31 and 32); querns and carbonised seeds show that cereals were processed and eaten, but these were probably imported from neighbouring Second Gravel Terrace settlements.

In contrast to low-lying sites at Claydon Pike, Mingies Ditch and Groundwell Farm, there was no evidence for four post structures, which are usually interpreted as above ground stores (Gent 1983, 243–267; Gingell 1981, 33–76). Since the type of four post structure found on these other sites had massive postholes, it is not likely that they would have been removed without trace at Watkins Farm. Their use does not seem to have been directly related to settlement size,

since while they were numerous at Groundwell Farm and there were five during the short occupation at Mingies Ditch, one four post structure sufficed for each of the larger settlement nuclei at Claydon Pike. All four sites appear to have similar economies, based on animal husbandry and imported grain; the absence of these structures at Watkins Farm is not reflected in a different mix of animals, so it is probably due to different methods of storage or may suggest that these structures are not related to the economy after all.

Water supply

In addition to the relict stream course there were a number of deep ramped wells on both sites. Feature 60 has been securely dated to the Iron Age; there were no steps and no ramp down into this well, which was perhaps straddled with the aid of the plank found within it. Deep features 498 and possibly 487 were probably other Iron Age wells, 498 having a ramp of sorts. In the Romano-British period such wells are common on local sites; larger examples have been excavated at Eagle Farm, Standlake, Farmoor and at Gravelly Guy (Allen 1986; Lambrick and Robinson 1979, 32–3 and 73; Lambrick 1985).

The stream course overlaid by ridge and furrow may have been active contemporary with the settlement (Fig. 1); otherwise watering the animals would have required driving them a kilometre to the rivers Thames or Windrush.

Livestock

The animal bones suggest a mixture of sheep and cattle, with rather fewer horses and pigs. Such mixed pastoralism is the norm in local Iron Age bone assemblages. Though sample sizes were small, the percentage of horses was slightly higher than those from arable sites in the region, perhaps indicating an emphasis on horse rearing. This has also been suggested for other low-lying pastoral settlements at Farmoor and Mingies Ditch (Robinson in Allen and Robinson forthcoming), and both this site and Mingies Ditch have produced foal bones. It is therefore possible that horse breeding provided one source of exchange. Butchery marks do not suggest intense exploitation of skins or hides, but other secondary products such as cheese or wool may well have been exported. Dogs were also present at Watkins Farm, and were eaten, though their main roles will have been as guard dogs, sheep dogs and pets.

Livestock were probably corralled within the interior during the Iron Age occupation. There was no area as blank as that at Tollard Royal, Wilts. (Cunliffe 1978, 160–161 and Fig. 11.6), where one half of the interior contained no features and was interpreted as having been used for animals, but the NE part of the interior at Watkins Farm was not dug into until late in the occupation, and appears never to have had domestic structures in it. The area outside, between ditches 479 and 550, was subdivided into several small enclosures which may have formed a group of paddocks similar to those added to the enclosure at Mingies Ditch; enclosure 17 etc. on the S and ditch 220 running off from it may suggest that a larger area of grazing was divided off between the main enclosure and the stream.

Evidence for small scale weaving, spinning, metalworking and possibly leather working suggests, as on other recently excavated sites in the Upper Thames Valley, that the site was operating largely at subsistence level and with a high degree of self-sufficiency. The pottery was generally more varied and of better quality than that at Mingies Ditch, similar to that from Farmoor, and a greater quantity of Droitwich briquetage was found at Watkins Farm than at either Farmoor or Mingies Ditch, but otherwise there is no indication of greater wealth or status. Despite the occurrence of the occasional decorative motif indicative of exchange, such as the 'Frilford swags' (Fig. 25), and 'saucepan pot' (Fig. 24 No. 9) the dissimilarity of pottery assemblages that are close in both space and time reinforces the view that most settlements were largely independent.

The Iron Age settlement at Watkins Farm fits into the pattern suggested by Farmoor, Mingies Ditch and Claydon Pike, Fairford, in which Middle Iron Age settlements practising animal husbandry expanded onto the low-lying First Terrace and floodplain and were only part of a larger agricultural network which also involved arable sites on the higher and better drained terraces. The possibility of specialised breeding, particularly of horses, has been raised in connection with several of these sites, and the seasonally occupied enclosures at Farmoor suggest that the Iron Age economy was both developed and diverse.

Unfortunately, concrete links between these pastoral settlements and their presumed arable counterparts in terms of pottery or other finds have not yet been found; close partners for Farmoor or Claydon Pike have not been identified, and for Mingies Ditch the character of the pottery from arable settlements at Beard Mill and Gravelly Guy only 1.5 km away is not particularly similar (D H Wilson in Allen and Robinson forthcoming; Williams 1951, 5–22; D Duncan pers. comm.). For Watkins Farm the settlement on the edge of the Second Terrace at Linch Hill (SP 4104), extracted for gravel before the Second World War, is the most likely complementary arable site (see Benson and Miles, 1974, Map 22).

THE LATE IRON AGE HIATUS

The pottery suggests a break in occupation between the Iron Age and early Roman occupations. Abandonment or settlement shift at the end of the later Middle Iron Age is common to many settlements in the Upper Thames valley, for instance Mingies Ditch, Hardwick, and Gravelly Guy, Stanton Harcourt (Allen and Robinson forthcoming; G Lambrick pers. comm.). Many sites are occupied for the first time in the 1st century AD, for example Linch Hill (Grimes 1943) and Barton Court Farm (Miles 1986), or are the early Roman successors of Iron Age settlements, as at Smithsfield adjacent to Mingies Ditch (Allen forthcoming), but concrete evidence of continuity is rare. This apparent hiatus in the settlement record may be partly illusory, caused by the survival of Middle Iron Age pottery styles and economy right up to the Roman conquest, with only a very brief 'Late' or 'Belgic' Iron Age.

Cunliffe has argued for a major settlement dislocation in the 1st century BC in Wessex, and has linked this to the collapse of the flourishing Middle Iron Age social and economic system (Cunliffe in Cunliffe and Miles 1984, 30–38). Possibly a similar sequence, occurring at a slightly later date, is evident in the Upper Thames, with the abandonment of these peripheral areas for settlement in unsettled times, and recolonisation only occurring in the later 1st century AD when stability returned.

THE EARLY ROMANO-BRITISH OCCUPATION (Figs. 35, 36)

Roman pottery from just above the peat in the main enclosure ditch shows that the ditch was still open in the later 1st century AD. Immediately overlying the peat was a layer of very gravelly clay, thickest down the ditch sides. The clay contained aquatic molluscs, indicating an alluvial origin, but Mark Robinson believes that it was not deposited by flooding, as there was no sign of alluvium in any other features during the subsequent Roman occupation. While a short episode of alluviation during the 1st century AD cannot be ruled out, it is more likely that this material is redeposited, perhaps dug out from the stream channel to the S. The alluvium and gravel layer is followed by a thick layer of clay silting (Fig. 5) which appears to have accumulated gradually, so the gravelly clay does not appear to have been deliberate backfill. Possibly it represents the partial collapse of an upcast bank adjacent to the ditch, which had been augmented by clay from the nearby stream channel. Some of the gravel may have derived from the sides after cleaning out the upper part of the ditch.

The clay silting layer shows that the main enclosure ditch remained open for some time before it was backfilled with more gravelly soils and cut through by later Romano-British ditches 155, 415, 450 and 451. Finds from these ditches suggest that this had occurred by the end of the 2nd century AD.

Ditches inside the main enclosure and roughly concentric to it, 4, 134–405, 411 and 57, were also cut by 155 etc., as were ditches 13, 14 etc. outside forming small rectilinear enclosures. Whether these were contemporary with use of the main enclosure ditch, and if so for how long, is difficult to determine. The pottery was not sufficiently distinctive to provide more accurate phasing within a broad late 1st and 2nd century bracket. The similar character and curve of ditches 134 and 4 suggests that they were opposite terminals of the same phase; both also had two phases of cut. 134 cut a Romano-British gully 132, so these features were clearly a secondary addition.

Between 134–405 and the main enclosure on the N and W were ditches 411 and 57, probably contemporary lengths of one circuit. These were probably earlier than 405, as this was filled with a dark occupation soil on both the NW and W, while they were not. Since this was a widespread fill, presumably derived from the contemporary occupation surface, it is likely to have found its way into 411 and 57 had they been contemporary with, or indeed later than, 405. The later Roman ditches tended to have darker fills, presumably reflecting the increasing buildup of occupation soil throughout the Roman period.

These ditches may simply have been lengths dug inside an existing hedge or bank around the main enclosure to heighten the barrier, perhaps similar to the enclosure at Blackthorn, Northants. (Williams and McCarthy 1974, 44–65), or to the early Roman banjo

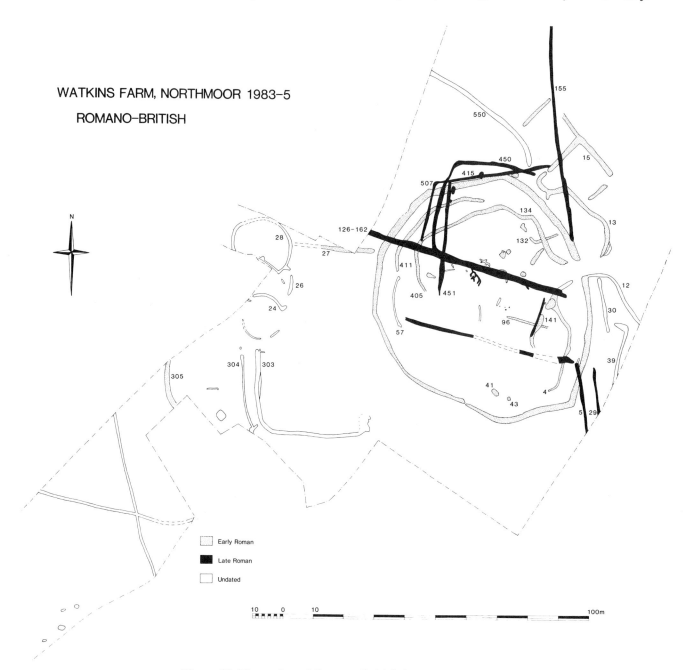

Figure 35 Phase plan of Romano-British features on Site A

enclosures of Hampshire, where the bank lay outside the enclosure ditch. Alternatively they may have formed complete double ditch circuits (see Fig. 36, 2b and 3b). No ditches corresponding either to 57 or to 134 and 4 were seen on the S side of the enclosure, but since both 4 and 134 petered out further ditches may have been machined away. 134 may even originally have been only as long as ditch 4, and 411 and 57 a continuation of it, later replaced by 405 inside (Fig. 36, 2a and 3a). Not enough of 134–405 was dug to substantiate or disprove this.

For much of their length the inner circuits are only 3.0–6.0 m from the main enclosure ditch, which is too narrow to use for corralling animals between the ditches. At Mingies Ditch, where this type of use is known to have occurred during the Iron Age, the distance between the ditch circuits averaged 13 m, which even allowing for hedges alongside both ditches left a strip 9.0–10.0 m wide. If, however, 134–405 and 4 were dug while the main enclosure ditch was still open, there would have been space to corral animals between the ditch circuits, as was suggested to have occurred at the enclosed site at Burradon, Northumberland, when an inner concentric ditch was added (Jobey 1970, 90).

The external ditched enclosures made up of features 13–261, 14, 15 etc. and the undated lengths of ditch further S, 30, 12 and 39, may also have been added up against the main enclosure ditch (Fig. 36, 2b and 3b). However, the way that some of these mirror the course of 134 and 4 may indicate that the main enclosure had been filled in by the time they were dug. Both ditches 13 and 134 kink sharply to the W opposite one another, and 39 ends at the N opposite a change in the alignment of 4 (Fig. 36, 2a and 3a). Nevertheless, the fact that later enclosure ditches 451 and 415 follow the line of the main enclosure on their N sides suggests that some parts of ditch 1, or the hedge alongside it, remained in use. Fig. 36 offers some alternative conjectural developments.

Continuity

Despite the apparent break in occupation, the character of both the Iron Age and early Romano-British settlements was very similar (compare Figs. 34 and 35). The essential elements of the Iron Age settlement were three: a large enclosure containing domestic structures, a smaller enclosure attached to a boundary ditch on the S and an area on the N between two large boundary ditches, 479 and 550, subdivided into several smaller enclosed areas. The purpose of the smaller enclosures was probably stock control and stock rearing.

The early Romano-British layout was substantially the same. The southern small enclosure 17 etc. was replaced by a group of interconnected enclosures on the W, 24, 26, 28 etc., linked to boundary ditches defining a large open area between them and the large enclosure. This area probably corresponded to that previously defined between the main enclosure ditch and 320–321 to the S. Ditch 1 was supplemented and probably eventually replaced by ditch circuits 134, 405, 411 and 4 inside it; these, however, were concentric to the Iron Age enclosure, though the area they enclosed was only 75% as large. A new series of small enclosures was added just outside the main enclosure entrance, but these probably replaced the Iron Age enclosures between 479 and 550, which do not appear to have continued in use in the Romano-British period.

The basic continuity in layout on Site A in the early Romano-British period is mirrored in the environmental remains and the limited animal bone evidence, which suggests that a 'Celtic' form of animal husbandry persisted. No Romano-British structures were found, but the indirect evidence of woodworm and bread beetles and the quantity of pottery recovered suggests more than mucking out from a settlement elsewhere. Structural evidence for the 1st and 2nd centuries AD is scarce on rural sites in this area; even where domestic enclosures have been identified by the characteristic concentrations of rubbish in their terminals, as at Smithsfield, Hardwick (Allen 1981, 28–31), little or no evidence of the structures themselves has survived. Excavation at Claydon Pike, Fairford (Miles 1984, 191–211) suggests that buildings may have been timber-framed resting on sill beams. Domestic occupation in the Romano-British period, however, as at Barton Court, Abingdon or Claydon Pike, Fairford, is generally marked by a greater intensity both of occupation debris and of synanthropic beetles and other environmental remains in comparison to Iron Age settlements (Robinson pers. comm.). At Watkins Farm the reverse was true, if anything; it is possible that the centres of Romano-British occupation were not found, but more probably occupation was only seasonal or sporadic.

SITE B (Figs. 2, 18)

It is possible that the Romano-British enclosures on Site A were being run from Site B, where one house-sized oval enclosure and several large concentrations of pottery strongly suggest domestic occupation. The pottery from here is broadly contemporary with that on Site A, and has a higher proportion of finer tablewares, perhaps indicating that this was the more important focus. Unfortunately, too little animal bone was recovered from Site B to permit valid comparisons between the sites.

On Site B the occupation appears to have been confined between parallel ditches on a WNW alignment. Smaller gullies and cross ditches run at right-angles to them, dividing up this swathe of land into smaller plots, and several of the wells also appear to be aligned upon these cross ditches.

Late Roman sherds came from two of the WNW ditches, 35 and 36, which should imply that much of the

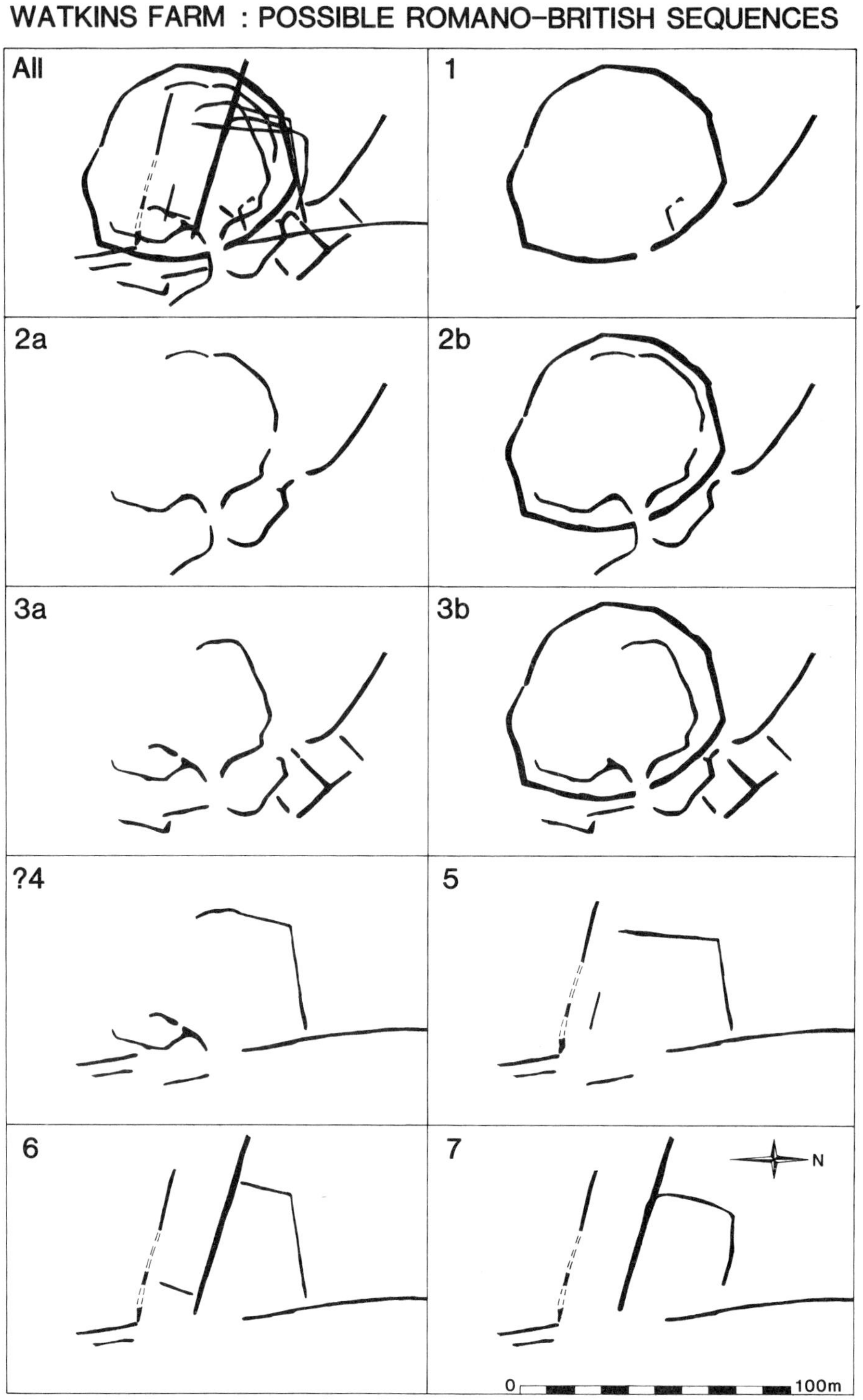

WATKINS FARM : POSSIBLE ROMANO-BRITISH SEQUENCES

Figure 36 Possible development of Romano-British enclosures on Site A

occupation was also of this date, but nearly all of the pottery from this site, including 95% of the sherds from 35 and 36, was 2nd-century. While it is possible that almost all the pottery except that from enclosure 34–220 was residual, and that the late Romano-British occupation generated virtually no rubbish, it seems more likely that the WNW ditches and associated features are 2nd

century in origin, but that these boundaries remained in use into the 4th century AD.

The WNW ditches are clearly not contemporary with a possible trackway running NNW (Fig. 18). Although the trackway ditches were undated and too shallow to establish any relationships, they are running towards a large Romano-British cropmark complex just W of

Pimm's Farm (SP 425 049; Benson and Miles 1974, 49–50), where a number of trackways meet at a crossroads. It seems most likely that the trackway is a late Roman development, cutting across some of the small enclosures, but alongside which occupation in the E part of the site continued.

The pattern of features on Site B is perhaps an example of land definition and infilling as described by Fowler (Fowler 1981), in which regular linear divisions are first subdivided and then gradually infilled and overridden. The wells, cross ditches and gullies forming small rectilinear enclosures are followed by modifications which cut across them and produce more rounded enclosures. This pattern is similar to that at Gravelly Guy nearby, where early Roman cross ditches and enclosures divided up a long strip of occupied land (Lambrick 1986, 112–4 and Fig. 30); at Gravelly Guy, however, land divisions may well have been first defined in the Iron Age.

THE LATER ROMANO-BRITISH OCCUPATION
The early Romano-British layout on Site A was probably superseded in the late 2nd or 3rd century AD by one based upon a trackway and boundary ditches running up to it. Several successive ditches delineated a large rectangular enclosure up against them, still largely overlying the previous enclosed area. The trackway runs NNW past Site B, and is heading towards the same Romano-British cropmark complex just W of Pimm's Farm. Several ditches and gullies on Site B are either on a similar alignment or at right angles to it; two, converging north-westwards towards the track from Site A, may form a second track heading for Pimm's Farm.

Running obliquely to these trackways are boundary ditches on a WNW alignment. The same alignment is evident on both Sites A and B, and indicates large scale land division at some stage in the Romano-British period (Fig. 2). S of the present day village of Northmoor, approximately 1.0 km SW of Watkins Farm, cropmarks of another Romano-British settlement at a trackway junction (SP 417 026; Benson and Miles 1974, 48–9) are surrounded by a grid of parallel boundary and trackway ditches covering several square kilometres, probably part of the same process (Air photographs RCHME NMR 3117/2186–8). Since the boundary ditches 126–162 and 31 appear to respect the trackway this is likely to have been late 2nd century AD or later; finds from 35 and 36

on Site B may show that ditches on this alignment were still in use in the late Roman period, 3rd–4th century AD. The land division may, however, have originated earlier than the trackway ditches 5 and 155, as long-established trackways were sometimes not defined by ditches until the later 2nd century AD, as at Rough Ground Farm, Lechlade (Allen et al. forthcoming).

The absence of late 3rd- and 4th-century occupation on either site except for a very few sherds suggests that the area was by this time being managed from elsewhere. Some of the larger boundary ditches were still surviving, on Site B at any rate, but alluvium in the tops of the wells indicates wetter conditions by the end of the Roman period, and settlement may no longer have been possible. The absence of such occupation may be part of a wider change in the pattern of settlement, as early Roman sites at Smithsfield, Hardwick and at Gravelly Guy (Fig. 1) have also lacked later occupation. This may simply reflect another settlement shift, later Roman occupation was present at Vicarage Pit adjacent to Gravelly Guy (Thomas 1955, 1–28), and at Eagle Farm, Standlake. Late Roman pottery has been found in the next field to the early Roman settlement, but it is alternatively possible that some degree of settlement nucleation, to trackway junction sites like Pimm's Farm and Northmoor itself (SP 417/025; Benson and Miles 1974, 48–9 and Map 22), was occurring in the later Roman period.

MEDIEVAL
In contrast to the extensive evidence of late Roman settlement (Benson and Miles 1974, 48–9; Lambrick pers. comm.), little is known of the early medieval history of Northmoor. A late Saxon spearhead was dredged from the Thames just S of the village (Victoria County History Oxon., 1, 346–372), but the earliest documentary reference, confirming a grant of land by Edward the Confessor to the Abbey of St Denis at Paris in AD 1059 (Gelling 1954, 366–7) only refers to a moor, not a settlement, and Northmoor is also absent from Domesday. It is next mentioned in c 1200 and fairly frequently thereafter (Gelling 1954, 366–7), and Emery has suggested (Emery 1974, 81) that Northmoor was not colonised until the 12th century. The excavated evidence bears out the presence of arable fields and of occupation at just this time.

Bibliography

Allen, T. G. 1981: 'Hardwick-with-Yelford: Smithsfield'. *Counc. Brit. Archaeol. Group 9 Newsletter* 11, 28–31.

Allen, T. G. 1986: 'Standlake: Eagle Farm'. *Oxford Archaeol. Unit Newsletter*. Vol. XIV, No. 1, 6-7.

Allen, T. G. 1987: 'Eagle Farm'. *South Midlands Archaeology* 17, 96–7.

Allen, T. G. (forthcoming): *Early Roman settlement and later land use in the Windrush Valley at Smithsfield, Hardwick with Yelford, Oxon.*

Allen, T. G., Darvill, T., Green, L. S. and Jones, M. U. (forthcoming): *Excavations at Rough Ground Farm, Lechlade, Glos.; a prehistoric and Roman landscape.*

Allen, T. G., Miles, D. and Palmer, S. 1984: 'Iron Age buildings in the Upper Thames region'. *Aspects of the Iron Age in central southern Britain* (eds. B. W. Cunliffe and D. Miles), 89–101, Oxford.

Allen, T. G. and Robinson, M. R. (forthcoming): *The prehistoric landscape and Iron Age enclosed settlement at Mingies Ditch, Hardwick with Yelford, Oxon.*

Benson, D. and Miles, D. 1974: *The Upper Thames Valley: an archaeological survey of the river gravels.* Oxfordshire Archaeological Unit Survey no. 2, Oxford.

Blandino, B. 1984: *Coiled pottery: traditional and contemporary ways.* London.

Bowler, D. Robinson, M. and Case, H. J. 1980: 'Three round barrows at King's Weir, Wytham, Oxon.'. *Oxoniensia* 45, 1-8.

Britton, E. B. 1956: 'Coleoptera Scarabaeoidea'. *Royal Entomological Society Handbook* 5, xi, London.

Brodribb, A. C. C., Hands, A. R. and Walker, D. 1971: *Excavations at Shakenoak Farm, near Wilcote, Oxfordshire Part 2: Sites B and H.* Oxford.

Case, H. J. 1982: 'Cassington 1950-2: Late Neolithic pits and the big enclosure'. *Settlement patterns in the Oxford region: excavation at the Abingdon causewayed enclosure and other sites* (eds. H. J. Case and A. W. R. Whittle) Counc Brit Archaeol Res Rep 44, 118-151, London.

Case, H. J., Bayne, N., Steele, S., Avery, G. and Sutermeister, H. 1964: 'Excavations at City Farm, Hanborough, Oxon.'. *Oxoniensia* 29/30, 1-98.

Case, H. J. and Whittle, A. W. R. (eds.) 1982: *Settlement patterns in the Oxford region: excavation at the Abingdon causewayed enclosure and other sites.* Counc Brit Archaeol Res Rep 44, London.

Cherry, J. F., Gamble, C. and Shennan, S. 1978: *Sampling in contemporary British archaeology.* Brit Archaeol Rep British Series 50, Oxford.

Clapham, A. R., Tutin, T. G. and Warburg, E. F. 1962: *Flora of the British Isles.* Cambridge.

Clarke, D. L. 1972: 'A provisional model of an Iron Age society'. *Models in archaeology* (ed. D. L. Clarke) 801–869, London.

Cunliffe, B. W., 1978: *Iron Age communities in Britain* (2nd edition) London.

Cunliffe, B. W. 1984a: 'Iron Age Wessex: continuity and change'. *Aspects of the Iron Age in central southern Britain* (eds. B. W. Cunliffe and D. Miles) 30–38, Oxford.

Cunliffe, B. W. 1984b: *Danebury, an Iron Age hillfort in Hampshire; the excavations 1969-1978.* Counc Brit Archaeol Res Rep 52, London.

Cunliffe, B. W. and Miles, D. (eds.) 1984: *Aspects of the Iron Age in central southern Britain.* Oxford University Committee for Archaeology Monograph No. 2, Oxford.

De Roche, C. D. 1978: 'The Iron Age pottery'. *The excavation of an Iron Age settlement, Bronze Age ring-ditches and Roman features at Ashville Trading Estate, Abingdon (Oxfordshire) 1974-6* (M. Parrington), Counc Brit Archaeol Res Rep 28, London.

De Roche, C. D. and Lambrick, G. 1980: 'The Iron Age pottery'. 'Archaeological investigations at Appleford' (J. Hinchcliffe and R.Thomas) *Oxoniensia* 45, 9-111.

Drury, P. 1978: *Excavations at Little Waltham 1970-71.* Counc Brit Archaeol Res Rep 26, 119-124, London.

Durham, B. 1977: 'Archaeological investigations in St Aldates, Oxford'. *Oxoniensia* 42, 83-203.

Easton, A. M. 1966: 'The Coleoptera of a dead fox (*Vulpes vulpes* (L)); including two species new to Britain', *Entomologist's monthly magazine* 102, 205–208.

Easton, A. M. and Smith, K. G. V., 1970: 'The entomology of the cadaver'. *Medicine, science and the law* 10, 208-215.

Emery, F. 1974: *The Oxfordshire landscape*, Oxford.

Folk, R. L. 1974: *Petrology of sedimentary rocks*. Austin, Texas.

Fowler, P. J. 1981: 'Later prehistory'. *The agrarian history of England and Wales, 1, i: prehistory* (ed. S. Piggott) Cambridge.

Fowler, W. W. 1889: *The Coleoptera of the British Islands.* III, London.

Gelling, M. 1954: *The place-names of Oxfordshire.* Vol. 2, English Place-name Society 24, 1946-47, Cambridge.

Gent, H. 1983: 'Centralised storage in later prehistoric Britain', *Proc Prehist Soc* 49, 243–267.

Gillam, J. P. 1968: *Types of Roman coarse pottery vessels in northern Britain* (2nd edition) Newcastle-upon-Tyne.

Gingell, C. 1982: 'Excavation of an Iron Age enclosure at Groundwell Farm, Blunsden St Andrew, 1976–7'. *Wilts Archaeol Mag* 76 (1981), 33–75.

Girling, M. A. 1981: 'Beetle remains'. 'The burial of John Dygan, Abbot of St Augustines' (J. Copland Thorn), *Collectanea historica; essays in memory of Stuart Rigold* (ed. A. Detsicas), 82–4, Maidstone.

Girling, M. A. 1986: 'The insects associated with Lindow Man'. *Lindow Man: the body in the bog* (eds. I. Stead, J. B. Bourke and D. R. Brothwell), London.

Grant, A. 1983: 'The use of tooth wear as a guide to the age of domestic ungulates'. *Ageing and sexing of animal bones from archaeological sites* (eds. R. Wilson, C. Grigson and S. Payne) Brit Archaeol Rep British Series 109, 91–108, Oxford.

Green, L. S. (forthcoming): 'The Roman pottery'. *Excavations at Rough Ground Farm, Lechlade, Glos.: a prehistoric and Roman landscape* (T. G. Allen, T. Darvill, L. S. Green and M. U. Jones).

Greig, J. R. A. 1979: 'Seeds and pollen'. *Fisherwick* (ed. C. Smith) Brit Archaeol Rep, British Series 61, 185–6, Oxford.

Grigson, C. 1983: 'Sex and age determination of some bones and teeth of domestic cattle'. *Ageing and sexing of animal bones from archaeological sites* (eds. R. Wilson, C. Grigson and S. Payne) Brit Archaeol Rep British Series 109, 91–108, Oxford.

Grimes, W. F. 1943: 'Excavations at Stanton Harcourt, Oxon., 1940'. *Oxoniensia* 8-9, 19-63.

Hamlin, A. 1966: 'Early Iron Age sites at Stanton Harcourt'. *Oxoniensia* 31, 12–21.

Harde, K. W. 1984: *A field guide in colour to beetles.* London.

Harding, D. W. 1964: 'The west settlement: the pottery'. 'Excavations at City Farm, Hanborough, Oxon.' (eds. H. J. Case, N. Bayne, S. Steele, G. Avery and H. Sutermeister) *Oxoniensia* 29/30, 79–87.

Harding, D. W. 1972: *The Iron Age in the Upper Thames basin.* Oxford.

Henig, M. 1978: *A corpus of Roman engraved gemstones from British sites*, Brit Archaeol Rep British Series 8, 2nd edition, Oxford.

Hillman, G. C. H. 1981: 'Reconstructing crop husbandry practices from charred remains of crops'. *Farming practice in British prehistory* (ed. R. Mercer) Edinburgh.

Hillman, G. C. H. 1984a: 'Traditional husbandry and processing of cereals in recent times: the operations, products and equipment which might feature in Sumerian texts, Part I: the glume wheats'. *Bulletin on Sumerian agriculture*. vol. 1.

Hillman, G. C. H. 1984b: 'Interpretation of archaeological plant remains: the application of ethnographic models from Turkey'. *Plants and ancient man* (eds. W. van Zeist and W. A. Casparie) Groningen.

Hinchcliffe, J. and Thomas, R. 1980: 'Archaeological Investigations at Appleford'. *Oxoniensia* 45, 9-111.

Hingley, R. and Miles, D. 1984: 'Aspects of Iron Age settlement in the Upper Thames Valley'. *Aspects of the Iron Age in central southern Britain* (eds. B. W. Cunliffe and D. Miles) 52–71, Oxford.

Hooper, M. D. 1971: *Hedges and local history* (National Council of Social Services), 6–13, London.

Isings, C. 1957: *Roman glass from dated finds*. Groningen.

Jobey, G. 1970: 'An Iron Age settlement and homestead at Burradon, Northumberland'. *Arch. Aeliana* (4th series) 48, 51–96.

Jobey, G. 1973: 'A native settlement at Hartburn and the Devil's Causeway, Northumberland'. *Arch. Aeliana* (5th series) 1 (1971), 11–54.

Jones, M. (ed.) 1983: *Integrating the subsistence economy*. Brit Archaeol Rep International Series 181, Oxford.

Jones, M. 1985: 'Archaeobotany beyond subsistence reconstruction'. *Beyond domestication in prehistoric Europe* (eds. G. Barker and C. Gamble) 108-128, London.

Kemp, R. A. 1985: *Soil micromorphology and the Quaternary*. Quaternary Research Association Tachnical Guide No. 2, Cambridge.

Kerney, M. P. 1976: 'A list of fresh and brackish-water Mollusca of the British Isles'. *Journ Conchology Lond*, 29, 26-8.

Kimmings, D. E. 1962: *Keys to the British species of aquatic Megaloptera and Neuroptera*, Freshwater Biological Association Scientific Publication 8, Ambleside.

Kloet, G. S. and Hincks, W. D. 1964: *A check list of British insects (revised): small orders and Hemiptera*. Royal Entomological Society handbook for the identification of British Insects 11, pt. 1.

Knorr, R. 1952: Terra-Sigillata-gefässe des erstenjahrhunderts mit Töpfernamen. Stüttgart.

Lambrick, G. 1984: 'Pitfalls and possibilities in Iron Age pottery studies — experience in the Upper Thames Valley'. *Aspects of the Iron Age in central southern Britain* (eds. B. W. Cunliffe and D. Miles), 162-77, Oxford.

Lambrick, G. 1985: 'Stanton Harcourt: Gravelly Guy'. *Counc Brit Archaeol Group 9 Newsletter* 15 (1984), 107-110.

Lambrick, G. 1986: 'Stanton Harcourt: Gravelly Guy'. *Counc Brit Archaeol Group 9 Newsletter* 16 (1985), 112–115.

Lambrick, G. (forthcoming): *Archaeological investigations at Mount Farm*, Dorchester, Oxon.

Lambrick, G. and Robinson, M. 1979: *Iron Age and Roman riverside settlements at Farmoor, Oxfordshire*, Counc Brit Archaeol Res Rep 32, London.

Leeds, E. T. 1939: 'Anglo-Saxon remains'. *The Victoria history of the county of Oxford* (ed. L. F. Salzman) 346-372.

Levine, M. 1983: 'The use of crown height measurements and eruption-wear sequences to age horse teeth'. *Ageing and sexing of animal bones from archaeological sites* (eds. R. Wilson, C. Grigson and S. Payne) Brit Archaeol Rep British Series 109, 223–250, Oxford.

Levitan, B. and Wilson, R. (forthcoming): 'The animal bones'. *Roman and native in the Cotswold Water Park* (D. Miles and S. L. Palmer).

Macgregor, A. 1985: *Bone, antler, ivory and horn*. London.

Mellor, M. 1980: 'The pottery' in 'A Beaker burial and medieval tenements in the Hamel, Oxford' (N. Palmer) *Oxoniensia* 45, 160–182.

Miles, D. 1984: 'Romano-British settlement in the Gloucestershire Thames Valley'. *Archaeology in Gloucestershire* (ed. A. Saville), 191–211, Cheltenham.

Miles, D. (ed.) 1986: Archaeology at Barton Court Farm, Abingdon, Oxon., Council Brit Archaeol Res Rep 50, London.

Miles, D. and Palmer, S. L. (forthcoming): *Roman and native in the Cotswold Water Park*.

Moffett, L. Robinson, M. A. and Straker, V. 1989: 'Cereals, fruit and nuts: charred plant remains from Neolithic sites in England and Wales and the Neolithic economy'. *The beginnings of agriculture* (eds. A. Miller, D. Williams, and N. Gardener) Brit Archaeol Rep British Series 496, 243-261, Oxford.

Morris, E. L. 1985: 'Prehistoric salt distributions: two case studies from western Britain'. *Bulletin of the Board of Celtic Studies*. University of Wales, Cardiff, 336–379.

Morris, E. L. (forthcoming): 'Petrological report on the non-local Iron Age pottery and Droitwich salt containers found at Claydon Pike, Lechlade'. *Roman and native in the Cotswold Water Park* (D. Miles and S. L. Palmer).

Oswald, F. and Pryce, T. 1920: *An introduction to the study of terra sigillata treated from a chronological standpoint*, London.

Page, P., Smithson, S. and Baker, H., (forthcoming): 'Excavations on the site of the medieval moated manor at Harding's Field, Chalgrove, Oxon.'. *Oxoniensia*.

Parrington, M. 1978: *The excavation of an Iron Age settlement, Bronze Age ring-ditches and Roman features at Ashville Trading Estate, Abingdon (Oxfordshire) 1974–76*. Counc Brit Archaeol Res Rep 28, London.

Paulian, R. 1959: *Coleopteres Scarabeides*. Faune de France 63, Paris.

Pearson, G. W., Pilcher, J. R., Baillie, M. G. L., Corbett, D. M. and Qua, F. 1986: 'High-precision C^{14} measurement of Irish oaks to show the natural C^{14} variation from AD 1840-5210 BC'. *Radiocarbon*, 28, No. 2B, 911-934.

Pearson, G. W. and Stuiver, M. 1986: 'High precision calibration of the radiocarbon time scale, 500-2500 BC'. *Radiocarbon*, 28, No. 2, 839-862.

Rackham, O. 1986: *The history of the countryside*. London.

Robinson, M. 1978: 'Roman trinket-rings from Oxfordshire'. *Oxoniensia* 43, 249–51.

Robinson, M. 1981: 'The Iron Age to early Saxon environment of the Upper Thames terraces'. *The environment of man: the Iron Age to the Anglo-Saxon period* (eds. M. Jones and G. Dimbleby) Brit Archaeol Rep British Series 87, 265-268, Oxford.

Robinson, M. 1983: 'Arable/pastoral ratios from insects'. *Integrating the subsistence economy* (ed. M. Jones) Brit Archaeol Rep British Series 181, 34, Oxford.

Robinson, M. 1984: 'Landscape and environment of central southern Britain in the Iron Age'. *Aspects of the Iron Age in central southern Britain* (eds. B. W. Cunliffe and D. Miles) 1-11, Oxford.

Robinson, M. (forthcoming): 'Possible models for the pastoral economy'. *The prehistoric landscape and Iron Age enclosed settlement at Mingies Ditch, Hardwick with Yelford, Oxon.* (T. Allen and M. Robinson).

Robinson, M. A. and Lambrick, G. H. 1984: 'Holocene alluviuation and hydrology in the Upper Thames basin'. *Nature* 308, 809-814.

Rogers, G. B. 1977: 'Les motifs non figures'. *Poteries sigellées de la Gaule Centrale*. Part I, 28 Supplement à Gallia.

Silver, I. A. 1969: 'The ageing of domestic animals'. *Science in archaeology* (eds. D. Brothwell and E. Higgs) 283–302, London.

Silverside, A. J. 1977: *A phytosociological survey of British arable-weed and related communities* (unpublished PhD thesis, University of Durham).

Smith, K. G. V. 1973: 'Forensic entomology'. *Insects and other arthropods of medical importance* (ed. K. G. V. Smith) London.

Stanfield, J.A. and Simpson, G. 1958: *Central Gaulish potters*. London.

Stuiver, M. and Pearson, G. W. 1986: 'High-precision calibration of the radiocarbon time scale, AD 1950-500 BC'. *Radiocarbon* 28, No. 2b, 805-838.

Stuiver, M. and Reimer, P. J. 1986: 'A computer program for radiocarbon age calibration'. *Radiocarbon* 28 No. 2b, 1022-1029.

Terrisse, J-R. 1968: *Les ceramiques sigillées gallo-romaines des Martre-de-Veyre, Puy-de-Dome*, 19 Supplement à Gallia.

Thomas, N. 1955: 'Excavations at Vicarage Field, Stanton Harcourt, 1951'. *Oxoniensia* 20, 1–28.

Wacher, J. S. and McWhirr, A. D. 1982: *Cirencester excavations 1: early Roman occupation at Cirencester*, Cirencester.

Wainwright, G. J. 1968: 'The excavation of a Durotrigian farmstead near Tollard Royal in Cranbourne Chase, southern England'. *Proc Prehist Soc* 34, 102–147.

Walden, H. W. 1976: 'A nomenclatural list of the land Mollusca of the British Isles'. *Journ Conchology Lond*, 29, 21-25.

Whitbread, I. K. 1986: 'The characterisation of argillaceous inclusions in ceramic thin sections'. *Archaeometry* 28, 79-88.

Williams, A. 1951: 'Excavations at Beard Mill, Stanton Harcourt, Oxon., 1944'. *Oxoniensia* 16, 5–22.

Williams, D. F. and Peacock, D. P. S. 1983: 'The importation of olive oil into Roman Britain'. *Producción y comercio del aceite en la antigüedad* (II Congresso) (eds. J. M. Blazquez Martínez and J. Remesal Rodríguez), 263–280, Madrid.

Williams, J. H. and McCarthy, M. R. 1974: 'A double ditched enclosure at Blackthorn'. *Two Iron Age sites in Northampton* (J. H. Williams) 127-169, Northampton.

Wilson, C. E. 1981: 'Burials within settlements in southern Britain during the pre-Roman Iron Age'. *Bulletin No. 18 of the Institute of Archaeology*, 127-169, London.

Wilson, D. H. (forthcoming): 'The Iron Age pottery'. *The prehistoric landscape and Iron Age enclosed settlement at Mingies Ditch, Hardwick with Yelford, Oxon.* (T. G. Allen and M. Robinson).

Wilson, R. 1978: 'The animal bones'. *The excavation of an Iron Age settlement, Bronze Age ring-ditches and Roman features at Ashville Trading Estate, Abingdon (Oxfordshire), 1974–76* (M. Parrington) Counc Brit Archaeol Res Rep 28, 110–13, London.

Wilson, R. 1979: 'The vertebrates'. *Iron Age and Roman riverside settlements at Farmoor, Oxfordshire* (G. Lambrick and M. Robinson) Counc Brit Archaeol Res Rep 32, 128–133, London.

Wilson, R. 1985: 'Degraded bones, feature type and spatial patterning on an Iron Age occupation site in Oxfordshire'. *Palaeobiological investigations research design, methods and data analysis* (eds. R. J. Fieller, D. D. Gilbertson and N. G. A. Ralph) Brit Archaeol Rep International Series 266, 81–93, Oxford.

Wilson, R. (forthcoming): 'Bone and shell evidence'. *The prehistoric landscape and Iron Age enclosed settlement at Mingies Ditch, Hardwick with Yelford, Oxon.* (T. G. Allen and M. Robinson).

Wilson, R. (forthcoming): 'The animal bones'. *Archaeological investigations at Mount Farm, Dorchester, Oxon.* (G. Lambrick).

Wilson, R. (forthcoming): 'The animal bones'. *Early Roman settlement and later land-use on the Windrush floodplain at Smithsfield, Hardwick with Yelford, Oxon.* (T. G. Allen).

Wilson, R. (forthcoming): 'Animal bones, fish bones and shells'. *Excavations on the site of the medieval moated manor at Harding's Field, Chalgrove, Oxon.* (eds. P. Page, S. Smithson and H. Baker) *Oxoniensia*.

Young, C. J. 1977: *The Roman pottery industry of the Oxford region*. Brit Archaeol Rep British Series 43, Oxford.

Technical appendix

SECTION 1: THE EXCAVATION

Romano-British and later shallow gullies and animal burrows (Fig. A1)

459 was only the easternmost of four shallow curving gullies which appeared to be forming small and very shallow enclosures open on the SW side.

459 and 467 were slots with near-vertical sides and a flattish bottom. 469 was of similar character except at the S end, where it dived down beneath the top fills of 402, extending further than was apparent on the surface. This part of the gully must be the result of animal burrowing. Just S of 433 gully 457 also deepened, but here the deeper part was irregular, and was apparently cut by 433. 467 was later than both 469 and 459, and since it only cut the very end of each was perhaps blocking the gap between them. Feature 457 just E of and parallel to 469 may represent another phase, but could not be traced through the top of 433. Romano-British finds in the top of 433 here, however, suggest that it did run through.

At its N end 459 cut a possible posthole 458, and was itself cut by a shallow scoop 454. Adjacent to it and also cut by 454 was another short gully 441, which turned into gully 466. 441 cut other even shallower gullies 475 and 474 running NW, both of which petered out short of 459. 466 was recut as a shallower gully 472, which turned NW at its N end and was cut by 454. Neither 441 nor 472 continued beyond 454. These features may have been connected with gullies 459 etc., as may 493 and 502, which were cut into the top of 433 (see Fig. 8), but may all result from animal disturbance.

Opposite 457 etc. on the N side of 126–162 were several other short lengths of sinuous gully 473, 476 etc. These were deeper and wider than 457, but though their sides were near-vertical and the bottoms flattish, they were of irregular depth. Below the top clayey silt fills were very gravelly, with mixed streaks of pure gravel and of silty clay interspersed. 473 cut ditch 416, and possibly also 476. These features were probably animal burrows beneath the medieval headland.

Another possible animal hole was an irregular patch of dark loamy silt just E of gully 197 and S of 126. This bottomed on gravel, and produced one sherd of Romano-British pottery.

SECTION 2: THE FINDS

Fabric descriptions of Iron Age pottery
by T G Allen

a) Definitions: quartz inclusions are defined as —

Coarse	>1 mm across
Medium	1 mm, and >0.5 mm
Medium-fine	<0.5 mm, readily visible macroscopically
Fine	hardly visible macroscopically, clear x10 magnification
Very fine	hardly visible x10, clear x20 magnification

For calcareous inclusions and ferrous lumps the same terms are used, but all refer to coarser particle sizes. Ranges are given, but

Coarse	is approximately >3 mm
Medium	3 mm down to 1 mm
Fine	<1 mm

Fabrics arranged into major fabric groups
(see Chapter 3: Iron Age pottery: Fabrics)

Group 1

Fabric 13a Abundant organic inclusions, usually grass or straw. The paste generally contains common medium to fine translucent and opaque quartz grains, rounded and sub-rectangular. These are often multicoloured.

13b Common to abundant organic grass/straw inclusions. Fine and very fine translucent angular and rounded quartz grains, sparse to common. A finer version of 13a.

Group 2 Sandy

Fabric 7 Black shiny rounded grains, medium to fine, common to abundant. Possibly limonite. Invariably accompanied by translucent and opaque quartz grains, rounded or sub-angular, sometimes multicoloured, i.e. white, red and yellow or orange. Sometimes medium or fine red ferrous lumps, and/or sparse medium to fine calcareous inclusions.

Fabric 2 Quartz, translucent and opaque, grains usually rounded or sub-rectangular, often multicoloured i.e. white, pink, red, yellow, orange and grey/black. Coarse to medium-fine, common to abundant. Sometimes includes sparse black shiny grains and/or coarse to medium red or brown/black ferrous lumps. Very occasionally contains lumps of limestone or flint. This fabric has a wide variation and includes a number of sub-groups, none of which was numerous. The following were separated out:

2a Coarse and medium multicoloured quartz, rounded, sub-angular, abundant. Also medium, fine red ferrous lumps, common, with occasional larger lumps. Organic impressions, sparse. Hard.

2b Fine quartz, usually translucent or milky white, common to very abundant. Usually has red or brown ferrous lumps, coarse-medium, and sometimes fine black shiny grains. Occasional coarse or medium quartz or other inclusions.

16 Red quartz, medium to fine, common to abundant, rounded and sub-angular. Contains black shiny grains and translucent clear quartz, medium to fine. This is a variant of 2a. Hard.

Fabric 8 Fine and very fine angular and rounded quartz grains, mostly translucent, multicoloured, common. Sometimes fine and very fine red ferrous inclusions. Very occasionally larger quartz, ferrous or other inclusions.

Group 3
Coarse sand and other mixed inclusions.
Fabric 2c   Rounded and angular medium quartz grains, common to abundant, multicoloured. Larger rounded grains and small quartz pebbles are common, as are coarse and medium ferrous lumps, limestone gravel, flint and black shiny rounded quartz. Occasionally bone and charcoal lumps occur.

5a   Coarse and medium-coarse sub-angular and rounded quartz, multicoloured, abundant to very abundant. Other coarse inclusions as for Fabric 2c with the exception of charcoal, but more common.

5b   Very coarse limestone gravel, common to abundant, rounded and sub-angular quartz as in 5a, common to abundant, and sparse flint etc. as in Fabric 2c.

Fabric 21   Coarse limestone gravel, common to abundant, common organic cereal and chaff inclusions, coarse and medium rounded and sub-angular multicoloured quartz. Also includes red or brown/black medium ferrous lumps, sparse to common.

Group 4
Ferrous inclusions
Fabric 1a   Abundant large red or brown ferrous lumps, up to 7 mm in length, with common, medium and coarse rounded and sub-angular quartz grains. These can be translucent or opaque and occur in several colours, with some black shiny grains. Occasional lumps up to 8 mm across. Also infrequent coarse to fine calcareous shelly lumps and organic impressions, grass or straw. Smooth feel.

1b   As 1a but medium to fine quartz with only very occasional larger lumps. Sometimes more common quartz and less ferrous inclusions. Smooth feel.

1c   Fine quartz, occasional medium quartz, common ferrous inclusions, organic impressions. Has a more dusty feel. (This fabric group is usually oxidised on the exterior and reduced in the interior.)

Group 5
Mixed sand and calcareous inclusions
Fabric 12a   Medium to fine calcareous inclusions, often rounded, abundant, with sparse to common larger shelly or pebbly lumps. The inclusions are neither plate-like nor characteristically oolitic, and probably derive from the limestone gravel. Medium-fine to fine common quartz grains, sub-angular and rounded, multicoloured. Medium to fine red ferrous lumps, sparse to common generally, but in some cases common to abundant. Occasional organic grass/straw impressions.

12b   Fine and medium-fine rounded and sub-angular quartz grains, common to abundant, multicoloured. Calcareous inclusions as in 12a but less common and generally finer. Ferrous inclusions sparse.

Fabric 11   Fine calcareous inclusions, >0.5 mm, sparse to common. Very occasional larger lumps. Character of inclusions as in Fabric 12. Fine multicoloured rounded and sub-angular quartz grains, common. Medium and fine sparse red ferrous lumps. A finer version of Fabric 12.

Fabric 10   Coarse to fine shelly limestone, medium and fine angular and rounded sparse to common quartz, transparent and opaque, multicoloured. Occasional larger quartz grains. Common organic grass or straw impressions (in the break) and medium to fine red ferrous lumps. Hard. This fabric is invariably oxidised outside and reduced inside.

Group 6
Calcareous
Fabric 3a   Shelly limestone, coarse to fine, common to very abundant. Inclusions up to 12 x 12 mm   Common organic straw/grass and cereal impressions, sometimes several cms long. Occasional coarse or medium ferrous lumps.

Fabric 3   Abundant very coarse limestone inclusions 7–8 mm across, rough and irregular, possibly broken down from lumps of limestone. Alternatively, could derive from the gravel; there are abundant smaller calcareous gravel pebbles as well. This variant only occurs in one or two large storage jars.

Fabric 3b   Oolitic limestone with characteristic spherical particles generally <1 mm across, abundant to very abundant, and larger irregular and plate-like calcareous inclusions up to 8 mm across, common to abundant. Sometimes organic grass/straw impressions, sparse to common, and very occasionally sparse medium or fine red ferrous inclusions.

Fabric 3c   Fossil shell, coarse to fine, sparse to common. No other calcareous particles.

Group 7
Grog-tempered
Fabric 17   Coarse and medium pink and grey grog particles, 1–2 mm across, common. Medium and fine calcareous angular and sub-angular inclusions and voids. Occasional red ferrous lumps, medium to fine. Smooth soapy feel.

Fabric 19   Coarse and medium grog particles, 1–3 mm across, grey and pink/buff, common. Red ferrous lumps of similar size, also common, medium and medium-fine sub-angular quartz grains, multicoloured,, black shiny rounded grains, sparse, some very fine translucent quartz grains. There is only a single instance of this fabric.

Group 8
Flint
Fabric 20   Coarse to fine angular flint, mostly calcined white or grey, common to abundant. Sometimes red ferrous lumps, medium to fine, common, and organic grass/straw impressions. Hard.

Group 9
Micaceous
Fabric 14   Fine and very fine translucent angular and rounded quartz grains, common. Fine mica platelets. Very occasional larger ferrous lumps, calcareous inclusions and quartz grains. Hard, dusty feel.

Group 10
Shelly alluvium
Fabric 9 Snail shell, coarse to fine, common. Medium-fine and fine rounded and sub-angular quartz grains, multicoloured, sparse to common. Red ferrous lumps, medium to fine, sparse to common.

Iron Age - additional material about central roundhouse features
by T G Allen

Two features clearly related to the house were gully 430, which cut ditch 402 but respected or was respected by 477 and 433, and ditch 151, which ran from the house entrance to the main enclosure entrance (both features were filled from bottom to top with dark soil and occupation debris, which appeared to have accumulated rapidly). What may have been a corresponding gully to 430 on the other side of the house entrance, gully 424, was cut by 425 but cut 401 (Fig. 9). Numerous sherds of a globular bowl were found in the bottom of 430, and several others of this same vessel well down in 477. The sherds were not highly abraded, and are not likely to have been lying around for very long. On this evidence it is suggested that 430 belongs just after 477. 151 clearly belongs to a stage when the central house faced towards the NE enclosure entrance, and so postdates 402. Otherwise it cannot be firmly dated. However, a number of sherds of several vessels were common to 151 and the Phase 3 enclosure ditches 425 and 433, while none could be matched in Phase 2 features, and only one in the Phase 4 group. Given the relatively large assemblage in 151 and the impression of fairly rapid accumulation of rubbish, 151 probably belongs predominantly with Phase 3, and fabric percentages including it are given in brackets.

A comparison was made between proportions of burnished vessels (based on Estimated Vessel No.) in groups in the stratigraphic sequence and in other enclosure groups (Table T3). There is not a clear trend, although the earliest and latest groups in the sequence have the least and greatest proportions respectively. Among the other groups 496/512/513 has a very low percentage and 124 a very high one; this matches their proportions of sandy fabrics. 23 does not fit the pattern, but all the pottery from this enclosure was recovered from the lower ditch fills, which were very clayey and wet, and this affected the survival of surfaces; the upper part of this enclosure was scraped away before excavation began.

Romano-British pottery
by Sheila Raven

Fabrics

Method of classification
The sherds were examined macroscopically and with a binocular microscope (x10) and divided into fabric groups and sub-groups according to their inclusions and firing characteristics.

Peacock's scheme for standardizing fabric description was used. The Munsell Chart was used to describe colour in conjunction with a verbal description. Inclusions were categorised according to:

a) Frequency - sparse, moderate, common, or abundant
b) Sorting - well-sorted or ill-sorted
c) Size - Fine
- Medium - under 1 mm
- Coarse - 1 mm - 5 mm
d) Rounding - rounded, sub-rounded, or angular

As mentioned under the heading 'Method of study' (see Chapter 3) the sample of pottery analysed contained medieval and post-medieval pottery as well as Roman and a sample of Iron Age sherds. Fabric categories 11 (coarse mixed sandy) and 15 (calcareous inclusions) in this report included sherds which could be Iron Age or Romano-British. This coarse local pottery found on small Romano-British sites is sometimes so close to local Iron Age fabrics as to be indistinguishable.

Fabric category 15 (calcareous) is a multi-period category, containing one joint Iron Age and Roman sub-category, one Roman, and two medieval. The remaining medieval and post-medieval fabrics are separate sub-categories within the normal run of the fabric series.

The finer imported or decorated pottery types that were easily identifiable by their specialist characteristics, such as samian and mortaria, were extracted first for ease of reference and form the first five categories of the fabric series. Seventeen major fabric categories have been identified, and in Table 8 these are expressed as percentages of the total assemblage.

These 17 main groups were broken down into sub-categories; however, some of these are very similar, and had the assemblage been larger these might have been amalgamated. For instance, Category 10 (mixed sandy wheel-made) is almost identical to Category 8.2 (sandy grey) except in terms of colour. Some pots (or parts of pots) were fired buff or black, or patchy brown and red instead of pure grey. This was probably due to poorly reduced firing conditions rather than design, but it was thought better to separate out a definitely reduced grey group.

Fabric series
1 Amphorae
2 Mortaria
3 Samian
4 Fine ware - Colour coat:
    4.1 Red colour-coat Oxfordshire
    4.2 Brown colour-coat
5 Fine ware - Decorated:
    5.1 Poppy head beaker
    5.2 London ware
6 White wares:
    6.1 Fine cream
    6.2 Less fine cream
    6.3 Sandy cream
    6.4 Granulated cream
7 Oxidised:
    7.1 Fine oxidised
    7.2 Less fine oxidised
    7.3 Granulated oxidised
    7.4 Densely granulated oxidised (medieval)
    7.5 Quartz-gritted oxidised
    7.6 Soapy oxidised
    7.7 Hard orange oxidised (Post-medieval)

7.8 Pale orange/grey oxidised
8 Reduced - grey:
  8.1 Fine grey
  8.2 Sandy grey
  8.3 Granulated grey
  8.4 Coarse granulated grey
  8.5 Quartz-gritted grey
  8.6 Coarse, sandy grey
9 Reduced - black & brown:
  9.1 BBI (Black-burnished ware)
  9.2 Black, quartzy ware
  9.3 Fine black and brown quartzy ware
  9.4 Coarse black and brown quartzy ware
  9.5 Fine handmade brown/black ware
11 Coarse mixed sandy:
  11.1 Coarse sandy (IA & R/B)
  11.1 (reduced/oxidised)
  11.2 Very coarse sandy (IA & R/B)
  11.3 Fine sandy/black sand (IA & R/B)
  11.4 Coarse sandy/black sand (IA, R)
  11.5 Hard, mixed sandy (IA)
  11.6 Sandy/black organic
  11.7 Sandy/iron ore/shell silt mixed (IA & R/B)
  11.8 Coarse sandy/organic (IA)
  11.9 Sandy flint
12 Mica inclusions:
  12.1 Fine mica ware
  12.2 Mica/quartz-gritted
14 Grog inclusions:
  14.1 Sparse grog
  14.2 Grey speckled grog
  14.3 Coarse grey speckled grog
  14.4 Coarse grog
15 Calcareous inclusions:
  15.1 Very fine oolitic limestone
  15.2 Fine oolitic limestone
  15.3 Coarse shelly limestone (IA, R)
  15.4 Coarse shelly limestone/iron ore (IA)
  15.5 Coarse oolitic limestone (IA)
  15.6 Coarse sandy/limestone (IA)
  15.7 Sandy/shell silt (IA)
  15.8 Hard, oolitic limestone (medieval)
  15.9 Smooth shelly limestone (?Saxon)

Unless otherwise stated all these fabrics are Roman. Periods are indicated thus: IA = Iron Age; R/B = Romano-British; m = medieval; P/M = Post-medieval.

Romano-British pottery fabric descriptions

1 Amphora - Dressel 20
2 Mortaria - Oxfordshire White Ware (Young 1977, 56)
3 Samian - (See samian report)
4.1 Red colour-coated Oxford Ware
Fine orange ware, sparse fine quartz inclusions, sparse mica, occasional iron ore. Red colour-coat interior and exterior (Young 1977, 123).
4.2 Brown colour-coat
Fine, soft cream ware, no visible inclusions. Dark brown colour-coat interior and exterior. Exterior sprinkled with small clay particles?

5.1 Very fine grey decorated ware
(Poppy-headed beaker fabric)
Very fine, smooth pale grey ware, sparse well-sorted fine quartz inclusions.
5.2 Fine decorated grey ware
('London Ware' type fabric)
Fine grey-buff hard ware, common ill-sorted quartz inclusions, occasional dark rounded inclusions.
6 White Wares
6.1 Fine cream ware, hard, fairly smooth. Very fine quartz inclusions, occasional red iron ore.
6.2 Fairly fine cream ware, sparse medium quartz inclusions, hard, smooth-rough.
6.3 Sandy cream ware, common small quartz inclusions, medium hard, rough.
6.4 Granulated cream ware, fairly hard, rough, common multicoloured quartz inclusions. Colour of surface and core varies greatly (cream - pink - grey).
7 Oxidised Wares
7.1 Fine ware, hard, fairly smooth very fine quartz inclusions, occasional red iron ore.
7.2 Fairly fine ware, sandy, rough, frequent quartz inclusions, occasional red iron ore and grog. Colour is very variable red/orange - pale orange.
7.3 Granulated ware, hard, rough, abundant mixed quartz inclusions. Colour red/orange.
7.4 Densely granulated ware, hard, rough, very abundant medium quartz inclusions, occasional red grog. Colour pale orange-cream. Medieval.
7.5 Quartz-gritted ware, harsh, medium-hard, with small common quartz inclusions, occasional mica, surface peppered with larger quartz grains. Colour red-orange surfaces, grey or orange core.
7.6 Soapy ware, hard, ill-assorted medium quartz inclusions. Colour variable and uneven. Pink-yellow/orange-grey/buff.
7.7 Hard sandy orange ware, very hard, smooth, frequent small quartz inclusions. Very hard fabric. Orange fabric, interior surface has green or brown glaze. Post-medieval.
7.8 Pale, orange granulated ware, hard, rough, abundant mixed quartz inclusions, occasional red iron ore. Pale orange core, patchy grey exterior.
8 Reduced wheel-made wares - grey
8.1 Fine grey ware, fairly hard, smooth, very fine quartz inclusions. Colour pale to medium grey.
8.2 Sandy grey ware, hard, rough, common small quartz inclusions. Colour pale to dark grey with black exterior.
8.3 Granulated grey ware, hard, fairly smooth, abundant small to medium quartz inclusions. Colour dark grey, pale grey exterior.
8.4 Granulated coarse grey ware, fairly hard, rough, abundant medium to large quartz inclusions. Colour pale grey, occasionally dark grey surface.
8.5 Quartz-gritted grey ware, fairly soft, harsh, common small quartz inclusions, surface scattered with larger quartz grains. Colour buff-pale grey-dark grey.
8.6 Coarse sandy grey ware, hard, coarse, burnished exterior, common quartz inclusions, sparse red iron ore and black organic.
9 Reduced black and brown wares
9.1 BBI, abundant white quartz inclusions, hard, colour

dark grey to black, burnish survives on exterior of some sherds, hand-made.

9.2 Black quartzy ware, hard, rough, common mixed quartz inclusions. Colour dark grey or black. Similar to BBI but less densely tempered.

9.3 Brown and black quartzy ware, fine, hard and fairly rough, abundant small mixed quartz inclusions. Colour variable, pale brown to dark grey to black, exterior surface generally smoothed.

9.4 Coarse brown and black quartzy ware, hard, rough, common medium to large quartz inclusions, sparse red iron ore and grog. Colour variable, dark grey with patchy brown or orange surfaces.

9.5 Fine hand-made brown and black quartzy ware, fairly hard, rough, fine common quartz inclusions. Colour dark grey to black to brown.

10 Mixed sandy wheel-made ware. Sandy reduced/oxidised ware. Same as fabric 8.2, but in a range of colours, sometimes just on one sherd. Colour ranges from buff — grey/brown — yellow/brown — dull red — black. (This amorphous group would be generally classed as unsuccessful reduced ware).

11 Coarse mixed sandy hand-made wares

11.1 Coarse sandy ware, common, medium to large quartz inclusions, occasional red iron ore. Colour variable, dark grey to orange — buff — brown. (= Iron Age fabric 2a)

11.2 Very coarse sandy ware. Similar to 11.1 but with very large quartz inclusions as well as medium quartz, giving a harsher, grittier fabric, occasional limestone. (= Iron Age fabric 2c).

11.3 Fine sandy ware (black sand), fairly fine hard, even textured, ill-assorted quartz inclusions including some black quartz, occasional mica. Colour orange to buff, sometimes grey at core. (= Iron Age fabric 7).

11.4 Coarse sandy ware (black sand). Moderately hard coarse ware, common multicoloured quartz inclusions, including black quartz, occasional black iron ore. Colour dark grey with brown and orange exterior. (= Iron Age fabric 7).

11.5 Hard coarse fabric similar to 114 but with larger and more abundant quartz inclusions, including black quartz, occasional red and ?black iron ore, vegetable matter, and flint. Colour grey with grey-brown exterior.

11.6 Sandy and black organic ware, coarse, fairly soft, common ill-sorted quartz inclusions, moderate black organic, occasional flint. Colour grey, grey-brown surfaces.

11.7 Sandy/shell silt/iron ore mixed ware, moderately hard, coarse, common mixed quartz inclusions, very fine calcareous shell silt, occasional red iron ore. Colour dark grey and brown. (= Iron Age fabric 9).

11.8 Coarse sandy/organic ware, moderately hard, rough, common small to medium quartz inclusions, moderate organic inclusions. Dark grey to black. (= Iron Age fabric 13).

11.9 Sandy/flint ware, hard, fairly rough, abundant quartz inclusions, sparse flint. Colour black.

12 Mica wares

12.1 Fine mica ware,, fairly soft, smooth and soapy, common small muscovite mica inclusions, very fine quartz, occasional red iron ore. Colour variable, buff - grey - reddish brown.

12.2 Mica/quartz-gritted, hard, harsh, common small muscovite mica inclusions, surface scattered with large quartz.

Colour buff, buff or grey core and dull orange margins.

13 Flint-gritted ware. Medieval.

13.1 Flint-gritted ware, hard, soapy, hand-made, medium to large quartz inclusions. Colour variable, pale brown - dark grey.

14 Grog Wares

14.1 Sparse grog ware, fairly soft, rough, sparse small (some of grog may be clay pellets or possibly marmstone) grog inclusions, moderate small quartz. Colour variable, buff — grey — orange/brown.

14.2 Grey speckled ware, hard, smooth, fairly fine, common grey grog inclusions of darker tone than main fabric giving speckled look. Colour pale grey often with darker grey surface.

14.3 Coarse grey speckled ware, hard, rough, abundant grey grog inclusions, occasional flint, and black iron ore. Colour grey with noticeable speckled effect on surface from different coloured grog.

14.4 Coarse grog ware, moderately hard, soapy, common to abundant grog of varying size and colour, moderate quartz, coarse and thick-walled. Colour very variable, dark grey — brown — red/orange. Some sherds are wheel-made, others are probably hand-made.

15 Calcareous Wares

15.1 Very fine oolitic limestone ware, medium hard, fairly smooth, common small oolitic limestone inclusions (now voids). Colour pale grey.

15.2 Fine oolitic limestone, hard, rough, abundant small oolitic inclusions giving densely-speckled look, sparse white quartz. Colour grey, grey and orange/brown surface.

15.3 Coarse shelly limestone ware, fairly soft, abundant shelly limestone inclusions of varying size. (= Iron Age fabric 3a).

15.4 Coarse shelly limestone/iron ore, hand-made = Iron Age fabric (see Iron Age pottery report). (= Iron Age fabric 3a).

15.5 Coarse oolitic limestone ware, hand-made = Iron Age fabric (see Iron Age pottery report). (= Iron Age fabric 3b).

15.6 Coarse sandy/limestone ware, hand-made = Iron Age fabric (see Iron Age pottery report). (= Iron Age fabrics 5b & 21).

15.7 Sandy/shell silt ware, hand-made = Iron Age fabric (see Iron Age pottery report). (= Iron Age fabric 9).

15.8 Hard oolitic limestone ware, hard, matt smooth surfaces, abundant small oolitic limestone inclusions, sparse quartz and red iron ore. Colour dark grey, orange, buff or brown surfaces. Medieval.

15.9 Shelly-limestone ware, hard, fairly smooth, abundant shelly limestone inclusions, sparse quartz. Colour grey/brown or dull orange. This is a finer, smoother fabric than the known Iron Age fabrics of similar inclusions from the site, and is probably wheel-made. It may be a stray Saxon sherd.

16 Miscellaneous Wares

16.1 Dark grey granulated ware, hard, rough, abundant multicoloured small quartz inclusions, moderate black iron ore. Colour dark grey.

16.2 Grey coarse granulated ware, hard, rough, abundant white and grey medium quartz inclusions, occasional marmstone and iron ore. Colour pale grey.

16.3 Grey/brown hard sandy ware, hard, smooth, common medium quartz inclusions, common black iron ore, occasional red iron ore. Colour grey/brown with reddish brown margins.

16.4 Marmstone sandy ware, fairly hard, common ill-sorted white marmstone inclusions. Colour pale grey.

17 Salt-glazed Ware. Post-medieval

Form code

1 Closed vessel with long narrow neck, wide body and one or more handles, no pouring lip.

2 As above, but with a pouring lip.

3 Closed or open vessel - 150 mm + height, height as great as or greater than body diameter.

3.1 Necked jar with everted rim.

3.2 Necked jar with bead or plain rounded rim.

3.3 Necked jar with undercut rim.

3.4 Jars with everted rims and minimal or no necks. (Where there is insufficient rim to judge whether they are from necked jars, they have been classified under this general category.)

3.5 Jars with squat or folded back rims and minimal necks.

3.6 Large storage jars.

4 Beaker - closed vessel, height as great as or greater than the rim diameter, which is less than the body diameter.

5 Cup or tankard - open vessel, no neck. Usually with one or more handles.

5.1 Tankard with one handle.

5.2 Cup, samian form Dv 37 without handle.

6 Bowl - open vessel, height less than rim diameter. Height to diameter is no less than 3:8, and up to 1:1

7 Dish - open vessel, height to rim diameter is less than 1:4, but more than 1:8.

8 Lid - open vessel, with height to rim diameter less than 1:2, and handle/knob to hold vessel at top.

(6* in text = Mortarium bowl)

Decoration code

1 Grooves (horizontal)
    Single = 1
    Double = 1 (2)
    Over 2 = 1 (3 or 4 etc.)

2 Grooves (horizontal)
    Wide - Single = 2
Double = 2 (2) etc.

3 Cordons - narrow

4 Cordons - wide

5 Lattice - acute

6 Lattice - obtuse

7 Incised curvilinear lines - compass-drawn

8 Applied Barbotine dots

9 Relief moulding

10 Burnish

11 Glaze - interior

12 Grooves - vertical slanting

13 Rouletted zones - narrow horizontal bands of short vertical strokes

14 Burnished lines - vertical, slanting

15 Corrugation

Range of jar and bowl forms

Since there were very few complete profiles, it has proved impossible to produce a detailed typology of the jar and bowl forms represented. Where only a little of the wall of the vessel below the rim survives, bowls can rarely be distinguished from dishes — it is for this reason that in the assessment of major vessel forms, bowls and dishes are classed as one category. However, it appears from the more complete examples that there are far more bowls than dishes from both sites.

For the same reason jars can only be divided into generalised groupings such as 'necked jars with everted rims'. There was not time to calculate rim diameters for the whole collection. A test sample of rims from feature 34 contained both wide mouthed jars and narrow necked jars in fairly equal proportions.

The rim series shows how much of the profile was present (Fig. A3). This series does not follow any typological order: rims were simply given a number as they were recorded. The rim series does not reflect every slight variation present at Northmoor. A single rim code like R12 represents a number of similar, but not necessarily identical, rims. However, it illustrates the main variations.

Since the pottery did not come from sealed occupation layers no attempt was made to construct a detailed chronological typology of pottery forms. Within the jar and bowl categories only broad divisions have been possible. Comparisons of the proportions of these on Sites A and B are given in Table T5.

Catalogue of all samian sherds

Feature	Form	Fabric	Description
96/4M	DV 37	CG	A relief moulded piece featuring an anacanthus motif, a trifide, and rows of beads demarcating the compartments, the design of which is paralleled in the products of Drusus I at Les-Martres-De-Veyre in Central Gaul (No. 186 in Terrisse 1968). This dates the piece closely to AD 100-120. The acanthus motif can be matched to K13 in Rogers (1977) and the trifide motif to Roger's G.395. Date: AD 100-120
96/4M	?	SG	Plain body sherd, curved, (surface) showing the shining gloss of South Gaulish products. (AD 43-100)
96/4M	?	SG	Plain flake (AD 43-100)
96/5M	?	?SG	Plain flake from foot-ring
96/5M	?	?SG	Plain flake
128	?	?CG	Plain flake
131	?	SG	Footring fragment from ? dish. Date: c 2nd century AD
131 (north end)	?Knorr 78	SG	Plain, tiny rim sherd, possibly from Knorr 78 cylindrical decorated bowl. Date: AD 60-80
131(top)	?	?EG	Plain, curved body fragment. Date: AD 120-160
138/16M	?	?CG	Burnt flake
162		?SG	Dish or bowl bead rim fragment

406/A/1	?	CG	Body sherd with one fine groove on exterior
406/A/1	?	?CG	Flake
406/A/2	Dv 18/31	EG	Dish —one third of whole vessel. Probably East Gaulish. One dip gloss with finger mark near base. Rivet hole on shoulder denoting repair. Date: AD 130-160
34/Cut2	Dv 37	?CG	A very worn rim of a relief-moulded bowl ahowing an ?egg-and-tongue frieze above an indistinguishable design. Wavy lines demarcating the compartments, rosettes and ?foliage are present. Date: Late 1st or 2nd century AD
35/B/2	Dv 33	CG	Rim and joining rim fragment. Date: 2nd century AD
35/C/1	?	?EG	Flake. Date: ?AD 120.
35/D/1	?	SG	Small plain sherd. Date: AD 43-110
35/D/2	Cr 33	CG	Rim with groove midway down wall of the vessel. Date: 2nd century AD
35/D/2	?	CG	Teo plain sherds from two different vessels
35/D/3	?	?CG	Flake
36	Dv 18/31	SG	Plain rim sherd with fine shining gloss (AD 43-110)
36	?	?SG	Flake
36	Dish	SG	Sherd from ?dish — very abraded. (AD 43-110)
36/D	Dv 18/31	CG	Foot-ring base with internal (Lezoux) name stamp almost completely worn away. Date: AD 120-160
36/D	?	?SG	Worn sherd
201/A	?	?CG	Footring flake
202/!	?	SG	Sherd from near footring dish/bowl
202/D/3	?	?CG	Two flakes
225 (South end)	?	?CG	Flake

Medieval and post-medieval pottery

Site A

Total sherd no.: 47 sherds
Total sherd weight: 1 kilo
Sherd No.
Medieval/Calcareous Ware: 70% Fabric no. 15.8
Medieval/Flint-gritted: 19% Fabric no. 13
Medieval/Oxidised Ware: less than 1% Fabric no. 7.4
Post-medieval/Oxidised Ware: 10% Fabric no. 7.7
Post-medieval/Reduced: less than 1% (Salt-glazed)Fabric no. 17
In addition, 1 sherd of medieval/Calcareous Ware - Fabric no. 15.8, weighing 30 g., 7 sherds of Post-medieval/Oxidised Ware — Fabric no. 7.7, and 1 sherd of Post-medieval/Reduced (Salt-glazed) — Fabric no. 17, came from *unstratified* deposits on Site A.

Site B

Total sherd no.: 10 sherds
Total sherd weight: 260 g.
Sherd No.
Medieval/Calcareous Ware: 60% Fabric no. 15.8
Medieval/Flint-gritted Ware: 30% Fabric no. 13
Post-medieval/Oxidised Ware: 10% Fabric no. 7.7

Roman pottery samples

Material sampled by thin section and atomic absorbtion.

Thin section

Fabric 7.3 - Granulated oxidised
Fabric 8.2 - Sandy grey reduced
Fabric 8.5 - Quartz-gritted grey reduced
Fabric 9.4 - Coarse black and brown 'quartzy' ware
Fabric 14.3 - Coarse grey speckled 'grog' ware
Fabric 15.3 - Coarse shelly-limestone calcareous ware

Atomic absorbtion

Fabric 7.3 - Granulated oxidised (5 sherds)
Fabric 8.2 - Sandy grey reduced (4 sherds)
Fabric 9.4 - Coarse black and brown 'quartzy' ware (5 sherds)
Fabric 15.3 — Coarse shelly-limestone calcareous ware (6 sherds)

Comparable test material
from Oxfordshire medieval pottery

Coarse sandy (medieval Pottery Code *Y*)
'Brill' brick (medieval Pottery Code *AM*)
Shelly-limestone (medieval Pottery Code *B*)

These samples from the Oxford Archaeological Unit medieval pottery collection were all thin sectioned and tested by atomic absorbtion. They are not identical to the Roman pottery fabrics, but appear to contain common basic inclusions, most of which are readily available in the geological deposits of the Oxford Clay Belt and river gravels. The Roman fabrics taken for atomic absorbtion analysis were deliberately chosen with this particular medieval pottery in mind, so as to have some sort of control sample for the group.

Medieval fabric Y is comparable to Roman fabric 8.2.

Medieval fabric AM is comparable to Roman fabrics 7.3. and 9.4. Medieval fabric B is comparable to Roman fabric 15.3.

Fabrics identified in fired clay

A Calcareous, fine and very abundant, also many coarser pebbles. Limestone gravel, not shell. Common red lumps and streaks, probably ferrous. Dusty crumbly feel

B Fine translucent quartz, usually angular, 1–2 mm across, common. Sparse calcareous limestone gravel, generally fine to medium. Common red ferrous lumps and organic grass/straw impressions. Crumbly, soft dusty feel

C Very fine translucent quartz (angular and rounded), 1 - 2 mm or less, common to abundant, occasional larger quartz. Red streaks and lumps, and sparse calcareous inclusions and organic impressions. Hard, dense, with smooth breaks and sometimes laminae in the clay. Smooth or slightly sandy feel.

D Common to abundant medium and coarse calcareous

inclusions, probably limestone gravel. Sparse fine or medium quartz (rounded and angular). Dusty feel. Not common, possibly = Fabric B when highly burnt, but more calcareous inclusions.

E Many organic impressions, grog, some fine and medium quartz and occasional ferrous lumps. Very lumpy break, as if much of the body was dried-out lumps. A variant of this has no visible grog and larger voids. Crumbly soft feel.

F Mixed sand and calcareous limestone inclusions. Quartz fine to medium, common to abundant, calcareous inclusions frequent to abundant, fine and medium. Main variants:

a) Much fine calcareous inclusions, 1–4 mm and common medium and coarse gravel, mainly fine quartz, common.

b) Fine and medium quartz, common to abundant, gravel mainly medium, but very fine inclusions as well, common. Both have red lumps and streaks, common to abundant.

G Organic straw/grass impressions abundant, very fine quartz (x 20 magnification). Dense, hard feel.

H Organic straw/grass voids abundant, also ferrous/clinker burnt inclusions. Highly burnt, light, soft feel.

J As Fabric F but no ferrous lumps or streaks. Possibly due to different firing conditions.

Stone objects

33 pieces of stone which showed signs of use were recovered from both Iron Age and Romano-British contexts on Sites A and B, in addition to a large quantity of burnt limestone lumps and fragments. The utilised pieces were of three kinds: querns, pestles or pounders, with a single spindle whorl. For a table of these by context, rock type and object type see technical appendix Table T8.

Iron Age

There were five definite and three possible querns, of which the fragment from 127 and possibly that from 430 came from rotary querns. The range of rock types used is similar to that at Mingies Ditch nearby (Allen and Robinson, forthcoming). Two definite pestles and two possible examples were also found, both quartzitic pebbles from the Glacial Drift showing signs of wear at one or both ends. Such hand-sized pestles and pounders are commonly found in association with saddle querns on the continent. One stone spindle whorl 120–150 mm across and of elliptical cross-section was found in the terminal of ditch 23, but has subsequently been lost.

Romano-British

Seven definite querns and one further possible example were represented by fragments from Site A, consisting of much the same rock types as in the Iron Age, and in very similar ratios. Some of these may be residual from the Iron Age occupation. Several possible pestles or pounders were also found, and these are also likely to be residual. Site B, which was not extensively investigated, produced one definite and one possible quern.

Burnt limestone, almost always grey in colour, occurs on almost all Iron Age and early Roman sites in the area, and was clearly connected with some very basic function of these settlements, whether pastoral or arable. At Watkins Farm it occurred in quantity on both Sites A and B, demonstrating that it was still being used at the end of the 1st century AD.

Metalworking
Iron Age

Fragments of three crucibles were found, in enclosure ditches 23 and 485 and in ditch 96. A few fragments of slagged clay or 'furnace lining' were also found in 23 and in ditch 486, adjacent to and contemporary with 485. This evidence would suggest that very small-scale reworking of copper and iron was being carried out in these two enclosures. The crucible fragment from 96 was tiny, and was probably residual.

Romano-British

The sole evidence for metalworking was a single scrap of iron slag from ditch 134 and another from ditch 162.

SECTION 3: ENVIROMENTAL
The animal bones from Watkins Farm, Northmoor, Oxon. by R Wilson

General aims of the report

The 9,213 bones recovered provide the basis for a brief discussion of the economy, culture and environment of the settlement. The bones were studied chiefly to make a comparison with bones from other sites of this period in the region. Since a large area of this site was excavated and the Iron Age settlement had a coherent layout and a short occupation, effort was also concentrated upon the spatial distribution of debris within the settlement.

Some 1,000 of the bones came from a separate excavated area, Site B, a short distance from the main site. Results from both areas are considered together but those from Site B are indicated wherever necessary.

Investigation of
the general spread of bones: recording

Bones were initially recorded by feature number without other information on the feature context. Later when Tooth Wear Stages and other mandible data were recorded the information was drawn onto record sheets grouped by period in order to facilitate the calculation of Minimum Numbers of Individuals. Thus feature records of fragment number data should be free of preconceived bias.

The bones were often badly fragmented. Since identification was concerned only with the gathering of data essential to a reasonable site interpretation, no detailed reunification of broken fragments was attempted simply to increase the percentage of identified bones.

Predisposition of the course of investigation

Findings from previous regional sites as disparate as Iron Age Mingies Ditch, Hardwick, Oxon. (Wilson in Allen and Robinson, forthcoming) and medieval Harding's Field, Chalgrove (Wilson in Page et al., forthcoming) suggested that coarse debris should be found around the settlement periphery, in non-domestic areas of building foundations and in any demolition or construction deposits. Finer debris would be discovered mainly inside or near buildings, especially those connected with secondary or 'kitchen' butchery, cooking and eating. For the Iron Age period, findings from Mingies Ditch indicated that much of the smaller and finer debris would be found just outside the houses in occupation spreads and house gullies.

Brief examination of the site plan beforehand showed the potential usefulness of the excavation for examining spatial distributions in that only a few widely spaced house enclosures were apparently present (Fig. 34). All bones, however, were from features cut into gravel; neither occupation layers nor the Iron Age ground surface itself had survived ploughing.

After the feature group results had been tallied the settlement plans was re-examined, and it was seen that the centres of house enclosures lay 15 m apart or more. At Mingies Ditch some 80% of site debris was estimated to lie within 15 m of the centres of houses. Thus the pottery and other occupation debris around the central house at Watkins Farm could be treated as a discrete group of waste from that house — a difficult task at sites where house foundations overlap. The coarse debris present in a house group might, however, be redeposited, since one interpretation of results at Mingies Ditch was that the butchery of large carcasses took place at greater distances from houses than the butchery of smaller carcasses. At medieval Harding's Field much of the carcass disassembly of rabbits, hares, domestic fowl and fish probably occurred in the kitchen or at the meal table. In addition, burnt and worked bones were expected to be found with such domestic area groups of bones.

Primary analysis and the verification of expected trends

Analysis proceeded using the chronological and area groupings of features suggested by the excavator and also the site plan, which indicated how area groups could be made up of less readily assignable feature evidence, or where small groups could be usefully aggregated to increase sample size. Results are given in Table T9.

1 As expected, most debris was associated with Iron Age house enclosure ditches and other features inside the main enclosure ditch, despite comparable lengths of peripheral ditches being excavated.

2 Remains of sheep and pig were relatively common in the ditches around the most clearly identifiable houses especially the central round house. Burnt debris was relatively abundant there.

3 Remains of cattle and horse were most abundant in peripheral feature, e.g. the main enclosure ditch and the entrance way antennae ditches. This trend is unaffected by uncertainty about the nature of the Romano-British occupations and possible Roman contamination of the enclosure ditch group, since the percentage of Roman coarse debris elsewhere is smaller than that of the enclosure ditch.

4 Other feature groups contained sufficient sheep, pig and burnt bones and occasional worked bones to indicate strongly the presence of houses or site areas where domestic activity occurred; e.g. 22–23, the southern 'house', partly destroyed by stripping, the western enclosure 496–513 and the north-western enclosure. A small group of bones from the waterholes on Site B indicates coarse debris in that area.

5 Romano-British groups indicate debris which is mainly intermediate between the extreme Iron Age groups. There was a concentration of domestic debris just S of ditch 162 but this was probably residual material from the Iron Age central house enclosure. A small group of bones from the waterholes on Site B indicate coarse debris in that area.

6 The combined percentage of cattle and horse is larger in the Romano-British period than in the Iron Age. The absence of well defined Roman deposits or features of domestic origin or function makes a strict comparison suspect, although the presence of bones implies some domestic activity, unless more elaborate explanations are offered, i.e. non-self-contained site activity.

7 While the percentages of the species-based indicators of 'coarse' and 'fine' debris may differ from other sites, the qualitative trends of the Iron Age site material confirm the general spatial configuration of bone debris at regional sites of different periods. Although coarser than in some other assemblages, the 'finer' debris is still found around the predicted centres of domestic activity at this site.

Comparison of feature type deposits with those elsewhere

Any intersite comparison of overall fragment number results is made difficult by the clear differences in the spatial spread of bones, the completeness of excavations, and the amount of each type of deposit excavated at different sites.

Fig. A4 compares percentages of the medium-sized and large species in different Iron Age feature groups at Watkins Farm with a range of comparable feature groups from Ashville, Farmoor, Mingies Ditch and Mount Farm, Oxon. (Wilson in Parrington 1978, 110-138; Wilson in Lambrick and Robinson 1979, 128-133; Wilson in Allen and Robinson forthcoming; Wilson in Lambrick forthcoming).

Debris in the house gullies forms the best comparative feature group and appears generally similar to that in features at Mingies Ditch, Mount Farm, and perhaps Farmoor, though more sheep and pig bones occurred in the gullies of the main house at Ashville. If the coarseness of house gully debris at sites is roughly comparable and therefore results from similar site activities, can the suggestion that the bone collections from each site are different be sustained? Might the virtual absence of excavated debris from occupation layers and postholes be a source of bias, when at Mingies Ditch such deposits contained a high concentration of sheep and pig bones?

These questions can scarcely be answered. The postholes and other features inside house enclosures at Watkins Farm contained some bones which indicate a higher representation of finer debris, if articulated foot ones of cattle in pit 499 are treated as a single unit. Absence of evidence from occupation layers is more critical since the contribution from this group at Mingies Ditch was considerable.

Fragment frequency of species and other classes of bone

Tables 11, T10 and T11 give frequency results for overall period and area groups.

The chief observation is that the incidence of horse bones is greater than usual in all period groups, ranging from 20 to 23% at the main site and 27% at Site B. Comment is made later. (See Minimum Number of Individuals — MNI.)

A decline in the number of sheep bones and an increase in cattle bones occurs between Iron Age and Roman groups, and is found in similar comparisons at other sites. Phase differences of species representation with the Iron Age are probably unimportant. If results from phases 1 and 2 are added together to increase sample size, cultural change might be suggested: if, however, results from phases 2 and 3 are added there is little evidence of change.

Skeletal element representation

The representation of the skeletal elements in the major and best dated groups of cattle, sheep and horse bones was examined to measure the degree to which species bones had been degraded by site processes, and assess if bone degradation was sufficient to obscure the detection of site activities such as scavenging, rubbish clearance, and aspects of butchery. Skeletal element distributions might yield evidence of such activity in the relatively discrete groups of bones from house enclosures though few differences of this kind had been detected previously at regional sites of these periods. Overall percentage results are given in Tables T12 to T14 for sheep, cattle and horse.

The chief usefulness of the sheep bones is as an index of bone preservation, calculated as the overall percentage of loose teeth and fragments of mandible radius and tibia in a sample group of sheep bones (Wilson 1985, 83; Wilson in Allen and Robinson, forthcoming). Deposits in the house gullies and their immediate surroundings have an index ranging from 73–82% which indicates considerable bone degradation by human and natural processes. These figures are similar to those at Mount Farm, lower that those at Mingies Ditch and higher than at Ashville and on medieval sites (Wilson 1985, Fig. 2). A small sample from the main enclosure ditch indicates better bone preservation there.

Few small bones of the hock, carpal and phalangeal joints are present. This suggests either poor recovery of bones by excavation or that these bones were already destroyed by previous site processes. Little can be deduced about butchery patterns. The abundance of sheep mandibles and teeth suggests several explanations: that butchery was carried out close to the houses; that heads provided food such as brains and split skulls were dumped close to the houses; *or* that cranial debris served ritual purposes when placed close to the houses.

Skeletal evidence of cattle is not very revealing either, though again head debris is abundant in most deposits and close to the houses. Vertebrae appear much more abundant in the main enclosure ditch and in the early Romano-British group. These, however, mainly consisted of articulated vertebrae from 404 in the main enclosure and from ditch 405 Cut D. At Mingies Ditch, Smithsfield (Wilson in Allen forthcoming) and Mount Farm such articulated debris is believed to indicate places of cattle butchery which occurred at some distance from houses. Thus some slaughtering of cattle would seem to have occurred in the northern and western areas of the enclosure, though it is also clear that cattle debris was sufficiently widespread for butchery to have occurred elsewhere too.

Where the deposition of elements of horse in house gullies and the distant main enclosure ditch are compared, and allowance is made for recently broken cranial debris from the main enclosure ditch, the element distribution appears to correspond to the patterns seen elsewhere.

Articulated remains and moderately complete crania

Undated pig skeleton. Context 49

A fairly complete skeleton of 56 normally identified elements, 36 ribs and 30 other fragments. All major epiphyses are unfused including those of scapula, humerus, radius and one first phalanx. All parts of the axis are unfused as are the bodies and neural arches of other vertebrae. This evidence indicates a juvenile pig aged between 4 and 11 months. (Silver 1969).

The bones are noticeably more robust than expected for pig bones of the period. No adequate bone measurements are possible except for a least breadth of the parietal bones of 40–42 mm which appears broader than normal and may indicate a post-medieval breed.

Finally, while the outsides of the bones are stained brown the interiors are yellow or white and look fresh and recent in comparison to the best dated bones of the enclosure settlements which are stained or mineralised throughout. Though anomalies of better bone preservation do occur, it is suggested that this pig skeleton is a burial of recent date.

Post-medieval juvenile horse. Context 55

Associated with 18th-century pottery. Broken cranium and mandibles of 35 fragments; 10 body elements and 50 other fragments from skeleton truncated by machining of topsoil.

M1 at T.W.S and deciduous premolar and deciduous incisors 1 and 2 in wear. Epiphyses of atlas and distal metacarpal are unfused. Estimated age between 2 and 7 months and nearer the latter.

GL of unfused metacarpal is 245 mm and appears large enough to substantiate the presence of a post-medieval skeleton with the potsherds.

Horse. Context 464

Undated burial inside central Iron Age house. Buried on right side: upper parts truncated by machining. Seventy-nine identifiable elements of cranium, backbone and limbs, with an additional estimated 500 small fragments.

All teeth are in wear and all epiphyses are fused. This animal is difficult to age from the teeth but was probably aged between 9 and 21 years, perhaps 15 years old when it died.

GL of radius is 220 mm est., Bp is 88 mm est. and Bd of the humerus is 77 mm. Estimated shoulder height is 1.363 m. Again these bones appear large for an Iron Age horse and the skeleton may be Roman or later in date, but it is not possible to decide.

No marks of butchery or pathology were found.

Articulated leg bones

Occasionally amongst the bones two or three articulating elements were discovered: five instances of horse, two in 13 and 61 at the entrance to the site, and one each in 485 of the NW enclosure and in 126 and 411 which are Romano-British ditches; a lower hind leg of cattle in 499, inside the enclosure 496–513, and on Site B one instance of an articulated hock joint of sheep in Romano-British 34.

Articulated vertebrae

One group of atlas, cervical and thoracic vertebral fragments survived in 404 and probably were part of the same backbone. Another group of atlas, axis, cervical, thoracic and lumbar vertebrae, at least partly articulated, was excavated from 405.

Cranial remains excluding mandibles
Moderately complete crania of horse were noted in features 30 (male horse 4–4.5 years of age - the entrance-way ditch). 125 (2 crania - central area), 130 (horse of 5–6 years of age, and one other cranium in pit - in middle of trackway), 402 (central house) and 404 (with articulated cattle vertebrae - main enclosure ditch).

Sizeable parts of cattle crania were found in 450 (Roman-British) and 484.

Articulated dog bones
Context

1 100 m. Elements of cranium, backbone and metapodials probably of same dog. Molar teeth in wear. A mature or old dog.

16 (=1). 11 identifiable elements, 28 ribs and other fragments in good state of preservation. All epiphyses are fused and the teeth are worn. Femur GL 183 mm, tibia GL 183 mm and distal width of humerus 33 mm. Estimated shoulder height of 0.54–0.56 m.

This was a mature dog of larger size and indeterminate sex, of Iron Age or Roman date.

301 and 302 (SW enclosure). Parts of two separate dog skeletons.

425/2 (Central house). Parts of one cranium. Frequencies of dog bones found in adjacent features show clustering effects and indicate the burial of fairly complete carcasses.

Site B
Context

204 (Romano-British pit or well). Eight elements of the same dog. All epiphyses fused and teeth are in wear.

Humerus of Gl 138 mm. Estimated shoulder height of 0.44–0.45 m. A mature dog of average height.

Hare
172 (?Iron Age). A femur and tibia are almost certainly from the same animal.

Notes on butchery and the working of bones
No systematic study of butchery was made but any unusual marks were noted.

Horse
Context

120m/3 Transverse knife cut on posterior midshaft of metacarpal.

152m/1 Cuts on posterior pelvis (meat removal).

130/2 Cuts behind orbit on cranium.

151 3m On scapula, transverse cuts parallel to glenoid cavity on lateral side, with longitudinal cuts toward the spine on both lateral and ventral aspects. Trimmed through edge of proximal epiphysis. Meat removal appears certain but disarticulation may have occurred too.

410/E/1 Lateral and ventral cuts at base of ischial flare of pelvis (meat removal). Also one transverse and one longitudinal

cut on anterior edge of distal articulation surface of astragalus — the latter possible related to splitting of metatarsal for bone working near central house.

411/A/1 Another astragalus, from ditch of probable Roman date, also showing longitudinal cut with similar eroded marks on a calcaneum probably from the same joint. Possible splitting of tibial above for bone working.

433/D/2 Fragment possibly of deliberately split metacarpal from central house ditch.

442/A/3 Transverse cut on anterior distal shaft of humerus and on edge of distal articulation surface laterally and medially.

496 Transverse cut on distal anterior shaft of tibia.

Dog
Context

23 Transverse cuts on tibia below media proximal epiphysis. Could be skin or meat removal marks.

Cattle
Context

137 Chopping through one side of sacrum from anterior direction indicates that carcass butchery took place on the ground or on a chopping board and not on a hung carcass (Romano-British).

513/517 First phalanx with medial trimming of proximal end and longitudinal nick on anterior distal end. This indicates butchery of the hoof to divide the phalanges, perhaps to split the metapodial for bone working.

Sheep or goat
Context

13 Crudely trimmed tibial shaft; point, awl or gouge, undated.

124 Tibia shaft with unfused distal epiphysis polished except at epiphyses, grooved in two places approximately 55 mm apart, at matching positions on opposite sides, with similar marking on the two intervening sides but offset 5 mm. (Fig. 28, No.7).

485 Fragments of sawn horn core, possibly of goat. Saw cut width of 1.9 mm.

Antler
Four pieces of antler were found, a sawn tine in 23, the southern house, an antler base in 413 and two Romano-British pieces in 141 on Site B and in 155 on Site A: all are from red deer except the last, which may be roe.

Conclusions
The data usefully add to the evidence of the butchery of horse and dog at these periods. Although skinning and meat removal is evident, particularly for horse, some of the marks suggest that further disarticulation and splitting of skeletal elements took place for the purposes of manufacturing bone implements or ornaments. At least two horse metapodials, one cattle metapodial and one horse tibia were picked out for such purposes. In addition antler was worked by sawing and two tibia of sheep were used without splitting to make further implements.

Compared to the Roman butchery of bones from Claydon Pike, Lechlade, Glos. (Levitan and Wilson in Miles and Palmer forthcoming), the cattle and horse bones showed little evidence of vigorous trimming and chopping down the sides of limb bones which accompanied the removal of meat. Little evidence was found of the first phalanges of cattle bearing transverse knife cuts, which are thought to indicate the removal of skins from around the hooves and may indicate an intensified exploitation of leather (Macgregor 1985, 42). At Watkins Farm the butchery pattern appears to follow a typical Celtic pattern even during the Roman period.

Age data

Mandible Wear Stages and estimated MWS are presented for sheep, cattle and pigs in Fig. 30. These frequency distributions of the age stage of animals at death are typical of these species at Iron Age and less Romanised settlements of the later period. Samples are too small in size to compare for any significant differences between period groups.

Small one or two place differences in the frequencies of MWS are noticeable where results are compared with those at previous sites. Such differences result from differences in the method of estimating MWS and have no cultural significance; they are partly attributable to the increased information available to estimate the MWS of incomplete mandibles (Grant 1983, 91-108) and also due to self-imposed limits on how far an age stage can be estimated reliably. Comparison of site data obtained by different specialists should be in terms of general trends and not in detailed comparisons between adjacent stages of MWS.

The mortality pattern of horse is not easy to assess. Age estimates are based on work by Silver (Silver 1969, 283-302) and Levine (Levine 1983, 223-250). The percentages of fused epiphysis and the ages at death estimated from the mandibles are given in Tables T16 and T17.

Most horses died as mature or old individuals. Percentages of fused epiphyses at 90–93% are similar to or less than at other sites. The mandible remains indicate a higher percentage or horses dying young: 25%, n=11. Discrepancies in the percentage estimates, other than of sample size, may be due to unfused epiphyses surviving worse than fused epiphyses (Wilson 1985, 82-3).

A closer estimate of the horses dying at less than 2.5 years is about 6–12 months of age.

Minimum Numbers of Individuals (MNI)

Mandible tooth eruption and wear data from left and right sides of the head were sorted into Iron Age and Romano-British groups. A few mandibles from the main enclosure ditch were treated as of the Iron Age but other less well dated information was not used. The least number of individuals present was then determined. Results are given in Table T17.

The percentages of species MNI are quite different to the percentages of species fragment frequency given in Table T17 but conform to trends elsewhere. Individuals of cattle and horse are represented by at least twice as many fragments as sheep and pig. The mean numbers of fragments per individual for the Iron Age groups are: horse 39.5, cattle 20.5, pig 9.8, sheep 9.5 and dog 8.0

This is explained by the better survival and better recovery of the elements of large and also longer-lived species. (see also Wilson in Allen and Robinson forthcoming). In general,

fragment numbers give a less reliable estimate of species abundance since the mandibles and teeth survive better than most other skeletal material.

In order, therefore, to obtain the best idea of the relative abundance of pig and sheep, it is necessary to use the estimate of MNI. Even here the sheep appear under-represented, as it was more difficult to distinguish individuals from the age stage data, loose teeth and broken mandibles of sheep than from those of cattle and pig. In part this reflects variability of determining MNI according to the number of bones present in each species. Species represented by few bones are over-represented by MNI in comparison with species represented by large numbers of bones.

Inspection of the number of mandible wear stages given for each species indicates that the representation of sheep could have been as high as 60%; consequently, cattle 21%, pig and horse each 7%, and dog 4% would be disproportionately lower. These figures are only a crude adjustment and any site comparisons should be made with the previously given MNI.

Bone measurements

The most important measurements are given in Table T18. Others of horse and dog are listed in the description of articulated bones.

The results are similar to those at comparable Iron Age and Romano-British sites and confirm a general increase in the size of bones into the Roman period.

Determination of sex

Determinations of animal sex were determined from the robustness of the bones or other morphological criteria (see Table T19).

Invertebrate and waterlogged plant remains
by Mark Robinson

Supporting details are given here for the printed report on invertebrate and waterlogged plant remains from Watkins Farm, Northmoor, including full results of the identifications. Notes are also given on the identification of wooden objects from the site.

The samples

Samples were taken of the fills of a range of Iron Age and Roman archaeological features, mostly waterlogged. The locations of the contexts sampled are shown on Figs. 18, 31 and 32. Summary details of the samples are given in Table T24. Two sets of samples formed stratigraphic sequences. Ditch 1–S1 was from the lowest organic deposits in the main Iron Age enclosure ditch and ditch 1–S2 was from the overlying organic sediments. Pond 204 S1–S4 comprised a sequence from one of the Roman water holes or ponds, S1 being the earliest.

Methods and results

Biological remains were extracted from the samples using the methods described in Lambrick and Robinson (1979, 79–80). The waterlogged anaerobic samples were washed through a stack of sieves down to an aperture size of 0.2 mm. In the case of samples 1–S3, 1–S4, 1–S5 and 1–S7, the sieved residues were only sorted for macroscopic plant remains, scanning them for species presence rather than picking out every identifiable item. For the remainder of the waterlogged samples, sub-sample 'a' (Table T24) was processed for the full range of macroscopic plant and invertebrate remains, while sub-sample 'b' was processed for arthropod remains alone.

The non-waterlogged aerobic samples were washed onto a 0.5 mm sieve and the residues sorted for mollusc shells.

Specimens were identified with reference to the collections in the University Museum, Oxford, and the results have been given in Tables T25–T43. The tables either record the minimum number of individuals represented by the fragments identified from a sample or show presence/absence. Nomenclature follows Clapham et al. (1962) for the higher plant remains. Molluscan nomenclature follows Kerney (1976) for the freshwater molluscs and Walden (1976) for the land snails. The Royal Entomological Society's revised check lists of British insects (Kloet and Hincks 1964; 1977; 1978) have been used for the nomenclature of the entomological results.

The results have been grouped in four sequences of tables:

1	Site A	Iron Age	(Tables T25–29)
2	Site A	Iron Age Burial	(Tables T30–33)
3	Site A	Roman	(Tables T34–38)
4	Site B	Roman	(Tables T39–43)

Waterlogged seeds

Results are given in Tables T25, T30, T34, and T39. Seeds were only examined from sub-sample 'a' of the waterlogged samples (Table T24). Only a one-tenth sub-sample was examined from the contents of the first sieve, the fraction between 0.5 mm and 0.2 mm. The number of seeds recovered (mostly *Juncus* sp.) has been multiplied by ten for inclusion in the tables.

Waterlogged wood

Waterlogged wood was not systematically identified from the samples, although its presence or absence has been recorded in Tables T26, T35 and T40. A preliminary examination of the wood recovered during the excavation showed that both *Quercus* and other taxa were present in the waterlogged deposits at each of Site A Iron Age, Site A Roman and Site B Roman. Three wooden objects were also examined (see Table T44).

Other waterlogged plant remains

Results are given in Tables T26, T31, T35 and T40. The sample sizes were as for the waterlogged seeds.

Carbonised plant remains

The carbonised plant remains from these samples were passed on to L Moffett for inclusion in her report (see Chapter 4: The charred plant remains).

Coleoptera

Results are given in Tables T27, T32, T36 and T41. The total sample examined from each context was sub-sample 'a' plus sub-sample 'b' (Table T24).

Other insects

Results are given in Tables T28, T33, T37 and T42. The sample sizes were as for the Coleoptera.

Other arthropods

Cladoceran ephippia were present in all the waterlogged samples including Pit 498. Acari and Araneae were also present in some of the samples.

Mollusca

Results are given in Tables T29, T38 and T43. Molluscs were only examined from sub-sample 'a' of the samples (Table T24). Molluscs were absent from samples 498, 24 and 202/3.

Samples were also examined from the pre-Iron Age soil covering the gravel and the interface between this soil and the gravel, but shells were absent. The gravelly grey clay filling the top of the main Iron Age enclosure ditch of Site A (see Chapter 1: The main enclosure ditch) was found to contain numerous opercula of the flowing water mollusc *Bithynia tentaculata*. It is likely that this layer was a dumped deposit which had in part been derived from a former stream bed. It was not alluvium and *B. tentaculata* would not have lived in the top of the ditch.

Charcoal

Charcoal was not systematically investigated from the site. However, a preliminary examination of charcoal recovered during excavation showed that both *Quercus* and 'hedgerow' taxa such as *Prunus* and *Crataegus* type were present in both Iron Age and Roman features.

An Iron Age hearth, 151/2M, contained much charcoal, 160 g being recovered by flotation. It mostly comprised *Rhamnus catharticus*, but some *Prunus* cf. *spinosa* was also present.

Table T2. Iron Age Pottery: Instances of Burnishing and Smoothing by Fabrics

Fabric	No.	Burnished and Smoothed %	% by Fabric Groups	Burnished % Groups
Fabric Group 1				
13	10	4	4	5.3
Fabric Group 2				
7	39	16	60	68
2	108	43		
16	-			
8	2	0.8		
Fabric Group 3				
2c	5	2	3	3.3
5	2	0.8		
21				
Fabric Group 4				
1	6	2.4	2.5	2
Fabric Group 5				
12	21	8	8	8.7
11				
10				
Fabric Group 6				
3a	16	6	16.5	9
3b	25	10		
(3c)	1	0.4		
Fabric Group 7				
17			0.5	-
19	1			
Fabric Group 8				
20	1	0.4	0.5	0.7
Fabric Group 9				
14	1	0.4	0.5	-
Fabric Group 10				
9	7	2.7	2.5	3.3
Miscellaneous				
18	2	0.8		
6	2	0.8		
	Total 249			

Table T1. Iron Age Pottery: Proportions of all fabrics in successive phases of the Central Roundhouse Enclosure

Contexts:	402	401/477/ 438	430	430/477/ 438/401	433	425	425 433	151	433 425 151	410	495	488	488 410 495	413 416
Fabrics														
13	7	6	9	10	4	-	2.5	2	2.5	5	-	-	12.5	4.5
Fabric Group 1	7	6	9	10	4	-	2.5	2	2.5	5	-	12.5	12.5	4.5
7	-	12	9	14	4	9.5	6	4	5	5	6	-	4.5	13
2	21.5	18	36	20.5	26	21.5	25	42.5	37	32-	56	50	40	50
16	-	-	-	-	-	-	-	-	-	-	-	-	-	-
8	7	-	-	-	-	-	-	6	1.5	-	-	-	-	-
Fabric Group 2	28.5	30	45	34.5	30	31	31	52.5	43.5	37	62	50	44.5	63
2c	-	-	-	-	4	6	5	10.5	7	5	12.5	-	7	-
5	-	-	-	-	2	3	2.5	-	1.5	-	-	-	-	-
21	-	-	-	-	-	-	-	-	12.5[1	-	-	-	-	-
Fabric Group 3a	-	-	-	-	6	9	7.5	10.5	8.5	5	12.5[1	-	7	-
21	-	6	-	3.5	2	-	1	-	0.6	-	-	-	-	-
Fabric Group 3b	-	6	-	3.5	2	-	1	-	0.6	-	-	-	-	-
1	7	6	27	14	-	6	2.5	2	2.5	5	6	-	4.5	4
Fabric Group 4	7	6	27	14	-	6	2.5	2	2.5	5	6	-	4.5	4
12	-	18	-	10	14	21.5	17.5	12	15	10.5	6	12.5	10	-
11	7	-	-	-	4	-	2.5	2	2.5	5	-	-	2.5	-
10	-	-	-	-	4	3	4	2	3	5	-	-	2.5	-
Fabric Group 5	7	18	-	10	22	24.5	24	16	20.5	20.5	6	12.5	15	-
3a	43	23.5	18	24	30	18.5	26	17.5	22.5	16	19	25	19	22.5
3b	-	-	-	-	-	-	-	-	-	-	-	-	-	-
Fabric Group 6	43	23.5	18	24	30	18.5	26	17.5	22.5	16	19	25	19	22.5
17	-	-	-	-	-	-	-	-	-	-	-	-	-	4
19	-	-	-	-	-	-	-	-	-	-	-	-	-	4
Fabric Group 7	-	-	-	-	-	-	-	-	-	-	-	-	-	4
20	-	-	-	-	-	-	-	-	-	-	-	-	-	-
Fabric Group 8	-	-	-	-	-	-	-	-	-	-	-	-	-	-
14	-	-	-	-	4	3	4	-	2.5	5	-	-	2.5	4
Fabric Group 9	-	-	-	-	4	3	4	-	2.5	5	-	-	2.5	4
9	7	12	-	7	-	6	2.5	2	2.5	6	-	6	4.5	-
Fabric Group 10	7	12	-	7	-	6	2.5	2	2.5	6	-	6	4.5	-
Total	(14) 58	(17) 106	(11) 31	(29) 137	(49) 140 [149]	(32) 136	(81) 276	(52) 106		(19) 30	(16) 43	(8) 18	(43) 91	(23) 38
	Phase 1	Phase 2	Phase 3		Phase 4					Phase 5				Phase 6

Total EVN for the sequence is 178. Total sherd number is 569. Add contexts 430 and 151, EVN is 241
total sherd number is 706.

Table T3. Proportion of burnished sherds in selected context groups

Central Roundhouse Sequence			Other Enclosures – Unphased		
Context	Definite	+Uncertain	Context	Definite	+Uncertain
402	6.7%	27%	496/512/513	4%	4%
401/438/477	30%	36%	23	20%	20%
+430 (2424)	27%(30%)	40%	125	30%	33%
425/433	23.5%	30%	436/442	33%	38%
+151	31%	35.5%			
410/495/488	21%	28%			
413/416	42%	50%	124	52%	56%

Table T4. Rims and bases divided into Jars, Bowls and Unassignable

Fabrics	Jars	Bowls	Uncertain Form
13	3	3	5
7	6	4	6
2	23	30 (42%)	18
16	1	1	
8	1		
2c	5	4	1
5	2	1	
21			
1	6	3	4
12	15 (54%)	2	11
11	3		2
10	1		2
3a	8	2	7
3b	25 (68%)	3	9
17	1		
19			
20	1		1
14			1
9			
Total			
221	101	53	67
	46%	24%	30%

Table T5. Roman Pottery: Percentages of Types of Jars and Bowl Forms

JAR FORMS		% of all jar forms	
No.	Type	Site A	Site B
3.1	Necked jar with everted rim.	56	41
3.2	Necked jar with bead or plain rounded rim.	15	19
3.3	Necked jar with undercut rim.	6	22
3.4	Jar with short or no neck and everted rim.	12	15
3.5	Jar with short or no neck and squat or folded back rim.	8	0
3.6	Large storage jar (everted rim).	3	3
	Total of jar rims	94	70

BOWL FORMS		% of all bowl/dish forms	
No.	Type	Site A	Site B
6/7.1	Flanged bowl.	10	19
6/7.2	Straight-sided bowl/dish with out-turned rim.	40	25
6/7.3	Straight-sided dish with plain rim.	5	19
6/7.4	Curved-sided bowl – Dv 37 form.	30	13
6/7.5	Curved-sided bowl/dish with bead or triangular rim.	10	0
6/7.6	Carinated dish – Dv 18 or 18/31 form.	5	19
6/7.7	Reeded flanged ?bowl/dish.	0	5
	Total of bowl/dish rims	20	18

Table T7. Fired Clay: Fabric, Weight and Object Type by Context

Contex No	A	B	C	D	E	F	G	H	J	Total grams
23	70*	50(*)	60(~)	20	10					210
124-163	7	7			7	20				34
125	100-	7	30							137
127			35^							35
138				7						7
166						15				15
12	7	7								14
404	27	10	35-				150-			222
151 = 417	460-	7	10			370				847
402						25*				25
425	50	7			25	130*				212
410		37				7				44
433	600*		665-(~)							1265
438 = 477	2			15						47
488			40(^)			30(*)(~)				70
495		55(~)				30			45	130
430						1000(*)				1000
413		25				50(~)				75
436 = 442	63	7	7	7	20	40				137
441	10									10
481		7								7
485		10	2			2085*		7		2104
487	3				7					10
498	5									5
499		10-				7				17
496/512/513	17	5	133(~)			7				166
503						10*				10
510		7								7
%	20.7	3.3	15.1	0.6	1.25	56.5	2.3	0.1	0.7	
Total	1421	227	1034	42	86	3864	150	7	45	6858

* Wattle = 6 (9)   - Loom Weight = 6 (12)   ^ Spindle Whorl = 1 (2)
[A & F]   [C, A, G, ?F]   [C]

Table T6. Briquetage: Weight, Fabric Type and Date

Context	Site A.	Site B
# 124 1 m.	17 grams.	206/1 13 grams. F.T.1a.
(125/1 2 m.)	46	? 235/2 37 F.T.1.
* 131	8 F.T.1.	Total 50 grams.
* 133	65	
* 134/3 4 m.	13	
*# 137	30 (15 F.T.1 = F.T.2)	
# 140/2	28	
151	125	
417	70	
155	2 F.T.1.	
*# 170/1	35 F.T.1.	
402	35	
416	1	
422	2	
425/1	29	
433	123	
434/N	10	
442	51	
* 451/A/1	8	
* (464)	15	
473/B/1	12	
477	92	
485	17	
488/C/1	9	
495	98	

indicates a context associated with the central roundhouse.

* indicates an R-B context.

# indicates a context connected with enclosure 124-163.

F.T.1 - Fabric Type 1.
F.T.2 - Fabric Type 2.

24 contexts Total 931 grams.

Briquetage came from 4 enclosures:
402-433 etc. (the central roundhouse).
124-163
442 = 436
485 etc. (outside 1).

It was not present in 23/32 or in 496-512-513.
At least 5 containers (1 F.T.1. and 4 F.T.2.) are likely to be represented on Site A.

Total of F.T.1 is 110 grams. (60 on Site A, 50 on Site B).
Total of F.T.2 is 876 grams. (all Site A.)

(INDEX FOR POTTERY: BRIQUETAGE is 1:0.032)

Total for Sites A and B is 931 + 50 + 5 (U/S) = 986 grams.

Table T9. Primary Assessment of all the depositional context of bone groups at Watkins Farm in terms of their proximity to former centres of domestic activity

	Number of bones	Combined % of sheep & pig (High %s indicate greater domestic activity)	% index of burnt and worked bones	Vector assessment of domestic activity in rank order (High = 1)
I Iron Age groups				
a) Inside main enclosure				
S house 23-32	197	59	5.1	1
Central roundhouse Phases 1 & 2	163	52	4.3	3
Phase 3 + trackway	364	40	2.8	4
Phases 3/4 & 5	136	46	2.2	5
E house 124-163	100	42	1.0	7
W house 496, 513 etc.	108	33	5.5	2
N enclosure 436-442	41	32	2.4	6
b) Enclosures outside MED				
NW 485, 490 etc.	16	50	-	8
SW 17-20 etc.	26	23	-	14
II Early R-B groups				
Main enclosure ditch MED	111	12	-	15
Ditch-circuits inside MED: 405, 411 etc.	158	21	1.9	12
Internal Features on E: 96, 136, 141 etc.	123	36	-	13
External E entrance enclosure 12 - 13 etc.	86	15	2.4	11
External W enclosures 24, 28 etc.	45	36	-	13
III Later R-B groups				
All enclosures and trackway ditches.	179	34	1.1	9
Water holes or pits 412, 478 etc.	36	3	-	16
IV Site B - R-B period, all features	206	14	4.8	10

Groups within later chronological period could be reranked from 1.

Table T8. Utilised Stone Objects by Context, Type and Object Type

Context	Millstone Grit	Lower Greensand	Lower Calcareous Grit	Sarsen	Upper Greensand	Drift	Limestone	Sp W.
Iron Age.								
23	Qx 2	-	? Q	-	-	-	-	-
125	-	-	-	-	-	Pe.	-	-
430/3/1	Q	-	-	-	-	-	-	-
151	-	? Q	SQ	-	-	-	-	-
127	-	RQ	? Q	? Pe.	-	-	-	-
16	-	-	-	? Q	-	-	-	-
166	-	-	-	-	-	Pe.	-	-
Romano-British. Site A.								
131	-	-	Q	-	-	-	-	-
134	-	Q x 2	-	-	Q	Pe.? Po.-	-	-
43	-	Q	-	-	-	-	-	-
13	-	-	? Q	-	-	? Po.	-	-
5	-	-	-	-	-	-	-	-
155	Q	-	-	-	-	-	-	-
162	-	Q	-	-	-	-	-	-
Romano-British. Site B.								
34	Q	-	-	-	-	-	-	-
35	-	-	? Q	-	-	-	-	-

Table T10. Fragment frequency in Iron Age central roundhouse phase groups and the main enclosure ditch (MED)

Phase	1	2	3	3/4	5	Total	MED
Cattle	39	16	144	40	4	243	65
Sheep/goat	12	68	113	39	13	245	11
Pig	2	2	32	11	-	47	2
Horse	21	3	75	20	9	128	33
Dog	4	1	13	-	-	18	6(a)
Cat	-	-	-	1	-	1	-
Red deer	-	-	-	-	A	A	1
Unidentified	220	95	521	252	39	1127	449
Burnt	4	3	10	2	-	19	-

a = Excluding 30 bones from 2 part skeletons of dog in MED

11 elements of dog cranium in F425 included in Phase 3.

Table T12. Percentage representation of the elements of sheep

	Iron Age Central Roundhouse				Early R-B	
Phases	1 & 2	3	3-5	South Enc. 23-32	MED	Inside MED
N	80	113	52	89	11	59
	%	%	%	%	%	%
Head	61	36	37	58	nc	58
Feet	8	9	12	2	nc	5
Body	30	55	52	39	nc	37
Teeth	28	18	25	35	nc	36
Mandible	32	18	8	20	nc	19
Vertebra	1	1	2	6	nc	2
Small bones (carpal, hock & phalangeal)	-	-	-	1	nc	-
Degradation index %	79	82	73	73	36	76

Table T13. Percentage representation of the elements of cattle

	Iron Age Central Roundhouse				IA - Early R-B	
Phase	1 & 2	3	3-5	South house	MED	Inside MED
N	55	144	65	38	65	148
	%	%	%	%	%	%
Head	58	56	50	47	34	32
Foot	18	11	14	29	9	13
Body	24	33	36	24	57	55
Teeth	26	24	25	26	12	12
Mandible	26	22	18	16	10	12
Vertebrae	-	5	-	3	23	24
Scapula	7	8	9	5	2	6
Joints	4	1	7	8	3	1
Phalanges	-	-	2	8	2	4

Table T11. Fragment frequency in Iron Age Groups

	Iron Age features within the MED							Outside MED	
Phase	Central House 1 & 2	House 3 & 4	Tkwy ph 3	N encl. 436-442 (+Ph. 5)	S House 23-32	E House 124-163	W Encl. 512-496	NW Encs. 485 etc	SW 17 etc
Cattle	55	155	29	25	38	32	57	3	8
Sheep	80	119	33	41	89	38	29	8	4
Pig	4	34	9	26	27	4	7	-	2
Horse	24	85	10	16	43	26	15	5	12
Dog	5	11	2	-	3	-	-	-	13
Cat	-	1	-	1	-	-	-	-	-
Red deer	-	-	-	A	A	-	-	-	-
Unidentified	315	639	217	136	436	226	394	16	60
Burnt	7	7	5	1	9	1	5	-	-
Worked bone (excl. unworked antler)	-	-	-	1	1	1	-	1	-

Iron Age or early Romano-British groups

	MED	Features inside MED N 405, 411 etc.	SE 136 etc.	Outside MED E entr 12, 13 etc.	W encl. 24 etc.
Cattle	65	91	57	26	26
Sheep	11	25	37	8	16
Pig	2	8	7	5	-
Horse	33	34	22	47	3
Dog	6b	1	3	-	-
Red deer	1	-	1+A	-	-
Unidentified	449	383	203	537	149
Burnt	-	3	-	1	-
Worked	-	-	-	1	-

Table T14. Percentage representation of the elements of horse

	Iron Age Central House Phases 1-5	Main enclosure ditch	Early R-B inside MED
N	128 %	33 %	56 %
Head	44	39	57
Foot	17	21	18
Body	39	39	25
Teeth	25	18	36
Mandible	10	6	18
Vertebrae	2	-	2
Scapula	9	-	-
Joints	5	3	7
Phalanges	4	6	2

Table T16. Estimated ages of horse mandibles and maxillae

	Less than 2.5 years	4-6 yrs	6-10 yrs	15-20 yrs
Iron Age Mandibles	1	1	4	1
Roman Mandibles	2	-	2	1
?Intrusive Burials	1 (F55)	-	-	1 (F464)
Iron Age Maxillae	-	1	-	-

Table T18. Selected measurements of animal bones (mm)

		Iron Age				Romano-British		
		n	r	x	s.d.	n	r	x
CATTLE								
Tibia	Bd	6	50-60	55.2	(3.37)	1	60	-
	Gt	-				-	345	-
Radius	Bp	5	64-78	71.8	(6.72)	1	80	-
	Gt	3	239-261	246.7		-		
	Bd	2	24-61	57.5				
Metacarpal	Bd	3	51-59	56.4		3	50-53	51.8
	Gt	2	172-178	175.0		2	165-174	169.5
Metatarsal	Bd	3	44-47	45.0		1	50	
SHEEP								
Humerus	Bd	-				1	27	
Tibia	Bd	-				1	24	
Metacarpal	Gt	1	100			-		
HORSE								
Tibia	Bd	11	51-66	60.4	4.25	1	65	
Metacarpal	Bd	3	42-47	45.0		-		
	Gt	2	201-203	202.0		(F55)	245i	
Metatarsal	Bd	5	42-44	43.0	(1.0)	-		
	Gt	4	233-249	242.8		1	258	
RED DEER								
Tibia	Bd	1	47			?18th cent. burial		

Table T17. Frequencies and percentages of the minimum number of individuals

	Iron Age		Romano-British	
	f	%	f	%
Cattle	15	26.8	7	33.3
Sheep/goat	27	48.2	7	33.3
Pig	5	8.9	3	14.3
Horse	6	8.9	3	14.3
Dog	3	5.4	1	1.8
Cat	1	1.8	-	+
Red deer	-	+	-	+
	57		21	

Table T15. Frequency and percentage distribution of horse epiphyses

	Iron Age		Romano-British	
	F	U	F	U
Early fusing 12-18 months	36	1	21	3
Intermediate 18-24 months	15	1	4	-
Late fusing	4	2	12	1
Total	55	4	37	4
Percentage fused	93%		90%	

F = Fused; U = Unfused

Table T19. Sex identifications of cattle and horse by period

	Iron Age	Roman
Metapodial indices of cattle	4 female / 1 male/castrate	1 female / 1 male/castrate
Pelvis of cattle	4 indeterminate	1 female / 1 indeterminate
Pelvis of horse	1 female / 1 male/castrate	2 female / 1 male castrate

Table T20. Iron Age Samples
(Only samples containing charred remains shown)

	553	487	498/4	495/B2	410	425/1	425/2
Sample Size:	10L	27L	15L	15L	20L	10L	10L
CEREALS							
Triticum dicoccum/spelta rachises	-	2	-	-	-	-	-
T. dicoccum/spelta spikelet forks	-	3	7	-	-	-	-
T. dicoccum/spelta glume bases	2	46	14	3	16	-	-
T. spelta glume bases	-	9	-	1	-	-	-
T. cf. spelta grains	-	-	-	-	-	1	1
Triticum sp. grains	-	10	1	4	3	1	-
Hordeum vulgare rachises	-	1	-	-	-	-	1
Hordeum sp. rachises	-	8	-	-	-	-	-
Hordeum hulled grains	-	18	-	1	-	-	-
Hordeum indet. grains	-	55	-	-	-	6	-
Cereal indet. grains	1	1	4	4	6	6	2
Cereal/Large Gramineae culm nodes and bases	-	-	-	-	1	-	4
WEEDS							
Silene sp.	2	1	-	-	-	-	-
Montia fontana ssp. chondrosperma	2	-	-	-	-	-	-
Chenopodium sp.	-	63	-	-	-	-	-
Chenopodiaceae indet.	-	39	-	-	-	-	-
Medicago/Melilotus	-	2	-	-	-	-	-
Trifolium spp.	-	56	-	-	-	-	-
Vicia cf. hirsuta	-	-	-	-	-	-	-
Vicia/Lathyrus	-	9	-	-	-	1	-
Large Legume indet.	-	-	-	-	-	1	-
Rosaceae thorns	1	-	-	-	-	-	1
Hyoscyamus niger	-	-	-	1	-	-	-
Veronica hederifolia	-	-	-	2	-	-	-
Euphrasia/Odontites	-	-	-	3	-	-	-
cf. Lamium sp.	-	-	-	1	-	-	-
Galium spp.	-	10	-	-	-	-	-
Sambucus nigra	-	1	-	-	-	-	-
Cirsium/Carduus	-	1	-	-	1?	-	-
Compositae indet.	-	-	1	-	-	-	-
Eleocharis palustris/uniglumis	-	10	-	-	-	-	-
Carex sp.	-	1	-	-	-	-	1
Gramineae indet.	1	5	-	1	-	1	-
Ignota	3	16	3	-	2	1	1

Table T21. Iron Age Samples
(Only samples containing charred remains shown)

	129/W	124/1	124/2	124/3	166	125/3rd	125/6th
Sample Size:	20L	10L	20L	20L	20L	10L	17.5L
CEREALS							
Triticum dicoccum/spelta spikelet forks	-	-	-	-	-	-	-
T. dicoccum/spelta glume bases	-	-	-	-	2	-	-
Triticum sp. grains	1	1	-	1	-	2	-
Hordeum hulled grains	-	-	1	1	2	-	2
Hordeum indet. grains	-	-	1	-	1	-	1
Cereal indet. grains	1	-	1	1	3	-	1
WEEDS							
Vicia/Lathyrus	-	-	-	-	-	-	-
Urtica dioica	-	-	1	1	1	-	-
Galium sp.	-	-	-	1	-	-	-
Eleocharis palustris/uniglumis	-	1	-	7	-	-	-
Ignota	1	-	1	1	1	-	-

Table T22. Iron Age Samples
(Only samples containing charred remains shown)

Sample No.:	496/N end	496/3	513/517	413/2	151/ 4th	127/2	140/3
Sample Size:	16L	17L	22L	16L	10L	10L	10L
CEREALS							
Triticum dicoccum/spelta rachises	1	-	-	-	-	-	-
T. dicoccum/spelta spikelet forks	1	-	-	-	-	-	1
T. dicoccum/spelta glume bases	6	-	-	-	-	-	-
T. spelta/aestivum s.l. grains	1	-	-	-	-	-	-
Triticum sp. grains	-	2	1	1	1	-	-
Hordeum hulled grains	-	1	-	-	-	-	-
Hordeum indet. grains	8	-	-	-	-	-	-
Cereal indet. grains	14	2	2	-	2	1	1
WEEDS							
Stellaria media type	1	-	-	-	-	-	-
Chenopodium sp.	2	-	-	-	-	-	-
Trifolium spp.	6	-	-	-	-	-	-
Vicia/Lathrus	2	-	-	1	2	-	-
Potentilla sp.	2	-	-	-	-	-	-
cf. Crataegus sp.	-	-	-	-	1	-	-
Rosaceae thorns	1	-	-	-	-	-	-
Polygonum persicaria	-	-	-	-	1	-	-
P. lapathifolium/nodosum	2	-	-	-	-	-	-
Galium sp.	-	-	-	-	1	-	-
Compositae indet.	-	-	-	-	-	-	-
Eleocharis palustris/uniglumis	1	-	-	-	1	-	1
Gramineae indet.	1	-	-	-	-	-	-
Ignota	1	-	-	1	1	-	-

Table T23. Romano-British Samples
(Only samples containing charred remains shown)

Sample No:	131/2	134/3	138/1	411/A/2	412/4
Sample Size:	18L	10L	10L	16L	18L
CEREALS					
Triticum dicoccum/spelta spikelet forks	1	-	-	-	-
T. dicoccum/spelta glume bases	1	-	-	-	-
T. cf. aestivo-compactum	1	1	-	-	-
Triticum sp. grains	1	1	7	-	-
Hordeum hulled grains	1	-	-	1	-
Hordeum indet. grains	-	-	-	1	-
Cereal indet. grains	8	-	4	1	-
WEEDS					
Chenopodium sp.	-	1	-	-	-
Medicago/melilotus/Trifolium	3	-	-	-	-
cf. Trifolium sp.	-	-	-	1	-
Polygonum cf. persicaria	1	-	-	-	-
Urtica dioica	1	-	-	-	-
Galium cf. aparine	1	-	-	-	-
Galium sp.	-	-	1	-	-
Eleocharis palustris/uniglumis	2	-	-	-	-
Avena sp.	-	-	-	1	-
Large Gramineae indet.	-	-	-	-	1

Table T24. Waterlogged and Molluscan Sample Details

Context	Condition	Weight (Kg) a seeds molluscs insects	b insects	Description
SITE A IRON AGE				
Sump 23	W	1.0	2.5	Dark brown organic gravelly silt
Ditch 1-S1	W	1.0	2.5	Grey brown organic silt
Ditch 1-S2	W	1.0	2.5	Brown humified silty peat with gravelly loam
Ditch 1-S3	W	1.0	-	Black humified peat
Ditch 1-S5	W	1.0	-	Grey organic gravelly clay loam
Ditch 1-S4	W	1.0	-	Brown organic loam with much gravel
Ditch 1-S6	W	1.0	2.5	Brown humified silty peat
Ditch 1-S7	W	1.0	-	Brown somewhat humified woody peat
Pit 498	W	0.5	-	Grey gravelly organic clay
SITE A ROMAN				
Well 41	W	1.0	-	Dark grey organic gravelly clay loam
Sump 24	W	1.0	-	Grey brown organic silt with some gravel
Gully 28	W	1.0	1.0	Grey brown organic silt with some gravel
Well 412/5	W	1.0	-	Grey black organic silt with some gravel
Sump 51	W	1.0	-	Grey brown organic silt with some gravel
SITE B ROMAN				
Water Hole 206/8	W	1.0	-	Grey gravelly organic clay
Pond 205/S1	A	1.0	-	Grey and brown gravelly clay loam
Pond 204/S2	W	1.0	2.5	Grey brown organic silt and gravelly loam
Pond 204 S3	W	1.0	2.5	Brown organic clay with some gravel
Pond 204 S4	A	1.0	-	Dark grey clay with some gravel
Ditch 202/3	W	1.0	-	Grey organic gravelly clay loam

W, waterlogged anaerobic deposit.
A, aerobic deposit from which organic remains were absent.

Table T25. Site A Iron Age

WATERLOGGED SEEDS	Number or presence							
	23	1S5	1S1	1S2	1S3	1S4	1S6	1S7
Ranunculus cf. repens L.	2	+	4	2	-	-	+	-
R. sardous Crantz	3	-	-	-	-	-	-	-
Ranunculus S. Batrachium sp.	-	+	10	22	+	+	37	-
Papaver rhoeas tp.	-	+	-	-	-	-	-	-
P. argemone L.	2	-	-	-	-	-	-	-
P. somniferum L.	-	+	2	-	-	-	-	+
Capsella bursa-pastoris (L.) Medic.	1	-	-	-	-	-	-	-
Rorippa nasturtium - aquaticum (L.) Hayek	-	-	2	-	-	-	1	+
R. cf. islandica (Od.) Bor.	-	+	-	-	-	1	-	-
Cruciferae gen. et sp. indet.	-	-	1	-	-	-	-	-
Viola sp.	1	-	-	1	-	-	-	-
Hypericum sp.	-	+	-	-	-	-	-	-
Silene cf. alba (Mil.) Kr.	1	-	2	4	-	+	-	-
Stellaria media gp.	13	+	4	2	-	+	-	+
Moheringia trinerva (L.) Clairv.	-	-	-	-	+	-	-	+
Arenaria sp.	12	-	-	-	-	-	-	-
Montia fontana L.	-	+	10	4	-	-	1	-
Chenopodium polyspermum L.	5	+	8	4	-	1	-	-
C. album L.	1	+	3	1	-	-	-	-
C. ficifolium Sm.	1	+	2	7	+	-	-	-
Atriplex sp.	2	+	2	2	+	-	1	-
Chenopodiaceae gen. et sp. indet.	-	-	2	-	-	-	-	-
Malva sylvestris L.	1	-	-	-	+	6	+	-
Rhamnus catharticus L.	-	-	3	5	-	1	1	+
Rubus fruticosus agg.	2	+	-	-	-	-	-	-
Potentilla anserina L.	-	+	1	-	-	-	-	-
P. cf. reptans L.	1	+	1	-	+	+	-	-
Aphanes arvensis agg.	1	-	-	-	+	-	-	-
Prunus spinosa L.	-	-	2	1	-	1	-	+
Crataegus monogyna Jacq.	6	+	10	11	+	+	12	+
Epilobium sp.	-	-	1	-	-	-	1	-
Callitriche sp.	-	-	-	-	-	4	-	-
Thelycrania sanguinea (L.) Four.	-	-	1	-	+	1	-	+
Chaerophyllum temulentum L.	-	-	2	-	+	5	+	-
Anthriscus caucalis Bieb.	-	-	-	1	-	-	-	-
Torilis sp.	1	+	1	-	-	+	3	+
Conium maculatum L.	-	-	-	-	-	-	-	+
Apium nodiflorum (L.) Lag.	-	-	14	8	-	-	-	-
Sison amomum L.	-	-	-	-	-	+	+	-
Pastinaca sativa L.	2	-	-	-	-	-	-	-
Polygonum aviculare agg.	1	+	-	-	-	-	-	-
P. persicaria L.	59	+	-	-	-	-	-	-
P. lapathifolium L. or nodosum Pers.	12	+	-	-	-	-	-	-
P. convolvulus L.	-	+	-	-	-	-	-	-
Rumex conglomeratus Murr.	1	+	1	-	-	-	-	+
Rumex spp.	6	+	5	2	-	-	-	-
Urtica urens L.	4	+	2	-	-	+	1	-
U. dioica L.	319	+	60	61	+	+	54	+

WATERLOGGED SEEDS	Number or presence							
	23	1S5	1S1	1S2	1S3	1S4	1S6	1S7
Primulaceae gen. et sp. indet.	-	+	-	-	-	-	-	-
Hyoscyamus niger L.	17	-	-	-	-	-	-	-
Solanum cf. dulcamara L.	-	-	1	2	-	+	2	+
S. cf. nigrum L.	3	-	-	-	-	-	-	-
Scrophularia sp.	-	+	-	-	-	-	-	-
Veronica S. Beccabunga sp.	-	+	-	-	-	1	-	-
Mentha cf. aquatica L.	-	-	5	12	-	-	-	-
Lycopus europaeus L.	-	-	-	-	-	-	-	+
Stachys sp.	-	+	2	-	-	-	-	+
Ballota nigra L.	5	-	1	1	-	-	-	+
Lamium sp.	-	-	-	-	1	-	-	-
Galeopsis tetrahit agg.	-	+	2	-	-	+	2	-
Nepeta cataria L.	-	+	1	5	-	+	2	-
Glechoma hederacea L.	-	-	-	1	-	-	-	-
Plantago major L.	-	-	-	1	-	-	-	-
Galium aparine L.	-	+	-	-	-	-	1	-
Galium sp.	37	+	16	30	+	+	12	+
Sambucus nigra L.	1	-	-	-	-	-	-	-
Valerianella dentata (L.) Pol.	-	+	-	2	-	-	-	-
Valerianella sp.	-	-	-	-	-	-	-	-
Senecio sp.	-	+	-	-	-	-	-	-
Tripleurospermum maritimum (L.) Koch	+	+	-	-	-	-	-	-
Arctium sp.	-	-	5	3	-	-	-	-
Carduus sp.	4	+	1	3	-	+	2	+
cf. Cirsium sp.	1	+	2	-	-	+	+	-
Lapsana communis L.	-	-	-	2	-	-	4	+
Sonchus oleraceus L.	-	-	-	1	-	-	-	-
S. asper (L.) Hill	1	-	-	-	-	-	-	-
Zannichellia palustris L.	-	-	-	1	-	-	-	-
Juncus bufonius L.	55	+	10	10	-	+	-	-
J. inflexus L., effusus L. or conglomeratus L.	10	+	32	20	+	+	-	+
J. articulatus gp.	10	+	51	-	-	+	30	+
Juncus spp.	10	+	20	-	-	+	20	-
Lemna sp.	-	-	15	15	-	-	-	-
Eleocharis S. Palustres sp.	-	+	+	-	-	-	-	-
Carex spp.	2	+	3	2	+	+	1	-
Gramineae gen. et sp. indet.	6	+	1	1	+	+	1	+
Total	622		337	255		208		

Table T26. Site A Iron Age

OTHER WATERLOGGED PLANT REMAINS		Number or Presence							
		23	1S5	1S1	1S2	1S3	1S4	1S6	1S7
Bryophyta	stem with leaves	+	-	+	+	-	+	+	+
Bud scales (not Salix)		+	-	+	+	-	+	+	+
Chara sp.	oospores	1	-	1	-	-	+	-	-
Crataegus or Prunus sp.	thorny twigs	-	+	+	+	+	+	+	+
Deciduous tree leaf fragments		+	-	+	-	-	-	-	-
Leaf abscission pads		-	-	+	+	-	+	+	+
Rubus sp.	prickles	-	+	-	+	+	+	+	+
Rumex sp.	stem fragments with pedicels	-	+	-	-	-	-	-	-
Salix sp.	buds	-	-	+	+	-	+	+	+
Salix sp.	leaf fragment	-	-	-	+	-	-	+	+
Twigs and wood		-	-	+	+	+	+	+	+

Table T 27. Site A Iron Age

COLEOPTERA	Minimum number of individuals			
	23	1S1	1S2	1S6
Carabus sp.	-	1	-	-
Leistus fulvibarbis Dej.	-	-	-	1
Nebria brevicollis (F.)	1	1	-	1
Notiophilus sp.	1	-	1	-
Dyschirius globosus (Hbst.)	-	1	-	1
Clivina collaris (Hbst.) or fossor (L.)	-	1	1	-
Trechus obtusus Er. or quadristriatus (Schr.)	3	4	2	2
T. secalis (Pk.)	-	-	-	1
Bembidion lampros (Hbst.)	-	-	1	-
B. guttula (F.)	-	1	-	-
B. guttula (F.) or unicolor Chaud.	1	-	-	1
Bembidion sp.	-	-	1	-
Pterostichus cupreus (L.)	-	1	-	1
P. melanarius Ill.	2	1	1	1
P. nigrita (Pk.)	-	-	-	1
P. vernalis (Pz.)	1	1	-	-
P. cupreus (L.) or versicolor (Strm.)	-	1	2	2
Calathus fuscipes (Goez.)	-	2	1	1
C. melanocephalus (L.)	-	1	1	-
Agonum muelleri (Hbst.)	-	-	-	1
Agonum sp.	-	1	-	-
Amara anthobia Vill. or plebeja (Gyll)	1	1	-	-
Amara sp.	1	-	2	1
Harpalus S. Ophonus sp.	-	-	1	-
H. affinis (Schr.)	-	1	-	-
Bradycellus sp.	-	-	1	1
Haliplus sp.	-	1	-	-
Agabus bipustulatus (L.)	-	-	2	2
Agabus sp. (not bipustulatus)	-	-	-	1
Helophorus aquaticus (L.)	1	1	-	-
H. grandis Ill.	-	-	1	-
H. aquaticus (L.) or grandis Ill.	-	-	2	1
H. nubilus F.	1	-	-	-
Helophorus spp. (brevipalpis size)	4	4	5	2
Sphaeridium bipustulatum F.	1	1	-	-
S. lunulatum F. or scarabaeoides (L.)	-	2	1	-
Cercyon spp.	3	3	2	1
Megasternum obscurum (Marsh.)	12	8	3	2
Hydrobius fuscipes (L.)	-	-	1	-
Anacaena globulus (Pk.)	-	1	-	-
Onthophilus striatus (Forst.)	3	-	2	-
cf. Paralister carbonarius (Hoff.)	-	-	-	1
P. purpurascens (Hbst.)	-	-	1	1

COLEOPTERA	Minimum number of individuals			
	23	1S1	1S2	1S6
Athoulus duodecimstriatus (Schr.)	1	1	-	-
Ochthebius minimus (F.)	-	3	2	2
Ochthebius spp.	2	4	4	2
Hydraena testacea Curt.	-	2	10	-
Limnebius papposus Muls.	-	-	-	1
Ptenidium sp.	1	1	-	-
Ptiliidae gen. et sp. indet. (not Ptenidium)	-	2	4	1
Choleva or Catops sp.	-	-	1	1
Colon sp.	-	1	-	-
Silpha obscura L.	-	-	1	-
Scydmaenidae gen. et sp. indet.	-	-	1	-
Micropeplus fulvus Er.	-	-	1	-
Metopsia retusa (Step.)	-	-	1	-
Lesteva longoelytrata (Goez.)	-	4	1	2
Lesteva sp.	-	-	-	1
Omalium sp.	1	1	1	-
Carpelimus bilineatus Step.	-	2	-	1
C. cf. cortincinus (Grav.)	-	1	-	-
Platystethus arenarius (Fouc.)	2	1	-	1
P. cornutus gp.	1	-	-	1
P. nitens (Sahlb.)	1	-	1	-
P. nodifrons (Man.)	-	3	1	-
Anotylus nitidulus (Grav.)	2	2	2	-
A. rugosus (F.)	3	3	2	1
A. sculpturatus (Grav.)	1	2	3	2
Stenus spp.	1	3	5	2
Paederus sp.	-	1	-	-
Lathrobium sp.	-	1	1	1
Rugilus orbiculatus (Pk.)	1	-	1	-
Rugilus sp.	-	-	-	1
Gyrohypnus angustatus Step.	-	-	-	1
G. fracticornis (Mull.)	1	1	-	-
G. atratus (Heer) or fracticornis (Mull.)	-	-	1	-
Xantholinus linearis (Ol.)	-	2	2	-
X. longiventris Heer	-	1	-	-
X. linearis (Ol.) or longiventris Heer	1	4	-	1
Philonthus spp.	2	3	1	1
Gabrius sp.	1	2	-	1
Staphylinus sp.	1	-	-	-
Mycetoporus sp.	-	-	-	1
Tachyporus sp.	1	-	1	2
Tachinus sp.	1	1	2	1
Aleocharinae gen. et sp. indet.	3	4	4	3
Pselaphidae gen. et sp. indet.	1	-	-	-
Geotrupes sp.	1	2	1	2
Colobopterus erraticus (L.)	-	-	-	1
Aphodius contaminatus (Hbst.)	2	5	3	4
A. fimetarius (L.)	1	2	-	1
A. cf. fimetarius (L.)	-	1	1	1
A. foetidus Hbst.	-	2	-	-
A. cf. granarius (L.)	1	8	3	2
A. luridus (F.)	-	-	-	1
A. rufipes L.	1	3	2	1
A. cf. sphacelatus Pz.	1	3	1	3
Aphodius spp.	3	1	-	1
Oxymus sylvestris (Scop.)	3	2	2	-
Onthophagus coenobita (Hbst.)	-	1	-	-
O. nutans (F.)	-	-	-	1
O. ovatus (L.)	1	2	2	1
Hoplia philanthus (Fues.)	-	-	-	1
Phyllopertha horticola (L.)	2	6	2	3
Cetonia aurata (L.)	-	-	-	1
Dascillus cervinus (L.)	-	-	1	-
Byrrhus sp.	-	1	-	1
Agrypnus murinus (L.)	2	2	2	1
Athous hirtus (Hbst.)	-	-	1	1
Athous sp.	-	-	1	-
Agriotes lineatus (L.)	-	2	-	1
A. obscurus (L.)	-	1	-	1
A. sputator (L.)	1	-	-	1
Agriotes spp.	1	2	1	1
Cantharis rustica Fall.	-	1	-	-
Cantharis sp.	-	-	1	1
Rhagonycha fulva (Scop.)	-	1	-	-

COLEOPTERA	Minimum number of individuals			
	23	1S1	1S2	1S6
Anobium punctatum (Deg.)	3	-	-	1
Ptinus fur (L.)	1	-	-	-
Malachius sp.	-	1	-	-
Brachypterus sp.	2	6	2	1
Meligethes sp.	-	1	-	-
Monotoma sp.	1	-	-	-
Atomaria sp.	1	2	3	1
Cryptophagidae gen. et sp. indet. (not Atomaria)	1	-	-	-
Orthoperus sp.	2	1	2	-
Coccidula rufa Hbst.	-	1	-	-
Stethorus or Scymnus sp.	-	-	-	1
Adalia bipunctata (L.)	-	-	1	-
Enicmus transversus (Ol.)	1	2	2	-
Lathridius minutus gp.	3	-	-	1
Corticariinae gen. et sp. indet.	1	2	1	1
Anaspis sp.	-	1	-	-
Anthicus antherinus (L.)	1	-	-	-
Bruchus or Bruchidius sp.	-	-	1	1
Chrysolina polita (L.)	-	-	1	-
Gastrophysa viridula (Deg.)	2	-	-	-
Phyllodecta vulgatissima (L.)	-	-	1	-
Phyllotreta atra (F.)	1	1	-	-
Longitarsus spp.	2	4	3	2
Chalcoides sp.	-	1	-	-
Chaetocnema concinna (Marsh.)	3	4	2	1
Chaetocnema sp. (not concinna)	-	1	-	-
Sphaeroderma rubidum (Grael.) or testaceum (F.)	-	1	-	-
Psylliodes sp.	2	-	-	-
Apion aeneum (F.)	1	1	-	-
A. pisi (F.)	1	-	1	-
A. craccae (L.)	-	-	1	-
Apion spp.	-	5	3	2
Phyllobius pyri (L.)	-	1	-	-
Polydrusus sp.	-	-	1	1
Sitona spp.	2	2	1	1
Hypera punctata (F.)	-	2	1	1
Hypera sp. (not punctata)	-	1	-	-
Tanysphyrus lemnae (Pk.)	-	10	-	-
Acales turbatus Boh.	-	-	1	1
Bagous sp.	-	-	1	-
Ceuthorhynchinae gen. et sp. indet.	2	2	-	1
Anthonomus cf. rubi (Hbst.)	-	-	1	1
Mecinus pyraster (Hbst.)	1	1	-	-
Gymnetron labile (Hbst.)	-	1	-	1
Ramphus pulicarius (Hbst.)	-	1	-	1
Total	118	201	142	111

Table T28. Site A Iron Age

OTHER INSECTS	Minimum number of individuals			
	23	1S1	1S2	1S6
Forficula auricularia L.	2	-	1	-
Pentatoma rufipes (L.)	-	-	-	1
Heterogaster urticae (F.)	2	-	1	-
Drymus sylvaticus (F.)	-	1	-	1
Scolopostethus sp.	-	1	-	1
Anthocorinae gen. et sp. indet.	1	3	-	-
Lytocorinae gen. et sp. indet.	-	1	-	-
Philaenus or Neophilaenus sp.	1	2	1	1
Aphrodes cf. albifrons (L.)	1	1	-	-
A. bicinctus (Schr.)	-	1	-	1
Aphrodes sp.	-	1	1	1
Aphidoidea gen. et sp. indet.	2	1	1	3
Homoptera gen. et sp. indet.	1	-	-	-
Myrmica scabrinodis gp. worker	-	-	1	-
Stenamma westwoodi West. worker	-	-	2	-
Lasius fuliginosus (Lat.) worker	-	-	1	15
L. fuliginosus (Lat.) female	-	-	-	1
Lasius niger gp. worker	1	1	1	-
Hymenoptera gen. et sp. indet. (not Formicidae)	1	3	2	2
Chironomidae gen. et sp. indet. larval head capsule	-	+	+	-
Dilophus febrilis (L.) or femoratus (Meig.)	1	1	3	2
Dipteran adults (not Dilophus)	-	2	1	-
Dipteran puparia	1	1	1	2

Table T29. Site A Iron Age

MOLLUSCA	Minimum number of individuals			
	23	1S1	1S2	1S6
Carychium sp.	-	4	-	-
Aplexa hypnorum (L.)	-	-	3	-
Lymnaea palustris (Mull.)	-	6	2	-
L. peregra (Mull.)	-	-	1	-
Lymnaea sp.	-	1	-	-
Planorbis planorbis (L.)	-	8	16	1
Anisus leucostoma (Milt.)	-	1	-	3
Armiger crista (L.)	-	7	5	1
Cochlicopa sp.	2	3	-	-
Vallonia costata (Mull.)	-	2	5	-
V. pulchella (Mull.)	1	-	-	-
Vallonia spp.	2	2	2	1
Arion sp.	-	-	+	-
Limax or Deroceras sp.	-	1	-	-
Trichia hispida gp.	4	3	4	4
Cepaea sp.	1	1	1	-
Pisidium sp.	-	1	1	-
Total	10	40	40	10

Table T30. Site A Iron Age Burial

WATERLOGGED SEEDS	Number Context 498
Ranunculus cf. repens L.	4
R. sceleratus L.	1
Stellaria media gp.	11
Chenopodium album L.	1
C. ficifolium Sm.	8
Atriplex sp.	13
Chenopodiaceae gen. et sp. indet.	1
Linum usitatissimum L.	1
Rubus fruticosus agg.	1
Potentilla anserina L..	1
P. cf. reptans L.	4
Aethusa cynapium L.	2
Polygonum aviculare agg.	1
P. persicaria L.	1
P. lapathifolium L. or nodosum Pers.	1
Rumex conglomeratus Murr.	1
Rumex sp.	6
Urtica urens L.	1
U. dioica L.	29
Alnus glutinosa (L.) Gaertn.	1
Hyoscyamus niger L.	1
Solanum cf. nigrum L.	1
Mentha sp.	1
Lycopus europaeus L.	1
Prunella vulgaris L.	1
Lamium sp. (not album)	1
Galeopsis tetrahit agg.	1
Plantago major L.	1
Sambucus nigra L.	3
Onopordum acanthium L.	1
Sonchus asper (L.) Hill	4
Eleocharis S. Palustres sp.	1
Carex sp.	3
Gramineae gen. et sp. indet.	6
Ignotum	1
Total	116

Table T31. Site A Iron Age Burial

OTHER WATERLOGGED PLANT REMAINS		498
Bryophyta	stem with leaves	+
Bud scales (not Salix)		+
Leaf abscission pads		+
Linum usitatissimum L.	capsule fragments	1
Pteridium aquilinum (L.) Kuhn	frond fragments	+
Salix sp.	buds	+

Table T32. Site A Iron Age Burial

COLEOPTERA	Minimum number of individuals 498
Bembidion lampros (Hbst.)	1
B. biguttatum (F.)	1
Pterostichus melanarius (Ill.)	1
Agabus bipustulatus (L.)	1
Helophorus sp. (brevipalpis size)	1
Cercyon sp.	2
Cryptopleurum sp.	1
Onthophilus striatus (Forst.)	2
Ochthebius sp.	1
Silpha atrata L.	1
Lesteva longoelytrata (Gz.)	2
Coprophilus striatulus (F.)	1
Platystethus cornutus gp.	1
Anotylus rugosus (F.)	1
A. sculpturatus (Grav.)	1
Oxytelus sculptus Grav.	1
Paederus littoralis Grav.	1
Rugilus sp. (not orbiculatus)	1
Gyrohypnus fracticornis (Mull.)	1
Philonthus sp.	1
Tachinus sp.	1
Aleocharine gen. et sp. indet.	1
Geotrupes sp.	1
Aphodius contaminatus (Hbst.)	1
Aphodius sp. (not contaminatus)	1
Oxyomus sylvestris (Scop.)	1
Agriotes sp.	1
Anobium punctatum (Deg.)	1
Ptinus fur (L.)	1
Brachypterus sp.	1
Omosita discoidea (F.)	3
Atomaria sp.	1
Stephostethus angusticollis (Gyll.)	1
Corticariinae gen. et sp. indet.	2
Chaetocnema concinna (Marsh.)	1
Ceuthorhynchinae gen. et sp. indet.	1
Total	42

Table T33. Iron Age Burial

OTHER INSECTS	498
Dilophus febrilis (L.) or femoratus (Meig.)	1
Dipteran puparia	2

Table T34. Site A Roman

WATERLOGGED SEEDS	Number 41	24	28	412/5	51
Ranunculus cf. repens L.	1	-	10	-	5
R. flammula L.	1	-	-	-	-
Ranunculus S. Batrachium sp.	-	-	216	-	14
Thalictrum flavum L.	-	-	-	1	-
Fumaria sp.	-	-	-	1	-
Brassica or Sinapis sp.	6	-	-	-	-
Thlaspi arvense L.	5	-	-	-	-
Capselle bursa-pastoris (L.) Medic.	-	1	-	-	1
Rorippa nasturtium-aquaticum (L.) Hayek	-	-	1	-	-
R. cf. islandica (Od.) Bor.	-	-	-	-	11
Cruciferae gen. et sp. indet.	1	-	-	-	-
Hyperium sp.	-	1	-	7	1
Silene cf. alba (Mil.) kr.	2	-	-	-	-
Stellaria media gp.	62	3	2	2	19
Sagina sp.	-	10	10	-	-
Arenaria sp.	-	1	23	-	-
Montia fontana L.	-	3	3	-	-
Chenopodium polyspermum L.	10	6	-	-	-
C. album L.	-	-	1	-	-
C. ficifolium Sm.	2	2	3	-	1
Atriplex sp.	2	7	1	-	8
Chenopodiaceae gen. et sp. indet.	-	3	-	-	1
Malva sylvestris L.	-	-	1	-	-
Linum usitatissimum L.	-	-	-	-	1
L. catharticum L.	1	-	22	-	-
Rubus fruticosus agg.	-	2	17	-	-
Potentilla anserina L.	-	6	3	-	-
P. cf. reptans L.	2	18	34	-	1
Prunus domestica L.	1	-	-	-	-
Crataegus monogyna Jacq.	-	-	1	-	-
Epilobium sp.	1	-	-	-	2
Callitriche sp.	-	-	81	-	-
Chaerophillum temulentum L.	26	-	1	-	7
Anthriscus caucalis Bieb.	-	2	-	2	-
Torilis sp.	-	-	1	-	1
Apium nodiflorum (L.) Lag.	-	-	-	-	1
Oenanthe sp.	-	-	-	-	1
Aethusa cynapium L.	-	-	-	-	1
Daucus carota L.	-	-	-	1	-
Polygonum aviculare agg.	3	1	-	-	-
P. persicaria L.	6	-	-	-	2
P. lapathifolium L. or nodosum Pers.	1	-	-	-	-
Rumex crispus L.	5	-	-	-	-
R. conglomeratus Murr.	-	-	-	-	2
Rumex spp.	11	2	8	5	3
Urtica urens L.	1	6	2	-	3
U. dioica L.	67	61	13	6	45
Primulaceae gen. et sp. indet.	1	-	-	-	-
Solanum cf. dulcamara L.	1	-	-	-	-
S. cf. nigrum L.	-	2	-	-	-
Veronica S. Beccabunga sp.	-	-	-	-	1
Lycopus europaeus L.	-	-	-	1	1
Prunella vulgaris L.	1	1	11	-	1
Ballota nigra L.	-	-	1	-	-
Glechoma hederacea L.	5	-	1	-	8
Plantago major L.	4	2	1	-	-
Galium aparine L.	1	-	-	-	-
Galium sp.	1	-	-	-	-
Sambucus nigra L.	1	12	1	3	15
Valerianella dentata (L.) Pol.	-	1	-	-	-
Valerianella sp.	-	-	1	-	-
Senecio sp.	-	-	-	-	1
Artemisia sp.	1	-	-	1	-
Carduus sp.	2	-	-	1	6
cf. Cirsium sp.	-	1	14	3	7
Lapsana communis L.	-	-	-	-	1
Leontodon sp.	1	-	14	-	-
Sonchus asper (L.) Hill	-	-	7	10	6
Juncus bufonius L.	22	62	20	1	32
J. inflexus L., effusus L. or conglomeratus L.	-	20	-	-	10
J. articulatus gp.	21	31	63	10	145
Juncus spp.	10	30	31	-	61
Sparganium erectum L.	-	-	-	-	1
Eleocharis S. Palustris sp.	1	4	1	-	4
Carex spp.	2	2	3	1	3
Gramineae gen. et sp. indet.	26	1	10	19	4
Ignota	2	-	-	-	-
Total	320	304	633	75	438

.fi nmwf2.txt

Table T35. Site A Roman

OTHER WATERLOGGED PLANT REMAINS	Preserve or Number	41	24	28	412/5	51
Bryophyta	stem with leaves	-	+	-	-	-
Bud scales (not Salix)		+	-	+	-	-
Chara sp.	oospores	-	-	535	-	2
Crataegus or Prunus sp.	thorny twigs	+	-	-	-	-
Deciduous tree leaf fragments		+	-	+	+	+
Leaf abscission pads		+	-	+	-	+
Linum usitatissimum L.	capsule fragment	-	-	-	-	2
Rubus sp.	prickles	-	-	+	-	-
Salix viminalis L. or viminalis x	leaves	-	-	-	-	+
Salix sp.	buds	+	-	-	-	+
Salix sp.	capsules	-	-	-	-	2
Twigs and wood		-	-	-	-	+

Table T36. Site A Roman

COLEOPTERA	Minimum No. of Individuals	41	24	28	412/5	51
Carabus sp.		-	1	-	-	-
Nebria brevicollis (F.)		1	-	2	-	-
Notiophilus sp.		-	1	-	-	-
Dyschirus globosus (Hbst.)		-	-	-	-	1
Clivina collaris (Hbst.) or fossor (L.)		-	-	1	1	-
Trechus obtusus Er. or quadristriatus (Schr.)		1	3	1	1	-
Bembidion lampros (Hbst.)		1	-	-	-	-
B. properans Step.		-	-	1	-	-
B. gilvipes Sturm		-	-	-	1	-
B. biguttatum (F.)		-	-	-	-	1
B. guttula (F.)		-	1	-	1	2
Pterostichus cupreus (L.)		-	1	-	-	-
P. melanarius Ill.		1	-	-	2	-
P. nigrita (Pk.)		1	-	-	-	1
P. cf. nigrita (Pk.)		-	-	1	-	-
P. cupreus (L.) or versicolor (Strm.)		1	-	1	-	-
Calathus fuscipes (Goez.)		-	2	3	-	-
C. melanocephalus (L.)		1	-	1	-	1
Agonum muelleri (Hbst.)		-	-	1	1	-
Amara bifrons (Gyll.)		-	-	1	-	-
A. anthobia Vill. or plebeja (Gyll.)		1	-	-	-	-
Amara sp. (not bifrons)		2	1	1	2	-
Harpalus S. Ophonus sp.		1	-	-	-	-
Metabletus foveatus (Fouc.)		-	-	1	-	-
Haliplus sp.		-	-	2	-	-
Hygrotus inaequalis (F.)		-	-	3	-	-
Agabus bipustulatus (L.)		-	1	1	-	-
Helophorus aquaticus (L.)		-	1	6	-	1
H. grandis Ill.		1	3	5	-	-
H. aquaticus (L.) or grandis Ill.		2	1	-	1	1
H. nubilus F.		-	-	1	-	-
Helophorus spp. (brevipalpis size)		6	15	24	4	5
Sphaeridium bipustulatum F.		-	-	2	2	-
S. lunulatum F. or scarabaeoides (L.)		2	-	1	-	1
Cercyon spp.		1	1	2	2	1
Megasternum obscurum (Marsh.)		2	3	4	1	2
Anacaena sp.		-	-	2	-	1
Helochares sp.		-	-	1	-	-
Kissiter minimus (Aub.)		-	1	-	-	-
Onthophilus striatus (Forst.)		1	-	-	-	1
Athoulus duodecimstriatus (Schr.)		1	-	1	-	-
Ochthebius bicolon Germ. or dilatatus Step.		-	-	3	-	-
O. minimus (F.)		1	5	9	-	5
Ochthebius spp.		4	11	8	4	9
Limnebius papposus Muls.		-	2	2	-	-
Ptenidium sp.		-	1	-	1	-
Ptiliidae gen. et sp. indet.		1	1	-	-	1
Choleva or Catops sp.		-	1	-	1	-

Table T37. Site A Roman

COLEOPTERA	Minimum No. of Individuals				
	41	24	28	412/5	51
Metopsia retusa (Step.)	-	-	-	-	1
Lesteva longelytrata (Goez.)	-	2	2	-	6
Lesteva sp.	1	-	-	-	1
Omalium sp.	1	-	-	1	1
Coprophilus striatulus (F.)	-	-	-	-	1
Carpelimus bilineatus Step.	-	-	-	-	4
Aploderus caelatus (Grav.)	-	-	-	1	-
Platystethus arenarius (Fouc.)	1	1	-	1	-
P. cornutus gp.	-	2	7	-	4
P. nitens (Sahlb.)	-	1	2	-	1
Anotylus nitidulus (Grav.)	-	-	3	-	1
A. rugosus (F.)	2	1	-	2	-
A. sculpturatus (Grav.)	1	1	1	-	2
A. cf. tetracarinatus Black	-	-	1	-	-
Stenus spp.	1	1	1	-	4
Lathrobium sp.	-	2	1	-	-
Leptacinus batychrus (Gyll.)	1	-	1	-	-
Gyrohypnus fracticornis (Mull.)	1	1	1	-	-
Xantholinus linearis (Ol.)	-	2	-	-	2
X. longiventris Heer	-	-	1	-	-
X. linearis (Ol.) or longiventris Heer	1	-	-	1	-
Philonthus spp.	2	-	1	2	1
Gabrius sp.	-	-	1	1	1
Staphylinus aenocephalus Deg. or fortunatorum (Woll.)	-	1	-	-	-
Tachyporus sp.	1	1	2	-	-
Tachinus sp.	1	2	1	1	1
Aleocharinae gen. et sp. indet.	3	2	5	2	2
Geotrupes sp.	-	2	1	-	-
Aphodius contaminatus (Hbst.)	3	4	2	-	2
A. cf. fimetarius (L.)	1	-	1	-	-
A. foetidus Hbst.	-	-	2	-	-
A. cf. granarius (L.)	-	2	6	-	1
A. rufipes L.	1	1	2	1	-
A. cf. sphacelatus Pz.	2	3	3	1	1
Aphodius spp.	1	2	5	2	1
Oxyomus sylvestris (Scop.)	2	1	1	2	-
Onthophagus coenobita (Hbst.)	-	-	1	-	-
O. ovatus (L.)	1	-	1	-	-
O. similis (Scrib.)	-	1	-	-	-
Phyllopertha horticola (L.)	1	2	2	-	1
cf. Cyphon sp.	-	-	-	-	2
Byrrhus sp.	-	-	1	-	-
Agrypnus murinus (L.)	1	-	2	-	-
Athous hirtus (Hbst.)	-	1	-	-	1
Agriotes lineatus (L.)	1	-	2	-	-
A. obscurus (L.)	-	2	1	-	-
Agriotes spp.	-	2	1	-	-
Cantharis rustica Fall.	-	-	1	-	-
Cantharis sp.	-	1	-	-	-
Rhagonycha fulva (Scop.)	-	-	-	-	1
Dermestes sp.	-	-	1	-	-
Stegobium paniceum (L.)	-	1	-	-	-
Anobium punctatum (Deg.)	1	-	-	1	-
Ptinus fur (L.)	-	-	-	1	-
Malachius sp.	1	-	-	-	-
Brachypterus sp.	3	-	1	-	-
Atomaria sp.	1	1	-	1	-
Cryptophagidae gen. et sp. indet. (not Atomaria)	-	1	-	1	-
Stilbus sp.	-	-	-	-	1
Coccidula rufa Hbst.	-	-	1	-	1
Enicmus transversus (Ol.)	1	-	-	-	2
Lathridius minutus gp.	-	-	-	1	2
Corticariinae gen. et sp. indet.	1	-	1	1	-
Typhaea stercorea (L.)	1	-	-	-	-
Pyrochroa serraticornis (Scop.)	-	1	-	-	-
Gastrophysa viridula (Deg.)	1	-	1	-	-
Hydrothassa marginella (L.)	-	-	-	-	1
Prasocuris phellandrii (L.)	-	-	-	-	1
Phyllodecta vulagatissima (L.)	-	-	-	-	1

COLEOPTERA	Minimum No. of Individuals				
	41	24	28	412/5	51
Phyllotreta nigripes (F.)	1	-	1	-	-
P. nemorum (L.) or undulata Kuts.	1	-	1	-	-
Longitarsus spp.	-	4	3	1	2
Chalcoides sp.	-	-	-	-	1
Chaetocnema concinna (Marsh.)	1	2	2	1	-
Chaetocnema sp. (not concinna)	1	-	1	-	-
Psylliodes sp.	-	-	1	-	-
Apion radiolus (Marsh.)	1	-	-	-	-
A. urticarium (Hbst.)	-	-	-	1	-
A. craccae (L.)	-	-	1	-	-
Apion spp.	1	2	1	-	2
Trachyphloeus sp.	-	-	1	-	-
Phyllobius sp.	1	-	-	-	-
Sitona sulcifrons (Thun.)	-	1	-	-	-
Sitona spp.	-	1	2	-	-
Hypera puncta (F.)	-	1	1	-	-
Notaris acridulus (L.)	-	-	-	-	1
Ceuthorhynchinae gen. et sp. indet.	1	-	-	2	-
Tychius sp.	-	-	1	-	-
Mecinus pyraster (Hbst.)	1	1	-	-	1
Total	83	116	179	55	92
OTHER INSECTS	41	24	28	412/5	51
Forficula auricularia L.	-	-	1	2	-
Sehirus bicolor (L.)	-	-	1	-	-
Heterogaster urticae (F.)	2	-	-	-	1
Anthocorinae gen. et sp. indet.	-	1	-	-	-
Philaenus or Neophilaenus sp.	-	-	1	-	-
Megophthalmus sp.	-	-	1	-	-
Aphrodes bicinctus (Schr.)	-	1	5	1	1
A. histrionicus (F.)	-	-	2	-	-
Aphrodes sp.	1	-	2	-	-
Aphidoidea gen. et sp. indet.	-	-	1	-	2
Trichoptera gen. et sp. indet. larvel cases	-	-	3	1	2
Stenamma westwoodi West. worker	1	-	-	-	1
Lasius niger gp. worker	-	-	2	-	1
Hymenoptera gen. et sp. indet. (not Formicidae)	2	1	5	-	1
Chironomidae gen. et sp. indet. larval head capsule	-	-	+	+	+
Dilophus febrilis (L.) or femoratus (Meig.)	-	-	2	1	1
Dipteran adults (not Dilophus)	1	-	3	1	1
Dipteran puparia	1	2	2	1	3

Table T38. Site A Roman

MOLLUSCA	Minimum No. of Individuals			
	41	28	412/5	51
Valvata cristata Mull.	-	-	-	1
Carychium sp.	-	-	-	1
Aplexa hypnorum (L.)	-	-	-	1
Lymnaea truncatula (Mull.)	1	1	-	3
Lymnaea sp.	-	1	-	1
Anisus leucostoma (Milt.)	1	-	1	9
Vallonia costata (Mull.)	5	-	1	-
V. excentrica Sterki	-	1	-	-
Vallonia sp.	4	3	1	-
Arion sp.	+	-	+	-
Limax or Deroceras sp.	1	-	2	-
Trichia hispida gp.	13	-	1	2
Pisidium sp.	-	3	-	-
Total	25	9	6	18

Table T39. Site B Roman

WATERLOGGED SEEDS	Number			
	206/8	204S2	204S3	202/3
Ranunculus cf. acris L.	-	2	1	-
R. cf. repens L.	-	1	-	-
Ranunculus S. Batrachium sp.	-	128	54	-
Papaver somniferum L.	-	6	-	-
Fumaria sp.	-	-	-	1
Thlaspi arvense L.	9	-	-	-
Barbarea vulgaris R. Br.	2	31	1	-
Hypericum sp.	-	-	1	-
Silene cf. alba (Mil.) Kr.	-	1	-	-
Cerastium cf. holosteoides Fr.	-	12	-	-
Stellaria media gp.	3	-	1	23
Chenopodium polyspermum L.	10	1	-	-
C. album L.	3	-	-	1
C. ficifolium Sm.	7	-	-	6
Atriplex sp.	7	7	-	5
Chenopodiaceae gen. et sp. indet.	10	-	-	-
Malva sylvestris L.	-	-	1	-
Linum usitatissimum L.	-	4	-	-
Medicago lupulina L.	-	4	-	-
Rubus fruticosus agg.	2	1	10	-
Potentilla anserina L.	-	1	-	-
P. cf. reptans L.	1	4	-	-
Crataegus monogyna Jacq.	2	1	17	-
Epilobium sp.	-	44	1	-
Chaerophyllum temulentum L.	3	16	1	-
Torilis sp.	-	17	1	-
Conium maculatum L.	23	1	-	3
Apium nodiflorum (L.) Lag.	-	4	5	-
Aethusa cynapium L.	-	1	-	3
Silaum silaus (L.) S. & T.	-	17	-	-
Pastinaca sativa L.	-	-	-	1
Daucus carota L.	4	10	2	-
Polygonum aviculare agg.	-	-	-	14
P. persicaria L.	-	-	-	10
Rumex conglomeratus Murr.	-	26	30	-
Rumex spp.	15	3	33	1
Urtica urens L.	2	-	-	2
U. dioica L.	26	3	4	4
Primulaceae gen. et sp. indet.	-	7	-	-
Fraxinus excelsior L.	-	1	5	-
Myosotis sp.	-	6	-	-
Solanum cf. dulcamara L.	12	-	1	-
Mentha sp.	17	7	60	-
Lycopus europaeus L.	-	1	3	-
Prunella vulgaris L.	-	1	5	-
Stachys sp.	4	-	-	-
Lamium sp.	1	-	-	1
Galeopsis tetrahit agg.	2	-	1	-
Glechoma hederacea L.	2	2	-	-
Galium sp.	-	7	-	-
Sambucus nigra L.	14	3	5	-
Senecio sp.	-	3	2	-
Anthemis cotula L.	-	-	-	25
Arctium sp.	-	-	1	-
Carduus sp.	6	-	-	2
cf. Cirsium sp.	-	12	11	2
Centaurea cf. nigra L.	-	2	-	-
Sonchus arvensis L.	-	2	-	-
S. asper (L.) Hill	11	8	8	6
Alisma sp.	-	31	7	-
Juncus bufonius L.	73	23	-	-
J. inflexus L., effusus L. or conglomeratus L.	10	-	31	-
J. articulatus gp.	451	124	122	-
Juncus spp.	62	32	41	-
Iris pseudacorus L.	10	-	-	-
Lemna sp.	31	-	-	-
Eleocharis S. Palustres sp.	-	-	1	-
Carex spp.	3	8	11	-
Gramineae gen. et sp. indet.	1	23	12	1
Ignota	-	2	1	-
Total	839	651	491	111

Table T40. Site B Roman

OTHER WATERLOGGED PLANT REMAINS		Number or Presence			
		206/8	204S2	204S3	202/3
Bryophyta	stem with leaves	-	+	+	+
Bud scales (not Salix)		-	+	+	-
Chara sp.	oospores	-	11	1	-
Crataegus or Prunus sp.	thorny twigs	+	-	+	-
Deciduous tree leaf fragments		-	+	+	-
Leaf abscission pads		-	+	+	-
Linum usitatissimum L.	capsule fragment	-	1	-	-
Populus sp.	buds	-	1	14	-
Rubus sp.	prickles	+	+	+	-
Rumex sp.	stem fragments with pedicels	-	+	+	-
Salix viminalis L. or viminalis x	leaves	-	+	-	-
Salix sp.	buds	-	+	+	-
Salix sp.	capsules	-	1	3	-
Trifolium sp.	calyx	-	1	-	-
Twigs and wood		-	+	+	-

Table T41. Site B Roman

COLEOPTERA	Minimum No. of Individuals			
	206/8	204S2	204S3	202/3
Carabus granulatus L.	-	1	-	-
Carabus sp.	-	-	1	-
Nebria brevicollis (F.)	-	2	-	-
Dyschirus globosus (Hbst.)	-	1	-	-
Trechus obtusus Er. or quadristriatus (Schr.)	1	-	4	1
Bembidion properans Step. or lampros (Hbst.)	-	-	1	-
B. biguttatum (F.)	-	2	1	-
B. guttula (F.)	1	1	1	-
B. lunulatum (Fouc.)	-	2	1	-
Bembidion sp.	-	1	-	-
Pterostichus cupreus (L.)	-	1	2	-
P. melanarius (Ill.)	3	1	-	1
P. cf. nigrits (Pk.)	1	-	1	-
P. strenuus (Pz.)	-	1	-	-
P. vernalis (Pz.)	1	1	-	-
Calathus melanocephalus (L.)	-	-	1	-
Agonum muelleri (Hbst.)	-	1	1	-
A. viduum (Pz.)	-	-	1	-
Amara cf. aenea (Deg.)	-	1	-	-
A. bifrons (Gyll.)	-	1	-	-
Amara sp.	1	-	1	1
Harpalus rufipes (Deg.)	-	1	-	1
H. cf. punctatulus (Duft.)	-	2	-	-
Harpalus S. Ophonus sp.	-	1	1	-
H. affinis (Schr.)	-	-	2	-
Acupalpus sp.	-	-	1	-
Badister bipustulatus (F.)	-	1	-	-
Dromius cf. melanocephalus (Dej.)	-	1	-	-
Haliplus sp.	-	-	2	-
Hygrotus inaequalis (F.)	-	-	1	-
Hydroporus sp.	-	1	5	-
Graptodytes pictus (F.)	-	1	-	-
Agabus bipustulatus (L.)	1	4	2	-
Agabus sp. (not bipustulatus)	-	2	2	-
Colymbetes fuscus (L.)	-	1	1	-
Dytiscus sp.	1	-	-	-
Gyrinus sp.	-	-	1	-
Helophorus aquaticus (L.)	-	12	4	-
H. grandis Ill.	2	10	7	-
Helophorus spp. (brevipalpis size)	1	51	13	1
Cercyon sp.	-	2	6	1
Megasternum obscurum (Marsh.)	1	1	4	-
Hydrobius fuscipes (L.)	2	5	6	-
Anacaena globulus (Pk.)	-	1	3	-
Anacaena sp. (not globulus)	-	3	-	-
Laccobius sp.	-	-	2	-

Table T41: Site B Roman - cont.

COLEOPTERA	206/8	204S2	204S3	202/3
Helochares sp.	-	1	-	-
Onthophilus striatus (Forst.)	-	1	-	-
Ochthebius bicolon Germ. or dilatatus Step.	-	-	1	-
O. minimus (F.)	-	8	-	-
Ochthebius spp.	-	23	10	-
Hydraena cf. nigrita Germ.	-	-	1	-
H. cf. riparia Kug.	1	2	1	-
H. testacea Curt.	5	3	9	-
Limnebius papposus Muls.	-	9	4	-
Ptiliidae gen. et sp. indet.	-	2	1	-
Colenis immunda (Strm.)	-	-	1	-
Choleva or Catops sp.	-	1	-	-
Silpha obscura L.	-	1	1	-
Scydmaenidae gen. et sp. indet.	-	-	1	-
Micropeplus fulvus Er.	-	1	1	-
Metopsia retusa (Step.)	-	1	1	-
Anthobium atrocephalum (Gyl.)	-	1	1	-
Lesteva longoelytrata (Gz.)	-	-	5	-
Lesteva sp.	-	2	1	-
Phyllodrepa sp.	-	1	-	-
Omalium sp.	-	-	1	-
Xylodromus concinnus (Marsh.)	-	1	1	-
Carpelimus bilineatus Step.	-	-	1	-
Aploderus caelatus (Grav.)	-	-	1	-
Platystethus arenarius (Fouc.)	-	1	1	-
P. cornutus gp.	-	-	1	-
P. nodifrons (Man.)	-	1	-	-
Anotylus rugosus (F.)	3	1	2	1
A. sculpuratus (Grav.)	-	1	-	-
Stenus spp.	1	5	4	1
Paederus littoralis Grav.	-	1	1	-
Lathrobium sp.	-	1	1	-
Gyrohypnus fracticornis (Mull.)	-	-	1	-
Xantholinus linearis (Ol.)	-	1	4	-
X. longiventris Heer	-	1	-	-
Philonthus spp.	1	2	2	-
Gabrius sp.	-	1	-	-
Staphylinus brunnipes F.	-	1	-	-
S. aenocephalus Deg. fortunatorum (Woll.)	1	1	-	-
S. olens Mull.	-	1	-	1
Staphylinus sp.	1	-	-	-
Mycetoporus sp.	1	-	-	-
Tachyporus sp.	2	2	1	-
Tachinus sp.	1	2	3	-
Aleocharinae gen. et sp. indet.	-	3	2	1
Geotrupes sp.	1	-	-	-
Colobopterus erraticus (L.)	-	-	1	-
Aphodius contaminatus (Hbst.)	2	5	1	-
A. foetidus (Hbst.)	-	-	1	-
A. luridus (F.)	-	1	-	-
A. rufipes (L.)	-	-	1	-
A. cf. sphacelatus (Pz.)	2	2	-	-
Aphodius spp.	-	-	1	1
Oxyomus sylvestris (Scop.)	1	-	1	-
Phyllopertha horticola (L.)	-	-	1	-
cf. Cyphon sp.	-	1	4	-
Byrrhus sp.	-	1	-	-
Dryops sp.	1	1	1	-
Agrypnus murinus (L.)	1	1	1	-
Athous bicolor (Gz.)	-	1	-	-
A. cf. bicolor (Gz.)	-	-	1	-
A. cf. haemorrhoidalis (F.)	-	1	-	-
A. hirtus (Hbst.)	-	1	-	-
Agriotes lineatus (L.)	-	1	-	-
A. obscurus (L.)	2	4	3	-
A. sputator (L.)	-	3	1	-
Agriotes sp.	-	1	-	-
Adrastus pallens (F.)	-	1	-	-
Trixagus obtusus (Curt.)	-	1	-	-
Rhagonycha fulva (Scop.)	-	1	-	-
Rhagonycha sp.	-	1	2	-
Cantharis or Rhagonycha sp.	-	1	-	-
Anobium punctatum (Deg.)	-	-	2	-

Table T41: Site B Roman - cont.

COLEOPTERA	206/8	204S2	204S3	202/3
Brachypterus sp.	-	1	1	-
Meligethes sp.	-	-	1	1
Rhizophagus parallelocollis Gyll.	-	1	-	-
Rhizophagus sp.	-	1	-	-
Atomaria sp.	-	2	1	-
Cryptophagidae gen. et sp. indet. (not Atomaria)	-	2	-	-
Stilbus sp.	-	1	2	-
Coccidula rufa Hbst.	-	1	-	-
Tytthaspis sedecimpunctata (L.)	-	1	-	-
Lathridius minutus gp.	-	10	4	-
Enicmus transversus (Ol.)	-	2	1	-
Corticariinae	-	3	1	-
Anthicus antherinus (L.)	-	-	1	-
Bruchus sp.	-	-	1	-
Lema cyanella (L.)	1	-	-	-
Chrysolina polita (L.)	1	5	1	-
Phaedon tumidulus (Germ.)	-	1	1	-
Prasocuris phellandrii (L.)	1	-	-	-
Phyllodecta cf. laticollis Suff.	-	-	1	-
P. vulgatissima (L.)	-	1	-	-
Phyllotreta atra (F.)	-	1	-	-
P. nigripes (F.)	1	1	2	2
P. vittula Redt.	-	3	1	-
Longitarsus spp.	-	13	2	-
Chalcoides sp.	-	-	1	-
Chaetocnema concinna (Marsh.)	-	2	5	1
Psylliodes sp.	-	2	-	-
Apion spp.	2	11	15	-
Phyllobius sp.	1	-	-	-
Polydrusus pterygomalis Boh.	-	-	1	-
Sitona hispidulus (F.)	-	1	-	-
S. cf. lineatus (L.)	1	1	1	-
S. sulcifrons (Thun.)	-	1	1	-
Tanysphyrus lemnae (Pk.)	1	2	6	-
Acalles turbatus Boh.	-	1	1	-
Bagous sp.	-	1	-	-
Ceutorhynchus erysimi (F.)	-	-	2	-
Ceuthorhynchinae gen. et sp. indet.	2	5	1	2
Anthonomus cf. rubi (Hbst.)	-	1	1	-
Total	54	308	223	17

Table T42. Site B Roman

OTHER INSECTS	206/8	204S2	204S3	202/3
Forficula auricularia L.	1	3	1	-
Palomena prasina (L.)	1	-	-	-
Eurydema oleracea (L.)	-	1	-	-
Stygnocoris fuligineus (Geof.)	-	1	-	-
Drymus sylvaticus (F.)	-	1	-	-
Scolopostethus sp.	-	1	1	-
Berytinus sp.	-	1	-	-
Tingis ampliata (H.S.)	-	1	-	-
Physatochelia dumetorum (H.S.)	-	1	-	-
Anthocorinae gen. et sp. indet.	-	2	-	-
Saldula S. Saldula sp.	-	1	1	-
Philaenus or Neophilaenus sp.	-	1	-	-
Megopthalmus sp.	-	2	-	-
Aphrodes cf. albifrons (L.)	-	1	-	-
A. bicinctus (Schn.)	1	2	2	-
A. flaviostriatus (Don.)	-	6	1	-
Aphrodes sp.	-	1	3	-
Aphidoidea gen. et sp. indet.	-	1	6	1
Homoptera gen. et sp. indet.	-	1	5	-
Sialis fuliginosa Pict. or lutaria L.	-	1	-	-
Trichoptera gen. et sp. indet. larval cases	4	3	-	-
Myrmica rubra (L.) or ruginodis Nyl. worker	-	1	-	-
M. scabrinodis gp. worker	-	6	8	-
M. scabrinodis gp. female	-	1	-	-
Stenamma westwoodi West. worker	2	1	1	-
Lasius fuliginosus (Lat.) worker	-	1	-	-
L. niger gp. worker	-	12	-	-
Lasius sp. (not fuliginosus) female	-	2	-	-
Lasius sp. male	-	1	-	-
Hymenoptera gen. et sp. indet. (not Formicidae)	1	4	3	-
Chironimidae gen. et sp. indet. larval head capsule	-	+	-	-
Dilophus febrilis (L.) or femoratus (Meig.)	-	15	1	-
Dipteran adulta (not Dilophus)	-	4	5	-
Dipteran puparia	-	2	2	-

Table T43. Site B Roman

MOLLUSCA	206/8	204S1	204S2	204S3	204S4
Valvata cristata Mull.	-	-	-	-	2
Bithynia sp.	-	-	-	-	2
Carychium sp.	-	-	2	1	18
Aplexa hypnorum (L.)	14	-	1	-	1
Lymnaea truncatula (Mull.)	-	1	1	-	5
L. palustris (Mull.)	-	-	-	1	-
L. peregra (Mull.)	-	20	17	-	-
Lymnaea sp.	-	7	5	-	2
Planorbis planorbis (L.)	-	8	34	37	1
Anisus leucostoma (Milt.)	13	1	11	-	3
Bathyomphalus contortus (L.)	-	-	-	-	1
Armiger crista (L.)	-	30	128	14	-
Succinea or Oxyloma sp.	-	1	1	-	1
Cochlicopa sp.	-	3	4	-	1
Vertigo antivertigo (Drap.)	-	-	-	-	4
V. pygmaea (Drap.)	-	-	-	-	1
Vallonia costata (Mull.)	1	9	6	1	-
V. pulchella (Mull.)	-	2	13	-	1
V. excentrica Sterki	1	1	1	-	-
Vallonia spp.	-	29	7	4	17
Punctum pygmaeum (Drap.)	-	-	1	-	1
Arion sp.	-	+	-	+	+
Limax or Deroceras sp.	-	1	4	-	19
Trichia hispida gp.	5	15	12	5	59
Cepaea nemoralis (L.)	1	-	-	-	-
Cepaea sp.	-	-	1	-	1
Pisidium sp.	-	2	10	1	-
Total	35	130	259	64	140

Table T44. Waterlogged Wooden Objects

Context	Object type	Identification
Water Hole 60.	plank	Fraxinus
Pit 498.	board with possible batten	both of cf. Alnus or Corylus
Sump 202/B.	bowl	cf. Alnus or Corylus

Table T45. Features, their dimensions, fills and date

No.	Type of Feature	Level Bottom	Depth	Length	Width	Profile	Fills	Date
2	Gully	0.60	c.0.10m	-	-	Saucer	Gleyed clay + gravel	?
5	Ditch					Sloping U	Dark peaty loam clay. Gleyed clay + gravel.	
8	Gully	0.38	0.20m	-	0.30m	V	Dark gleyed clay + gravel	IA
12	Ditch	0.58	3.5					
13	Ditch	0.64	0.68			V		RB
14	Ditch	0.79	0.68			Bowl	Slow clean clay silting. Primary clay gravel silting.	
15	Ditch	0.82	0.61			Sloping U.	Slow clean clay silting. Clay + gravel silting. Peaty clay.	
17	Ditch	0.54	0.32	5.40	-	Bowl	Clay + gravel silting. Peaty clay.	IA
18	Ditch	0.69	0.22	3.20	-	V	Peaty clay + gravel.	IA
19	Ditch	0.59	0.35	4.50	-	V	Peaty clay + gravel.	IA
20	Ditch	0.58	0.18			Bowl	Clay + gravel silting. Peaty clay.	IA
21	Ditch	-	0.20		0.80	Bowl	Clay + gravel silting.	IA
24	Enclosure Ditch	0.68 / 0.49	0.24 (Sump 0.38m)			Sloping U	Clayey peat + gravel.	RB
25	Enclosure Gully	0.45	0.22		0.45	V	Grey clay + gravel. Peaty clay.	RB
26	Enclosure Ditch	0.61	0.30			Wide V	Slower clay or gravel silting. Clay silting & heavy gravel erosion. Peaty clay.	RB
27	Ditch	0.41	0.25		1.5	Sloping U	Slow clean clay silting. Clay + gravel silting.	RB
29	Trackway Ditch	0.33	0.30				Clay + gravel silting. Clay + gravel silting.	RB
30	Ditch	0.71					Mixed gravel + gravel. Slow clay silting, some gravel. Clay and gravel 50%. Peat.	?
31	Boundary Ditch = 9 & 7	0.25	c0.50			V and sloping V	Clay silting. Clay + gravel silting. Clay silting.	RB
32	Enclosure Ditch	<0.20	0.25			V	Primary clay + gravel silting.	IA
34	Ditch =220							
35	Ditch	-0.55	0.72			Sloping U		RB
36	Ditch	-0.43	0.50			Sloping U		RB
38	Pit	-	0.20	0.80	0.40	Sloping V	Clean clay silting. Clay and gravel. Peat.	
39	Ditch	0.54	0.54				Clay, sand and gravel. Clay and gravel. Gravel and clay silting.	?IA
40	Gully	0.39	0.22			Saucer	Clay and gravel	RB

No.	Type of Feature	Level Bottom	Depth	Length	Width	Profile	Fills	Date
61	Ditch	0.35	0.25			Sloping U	Loamy clay, and gravel.	
64	Sump?		Not Dug	2.30	1.40	-	Grey clay and gravel.	
87	Gully	+0.23	<0.15	2.65	0.45	Bowl	Silty clay loam	?
96	Gully	+0.03	0.25		0.54	U	Black clay loam and gravel.	RB
115	PH/Slot	+0.11	0.26	0.95		U	Dark gleyed clay and gravel.	?
129	Pit	-0.12	0.20			Bowl	Dark soil and occupation debris.	IA
130	Pit	-0.31	0.46	2.84		Sloping U	Dark gleyed clay. Clay and gravel silting.	IA
131	Ditch		0.45	6.75	1.15	Sloping U	Dark clay loam. Mottled clays and gravel in backfill? Clean black silty clay. Clay and gravel silting.	RB
133	Gully	+0.04				Bowl	Clay and gravel	?RB
139	Pit	+0.06	<0.20	0.85	0.58	Saucer	Silty clay loam ? + gravel.	?
150	Pit	-0.15	0.24	1.32	1.10	Bowl	Dark soil and occupation debris.	IA
161	Hollow (Part of 174)	-0.51	0.52	0.40		Saucer		RB
164	Ditch = 13 = 261					Sloping U	Gravelly clay. Slow clay silting.	RB
173	Pit or Sump	-0.94	0.55			U	Gleyed sticky clay and gravel layers.	RB

No.	Type of Feature	Level Bottom	Depth	Length	Width	Profile	Fills	Date
41	Well	0.84	0.66		1.68	Sloping U	Gravel (?Disturbed) Clay and gravel. Peat.	RB
43	Pit	0.68	0.48			Sloping U	Clay and gravel Clean clay. Peaty clay.	RB
44	Gully	-	0.18	-	0.55	Sloping U	Clay and gravel	-
46	Interrupted Ditch	0.56	0.30	-	0.60	V	Clay and gravel	?IA
48	Interrupted Ditch	0.50	0.22	2.0	0.55	Sloping U	Clean clay Primary clay and gravel.	?IA
49	Pit	0.25	0.17			Bowl		?
52	Sump	0.58	0.34	0.90	0.80	V	Clay and gravel	RB
54	Pit	0.63	0.25			V	Dark peaty loam clay.	-
55	Gully Sump	0.33 0.54	0.22			U and V	Clay and gravel silting.	-
57	Ditch	0.29	0.20		0.50	Sloping U	Clay and gravel silting.	-
58	Segmented Ditch	-	0.32	2.80	0.65	V		IA
59	Segmented Ditch = 3?	-						IA
60	Well/pit	1.35	1.15	3.40	2.80	V	Loamy clay and gravel. Gleyed clay and gravel. Peat. Fibrous silty peat. Clayey silt and fibrous soot layer. Gravel erosion.	RB

No.	Type of Feature	Level Bottom	Depth	Length	Width	Profile	Fills	Date
215	Ditch	-0.02	0.20			Sloping U	Gravel and gleyed clay. Clean gleyed clay. Gravel and gleyed clay.	?
216	Ditch		0.23			Wide V	Oxidised clay and gravel. Gleyed clay and gravel. Dark gravel and clay.	?
218	Ditch	-0.11	0.19				Oxidised clay and gravel. Gleyed clay + gravel pockets.	?
219	Ditch	Top-0.03	Not dug				Gleyed clay and gravel.	?
220	Ditch = 34	-0.02	0.25			Sloping U	Gleyed clay. Gleyed clay and gravel.	RB
221	Ditch? = 222		Not dug				Gleyed clay and gravel.	?RB
222	Ditch? = 221	-0.02	0.14			Sloping U	Gleyed clay	?RB
223	Ditch? = 224	-0.04	0.56			Sloping U	Mixed clay and gravel. Clean gleyed clay. Gleyed clay and gravel.	?RB
224	Ditch? = 223	0.00	0.15			Sloping U	Oxidised clay and gravel.	?
225	Ditch	-0.17	0.17			Sloping U	Gleyed clay and gravel.	?
226	Ditch = 225		Not dug			-	Gleyed clay and gravel.	?
227	Ditch = 225		Not dug			-	Gleyed clay and gravel.	?

No.	Type of Feature	Level Bottom	Depth	Length	Width	Profile	Fills	Date
180	Pit	+0.15				Saucer		RB
189	Pit?	-0.60	0.30		0.36	Bowl	Silty clay and gravel.	
196	Ditch/ Gully	-	0.30			Sloping U	Clay and more gravel. Clay and gravel.	RB
199	Layer	+0.06	0.05 - 0.10				Mixed subsoil and occupation debris.	
201	Ditch	-0.43	0.52			Sloping U		?Med.
202	Ditch Sumps	-0.21 -0.52 -0.70	0.30 0.66 0.75			U U U		?Med.
203	Ditch	-0.33	0.35			Sloping U		?Med.
204	Well	-0.88	0.96			U		RB
205	Pit Posthole	-0.30 -0.50	0.52 0.70			V U		?
206	Well	-0.84	0.92			U		RB
207	Gully/Pit	-0.10	0.20			Bowl or V		?
208	Ditch	-0.02	0.15					?RB
209	Ditch	-0.20	0.32			U		RB
210	Ditch	-0.14	0.24			Wide sloping U	Gleyed clay + gravel.	?
211	Ditch	+0.02	0.10			Bowl	Gleyed clayey gravel.	?
212	Ditch	-0.05	0.17			Saucer	Pale gleyed clay + gravel.	?
213	Ditch?	-0.05	0.12			Saucer	Pale gleyed clay + gravel.	?
214	Linear Pit or Ditch	+0.10	0.36			Bowl	Clean dark loamy clay. Gleyed clay and gravel. Clean gravel.	?

No.	Type of Feature	Level Bottom	Depth	Length	Width	Profile	Fills	Date
261	Ditch = 13		0.80			U	Pale gleyed sandy clay. Gleyed clay. Gleyed clay + gravel spills. Oxidised clay. Peaty sticky clay. Peat and gravel.	RB
262	Ditch		0.48				Gleyed clay. Gleyed clay and gravel.	
263	Linear Pit		0.35			V	Pale gleyed clay + gravel.	
264	Ditch = 415		0.30			Sloping U		
265	Ditch = 403		0.28			Sloping U	Gleyed clay and gravel. Silty subsoil spills.	
266	Pit		0.75			U	Dark clay and gravel.	
267								
301	Linear Pit		c0.60			V	Oxidised clean clay silting. Dark gleyed clay + gravel. Gleyed clay.	
302	Linear Pit		c0.60			V	Oxidised clean clay silting. Dark gleyed clay + gravel. Peaty clay.	
303	Ditch		0.32			Bowl		
304	Ditch		0.55			V		
305	Ditch Sump		0.47 0.73			Bowl Sloping U		?RB
306	Ditch		Not recorded				Dark gleyed clay. Gleyed clay and gravel.	

No.	Type of Feature	Level Bottom	Depth	Length	Width	Profile	Fills	Date
228	Ditch	-0.11	0.29			U	Brown clay. Dark gleyed clay + gravel.	RB
229	Ditch	+0.07	0.28			U	Clean clay. Dark gleyed clay + gravel.	RB
230	Linear Pit	-0.16	0.18			Sloping U	Gleyed clay and gravel.	?
231	Hollow?		Not dug				Gleyed clay.	?
232	Pit/PH	-0.47	0.45			V	Gleyed sticky clay. Gravel and gleyed clay.	RB
233	Ditch	-0.52	0.82			Wide V		
234	Well	-1.05	0.79			Sloping U	Oxidised clay. Gleyed clay. Peat. Clayey peat. Sandy gravel.	
235	Hollow	-0.46	0.46			Saucer		RB
236	Gully	-0.15				U	Brown clay. Gleyed clay and gravel.	
237	Gully?		Not dug				Gleyed clay.	?RB
238	Pit	-0.65	0.60				Gleyed clay and gravel. Peaty gleyed clay + gravel.	RB
239								
260	Ditch		0.60			U	Gleyed clay. Gravel + light gleyed clay. Peaty clay and gravel.	

No.	Type of Feature	Level Bottom	Depth	Length	Width	Profile	Fills	Date
320	Ditch		c0.25			Sloping U	Dark brown silty loam. Oxidised clay and gravel.	
321	Ditch		Not dug				Brown clay and gravel.	
403	Ditch/Gully	0.10	0.28		0.70	U	Slow clean clay - silting. Subsoil spill.	
407	Natural Subsoil							
408	Gully = 424							IA
409	Ditch = 425							IA
414	Gully	+0.02	0.16				Gleyed clay + gravel.	?
417	Ditch = 151							IA
418	Pit		0.26	1.09			Pale clayey silt.	RB
424	Gully		0.10	10.23	0.30	Bowl	Dark occupation IA soil.	
432	Gully		0.14		0.32	U	Dark occupation IA soil.	
437	PH		0.14		0.34	U	Brown silty clay loam and gravel backfill.	
438	Ditch						Dark occupation soil.	IA
441	Gully/Animal disturbance.	+0.25	0.11			U	Dark occupation soil.	
443	Gully		0.10				Dark silty clay loam (+ gravel).	IA?
444	?Stakehole		0.09	0.12			Dark silty clay ?IA loam (+ gravel).	
446	Layer	+0.037	0.05	c.1.50 x 1.00			Dark clayey silt.	IA

No.	Type of Feature	Level Bottom	Depth	Length	Width	Profile	Fills	Date
307	Pit/Well		0.82	2.75	1.45	U	Clean gleyed clay. Gleyed clay and gravel. Peaty clay. Peat and a little gravel.	?Med.
308	Pit/Well				2.15	Sloping U		
309	Gully		Not dug			Sloping U	Brown clay loam.	
310	Gully		0.11			Bowl	Gleyed clay and gravel.	
311	Gully/Slot		c0.10				Peaty clay and gravel.	
312	Pit/PH		Not dug	0.63	x 0.42		Gleyed clay and gravel.	
313	Ditch		Not dug				Gravel and gleyed clay.	
314	Pit		0.32	1.70	x 0.78	Bowl	Clay + gravel. Clean gleyed clay.	
315	Pit		0.32	1.52	x 0.65	Bowl	Pale gleyed clay and gravel. Clean gleyed clay.	
316	Pit		0.32	1.55	x 0.83	Bowl	Pale brown clay and gravel. Pale gleyed clay + gravel. Clean gleyed clay.	
317	Gully		>0.26		0.55		Oxidised clay and gravel.	
318	Pit/PH		Not dug	0.60	x 0.42		Loamy clay and gravel.	
319	Linear Pit		c0.55			V	Gleyed clay. Oxidised clean clay silting. Dark gleyed clay + gravel. Peaty clay.	

No.	Type of Feature	Level Bottom	Depth	Length	Width	Profile	Fills	Date
474	Gully/animal disturbance.		0.07			V	Pale gleyed clay loam.	
475	Gully/animal disturbance.		0.08			U	Pale gleyed silty loam.	
476	Gully/animal disturbance.						Mixed silty clay loam and gravel.	
481	?Gully		0.08		0.28	Sloping U	Gleyed silt and subsoil patches.	IA
482	PH		0.26	0.40 x	0.40	Sloping U		IA
486	Ditch	-0.38					As 485	IA
489	Gully		0.14		0.32	U	Gleyed silty loam. Eroded subsoil at the sides.	
493	Gully/animal disturbance.		0.18			U	Dark silty clay loam and gravel.	
500	PH	+0.07	0.30	0.28 x	0.28	U	Dark clay loam + black specking. Gleyed clayey loam + gravel.	IA
501	Ditch	-0.05	0.40			V	Black silty loam.	
502	Gully/animal disturbance.	+0.17	0.20		0.20	U		
504	PH	+0.16	0.16		0.27	U	Gleyed clayey silt and gravel.	
505	PH/Natural	+0.17	0.11		0.23	U	Pale gleyed clayey silt.	
506	PH/Natural		0.16		0.28	U	Pale gleyed clayey silt.	
508	PH	+0.25	0.10	0.14 x	0.14	U	Dark silty loam.	

No.	Type of Feature	Level Bottom	Depth	Length	Width	Profile	Fills	Date
447	Animal Disturbance							
448	Animal Disturbance							
452	Gully = 490							IA
454	Hollow	+0.30	0.11	0.054 x	0.54	Wide V	Pale gleyed clay loam and gravel.	
455	Stakehole?	+0.32	0.08	0.17 x	0.17	Bowl	Gleyed clay loam and gravel.	
456	= 457							
457	Gully?		0.16			V		RB
458	?PH					-	Gleyed clayey silt.	
459	Gully/Animal Disturbance.						Dark silty loam + gravel.	
462	Hollow					Irreg. Saucer	Gleyed silty clay + or subsoil flecks and mottles.	IA?
463	?Stakehole		0.16			W	Sandy loam + gravel.	
464	Horse burial	+0.16	0.20	1.85 x	1.10	Wide U	Clay loam + gravel.	
465	PHS		0.11	0.28 x	0.25	W	Gleyed loamy clay.	
466	Gully/Animal disturbance.		0.18		0.30	U	Dark clay loam. Light clay loam.	
467	Gully/ animal disturbance.	+0.22	0.18			U	Dark occupation RB? soil and gravel.	
469	Gully/Animal disturbance.						Dark occupation RB? soil and gravel.	
472	Gully/animal disturbance		0.10			U		
473	Gully/animal disturbance.					U	Mixed silty clay loam and gravel.	

No.	Type of Feature	Level Bottom	Depth	Length	Width	Profile	Fills	Date
509	Pit/Hollow	+0.22	0.12	0.44 x	0.35	Saucer	Dark silty loam + gravel.	
510	Layer		0.20				Reddish grey silt.	IA
511	Ditch = 501							
515	PH	-0.08	0.43	0.70		U	Pipe - Dark silty loam. Packing - Pale clay loam + gravel.	RB
518	Pit/Hollow		0.32			U	Mixed gravel and clean clay lenses. Gravel and pale gleyed clay.	RB
519	Gully/Pit		Not dug				Dark silty clay loam.	
550	Ditch		0.54		1.43	Sloping U	Oxidised clay and gravel. Oxidised mottled clay. Sandy clay and gravel. Peaty clay. Gravel spills.	
551	Ditch		Not dug				Gleyed clay and gravel.	
552	Pit		Not dug	2.70	0.85		Gravel and gleyed clay.	
553	Ditch		0.47		1.00	Sloping U	Oxidised clay and gravel. Gleyed clay, some gravel. Gravel and gleyed clay. Gleyed leached clay + gravel.	
554	Ditch		-				Gleyed clay and gravel. Charcoal hearth? Gleyed clay and gravel.	

No.	Type of Feature	Level Bottom	Depth	Length	Width	Profile	Fills	Date
601	Pit						Black clay loam + occupation debris.	RB
602	Ditch = 233						Nth cut - Brown loam clay. Sth cut - Black loam clay.	RB
603	Ditch						Gleyed clay and gravel.	RB
604	Gully					Sloping U	Pale gleyed clay + gravel.	RB
605	Ditch = 36						Dark gleyed clay + gravel.	RB
606	Ditch		Not dug				Dark gleyed clay + gravel.	
607	Pit		0.20			Saucer	Black clay loam and occupation debris.	Med.
608	Pit/Hollow						Oxidised clay loam + gravel.	
609	Ditch		Not dug				Gleyed clay and gravel.	
610	PH		Not dug	0.40			(NW) Pale gleyed clay + limestone.	
611	PH		Not dug	0.40			(NE) Pale gleyed clay + limestone.	
612	PH		Not dug	0.40			(Sth) Pale gleyed clay + limestone.	
613	Pit		Not dug				Black clay.	
614	Gully		Not dug		0.30		Gravel and pale gleyed clay.	?
615	Gully		Not dug		0.25		Gravel and pale gleyed clay.	?

No.	Type of Feature	Level Bottom	Depth	Length	Width	Profile	Fills	Date
616	Pit/Hollow		Not dug				Dark gleyed clay and gravel.	?
617	Ditch		Not dug				Dark gleyed clay or oxidised clay and gravel.	?
618	Ditch		Not dug				Gleyed clay and gravel.	?
619	Ditch		Not dug				Dark gleyed clay + gravel.	?
620	Ditch		0.25			Sloping U	Gleyed clay, a little gravel.	?
621	Ditch		<0.20			Sloping U	Gleyed clay and gravel (blue-grey).	?

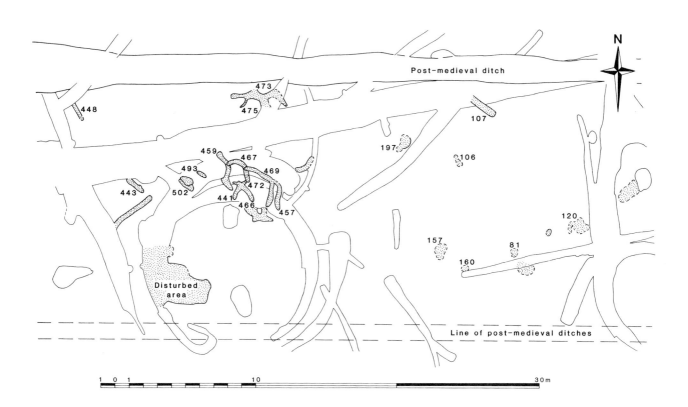

Figure A1 Plan of shallow gullies or animal burrows beneath the medieval headland

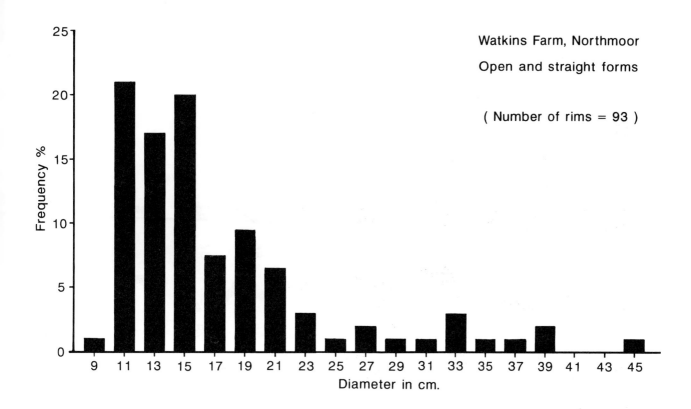

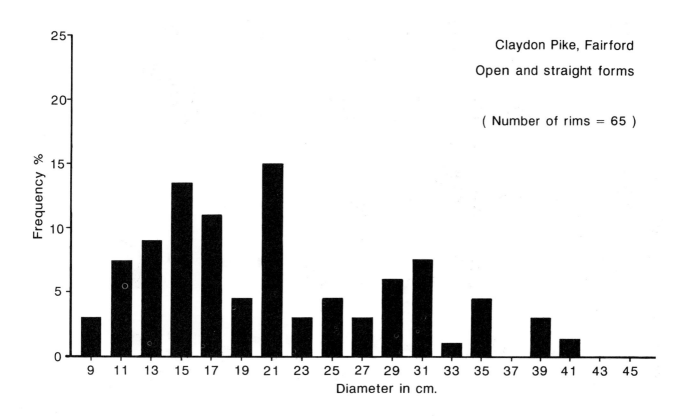

Figure A2 Iron Age pottery: histogram of rim diameters of open forms from Watkins Farm;
Iron Age pottery: histogram of rim diameters of open forms from Claydon Pike, Fairford

Northmoor/Watkins Farm 1983–4   Rim Series

Figure A3 Romano-British pottery: rim series

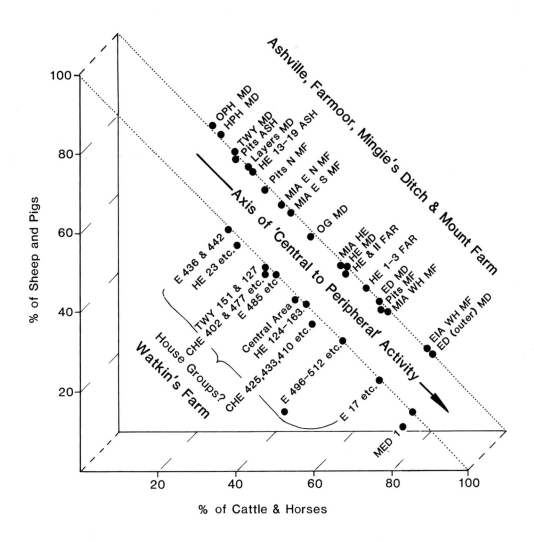

*Figure A4 Graph showing central to peripheral spread of bones
with data from excavations at Ashville, Farmoor, Mingies Ditch and Mount Farm*

E	Enclosure	H	House
ED	Enclosure Ditch	HE	House Enclosure
TWY	Trackway	OPH	Other Postholes
OG	Other Gullies	CHE	Central House Enclosure
OED	Outer Enclosure Ditch	EIA	Early Iron Age
WH	Waterhole	MIA	Middle Iron Age
ASH	Ashville	MD	Mingie's Ditch
FAR	Farmoor	MF	Mount Farm
N	North	S	South